221

PETER SCUDAMORE'S RECORD SEASON

Also by Dudley Doust:

IAN BOTHAM: THE GREAT ALL-ROUNDER
With Mike Brearley: THE RETURN OF THE ASHES
                   THE ASHES RETAINED
With Severiano Ballesteros: SEVE: THE YOUNG CHAMPION

221

PETER SCUDAMORE'S RECORD SEASON

DUDLEY DOUST

Hodder & Stoughton
LONDON SYDNEY AUCKLAND TORONTO

British Library Cataloguing in Publication Data

Doust, Dudley
   221 Peter Scudamore's record season.
   1. Great Britain. National Hunt racing. Jockeys:
   Scudamore, Peter
   I. Title
   798.4'5'0924

   ISBN 0-340-50888-4

First published in Great Britain 1989
Second impression 1989

Published by Hodder and Stoughton,
a division of Hodder and Stoughton Ltd,
Mill Road, Dunton Green, Sevenoaks, Kent TN13 2YA
Editorial Office: 47 Bedford Square, London WC1B 3DP

Photoset by Rowland Phototypesetting Ltd,
Bury St Edmunds, Suffolk

Printed in Great Britain by St Edmundsbury Press Ltd,
Bury St Edmunds, Suffolk

Bound by Hartnolls Ltd,
Bodmin, Cornwall

For Marilyn
and once again
for Jane

'Burnt horses bolt'
— *Anon*

Contents

List of Illustrations

Black and white illustrations used with the kind permission of: J. T. Ashley: p. 40; Trevor Jones: p. 120, p. 139; Bernard Parkin: p. 201; *The Racing Post*, John Crofts Photography: p. 158, A. Johnson: p. 35, Kicksports Foto: p. 176, Edward Whitaker: p. 196; George Selwyn: p. 86; Chris Smith: p. 66; Alec Spark: p. 172; Bob Thomas: p. xii, p. 101, p. 116; *The Times*, Adrian Brooks: p. 3, Hugh Routledge: p. 52; Colin Turner: p. 40, p. 76, p. 95, p. 142, p. 151, p. 176.

Colour illustrations

Between pages 116 and 117
On the gallops at Upland[1]
Martin Pipe and Peter Scudamore[1]
Chatam[3]
Sabin du Loir[2]
The junior Scudamores[2]
With Jonjo O'Neill[2]
Bonanza Boy after the Racing Post Chase[2]
Bonanza Boy at Aintree[3]
Desert Orchid[2]
David Nicholson[1]
Fred Winter[1]
Christies Fox Hunter Chase[3]
With Marilyn[2]
201 at Towcester[3]

Acknowledgments

1 Allsport
2 Trevor Jones
3 Bob Thomas Sports Photography

Acknowledgments

For help and advice in the preparation of this book, the author wishes to thank Peter's fellow jockeys, who were generous to a man; National Hunt trainers and owners, as well as a few race course officials, not least the best of them all, Edward Gillespie, general manager at Cheltenham. Among the generous racing journalists, my friend Brough Scott must be thanked (or blamed) for putting me onto the project. I should also like to thank John Oaksey for his kind, avuncular aid, Cherry Forbes for her cheerful research, Martin Trew for further research and advice, and, importantly, Paul Hayward who picked up mistakes in fact and phrase in the manuscript.

Who have I left out? Tons. My editor, Nick Sayers, who found order in chaos, is one and Dave Smith of Dave's Disc Doctor Service, Ltd, Paddock Wood, Kent, another. The admirable Smith recovered the book which, for three awful days, was lost in outer space.

Peter Scudamore

Sir Peter's Stirrups

Sir Peter Escudamor IV, of French descent, was a knight and a West Country landowner. He served Edward I or, by other accounts, Edward II, in wars on the Continent and it was Sir Peter, appropriate to the story of a jockey and kinsman, who made the first known use of the stirrup in the Scudamore arms. It appears on a seal which was attached to his charter of 24 August 1323.*

The seal looks like this:

'Nothing changes much,' smiles Peter Scudamore, champion jockey and A-level scholar of Medieval History. 'It looks a lot like the stirrups I use, only in those days I suppose they were made out of wood.' Peter and Sir Peter are collateral cousins.

*The Scudamores of Upton Scudamore: a Knightly Family in Medieval Wiltshire: 1086–1382, by Warren Skidmore. Privately printed, Akron, Ohio, 1982.

On the Road

1988, Christmas was coming and that night he had heard the angels sing. They were his two small sons, Thomas and Michael, in a school Nativity play. Later he had taken a glass of champagne with his wife Marilyn and his parents at the Black Horse Inn, a pub near his home in a pretty fold of the Cotswolds. He had slept well, too well, becalmed on a water bed. His wrist-watch alarm, unfortunately, had also slept well and when we met in the car park at Stow-on-the-Wold the following morning he was bent over the dashboard of his car, slowly rubbing his jaw with a portable razor. 'Congratulations,' I said, adding mine to the multitude. 'Well done at Haydock.'

The buzzing stopped and he grinned. He looked fresh but tired. 'Thanks. Very kind of you,' said Peter Scudamore who the previous day at Haydock Park, near Liverpool, had ridden his 98th, 99th and 100th National Hunt winners of the season. He packed away the portable razor and we set out in pursuit of number 101.

It was 8:10 on the morning of 16 December. The race meeting today was at Fakenham, a rural 'gaff' of a track in backwater East Anglia, eight miles from the North Sea. Fakenham is not a fashionable race course and, accordingly, Scudamore was dressed informally: a blue blazer, shirt and loosened tie, sharply creased trousers, loafers with tassels.

Scudamore said it would be a long journey to Fakenham: he thought about three and a half hours. 'Haven't a clue how far that is in miles.' His voice was clear and staccato, with just the aftertone of a West Country accent. 'Jockeys measure distance in time.'

2

The Scudamore family

Already that season Scudamore, we later estimated, had spent more than 240 hours – that's 10 full days – in his car as he drove to and from race meetings round England: from Newton Abbot in Devon where, on July 30, he rode a winner in the first race of the season, to Market Rasen in Lincolnshire, from Haydock Park in Lancashire to Folkestone in Kent. He would, before the term was over on June 3 at Stratford-upon-Avon, spend the equivalent of maybe three weeks behind the wheel of the car. I fastened my seatbelt.

It was my plan to observe the remarkable man, to meet some of the characters that surround him – among them horses, of course, other jockeys, trainers, owners, veterinarians, valets, farriers, stable lasses and lads, track officials, punters, a family genealogist, even the man who makes Peter's boots, lovely little things, soft and light and crafted from French calf and kid.

I would travel through the world of hurdling and steeple-chasing, known together as 'the winter game', and spend much

3

of the time alongside or, as they say in racing, 'upsides' Peter in the passenger seat of his car. I would watch the races, major and minor, and soak them up, whether he won, lost, fell, was brought down or pulled up. I would keep an account – more a random scrapbook than a diary – of Scudamore, his sport and his spectacular season of 1988–89.

I confess I knew very little about the technicalities of Peter's sport. But I had spent the whole of my professional life as a writer around sportsmen and women – I had been privileged to know many of the greatest of our time – and now I was fascinated to study a sport that was new to me, and the man who dominated it.

At 5 feet 8 inches, Scudamore is tallish for a jump jockey. His street weight of eleven stone, is about average but, on most days, he turns out at ten stone. If he must 'make light', which he doesn't have to do today, he'll use a sauna and sweat down to nine stone nine pounds. At that weight his ribs will show like a washboard but, dressed and seated on the scales with his saddle and leathers in his lap, he will make the National Hunt handicap minimum: ten stone.

'If I'm heavy I can lose a couple of pounds in a half hour,' he said. 'If not, it means a couple of hours in the sauna up at Nigel's.' I had seen Peter's cottage once and I could picture him on cold winter nights, towel in hand, climbing over the stone wall outside the back door and walking across a frosted field to Nigel Twiston-Davies's farmhouse, past the horses Nigel kept in, past the chickens, clucking in their sleep. Then into some sort of pine-board Scandinavian sauna. The image seemed bizarre, makeshift and strangely amateur.

'Chris Grant and Hywel Davies, I'd say, were the most dedicated wasters,' he said 'and we reckon Steve Smith Eccles works hard to keep his weight up!'

As for Peter's diet, it was already legend: steamed fish and spinach. Salt was to be avoided: it made you thirsty and since fluid means weight he often drank nothing until the day's racing was over. Perhaps a cup of tea before the fourth race. 'It's not hard to waste and keep to a diet,' he said. 'I'm not on a vanity kick. It's business.' In every way Scudamore looks after himself and, by design, is seen to be doing so. This, frankly, is for the owners, the Press, other observers.

4

'It's all great when you're getting the winners,' he said. 'But when the winners don't come through you start to leave yourself open to criticism. You're not trying hard enough. You're too fat. You're drinking too much. You're not training hard enough. I made up my mind early, I'll take the Piggott line. They'll have no comeback with me.'

Scudamore shrugged: it all went with the job.

Despite mention of Piggott, the job of National Hunt race-riding, apart from equal dedication, is a world apart from riding on the flat. My friend and colleague at *The Sunday Times*, Brough Scott, had put me up to the Scudamore book. Launching me on my way, he had spoken about the difference between the two forms of race-rider: the flat jockey and the jump jockey.

'A flat jockey's job is to make a horse go fast, purely and simply, but, because so much depends on this, the good ones – Piggott, Cauthen, Eddery – get incredible depths of knowledge in this tiny, limited discipline. You can see it in their eyes; speed is their only concern. They're quite incapable of doing much with a horse on a lateral-control basis but, because they're in such total command of their tiny discipline, they're better jockeys than jump riders.

'On the other hand, the jump jockey's disciplines encompass leaving the ground and getting a horse to manoeuvre much more. He may not be as good a jockey as a flat jockey, but he's a better all-rounder. He's a better horseman.'

Within the National Hunt game, of course, lie two forms of race: the hurdle, run over soft, sloping-away, gorse-packed obstacles which ideally are brushed and may even be flattened by the passing horse and the steeplechase, run over solid and upright birch-built fences and sometimes water, an altogether different proposition which demands that the horse clear the obstacles cleanly.

'With hurdlers, you're basically looking for speed all the time and can often get away with poor jumping,' Peter said. 'Not with a chaser. With a chaser you've got to have a horse brave enough to go for a fence and smart enough to respect it.' He laughed. 'As well as fast obviously. It's not an easy combination to find.'

Hurdling, I had read, was a manufactured race. It began, according to legend, in the early 19th century. 'It is said that hurdle-racing had its origin some years ago, when, in the absence of better sport,' according to the *Badminton Library*, 'a royal hunting party on the Downs near Brighton, when George IV was King, amused themselves by racing over some flights of sheep hurdles. The fun was thought to be so good that regular races over hurdles were organized.'

Steeplechasing, on the contrary, appears to have been more haphazard in its beginnings. It is widely, if not unshakably, taken that the first steeplechase was held in 1752 at Newmarket-at-Furness, not far from Limerick in the West of Ireland. The contestants were a Mr O'Calloghan and a Mr Edmund Blake, both possibly blotto with drink at the time. Who won the race, what wagers were laid, or how well the race proceeded, is not on record.

The course they raced was. It ran from the steeple in Buttevant to the steeple in Doneraile, both Protestant churches, for the Anglo-Irish were the riding gentry of the day. The distance was four-and-a-half miles, which in itself is interesting, for it is the same distance as the Grand National, the most famous steeplechase race in the world.

Anyway, at Fakenham, Scudamore would ride in one of each form of National Hunt race: a hurdle and a steeplechase.

The son of Michael Scudamore, a celebrated jockey of his day and now a trainer, Peter Michael Scudamore was born on June 13, 1958. He was brought up in the rolling hills of Herefordshire, not far from the Welsh Mountains and with a trout stream at the bottom of the fields. 'I think I once caught a trout,' he said, 'but I don't much like killing things.'

His attitude towards living creatures was then, and still is, something of a paradox. He neither fishes nor shoots and as a little boy, according to his father, had a soft-spot for the house fly. 'His mother swatted one once,' recounted Michael, 'and he went crazy: "what did you do that for, what did he ever do to you?" He got very upset when I killed a pigeon that was hurt.'

On the other hand, Peter was a hard-driving Pony Club stalwart. Twiston-Davies, his friend and business partner in a 390-acre Cotswold farm, remembers Peter as an unexceptional rider as a boy. His mother recalls the same thing. 'You didn't look at him,' she once recalled, 'and say "what marvellous inbuilt talent." They don't realise what effort and determination he's had to put in.'

Peter, no Mozart of the mounting block, does not disagree. 'I've found in life that I've never been a "natural" at things,' he now said candidly. 'I'd make mistakes. Then I'd systematically cut them out. I'm not a natural. But I'm good at practice, and I've always become quite good at things if I practise hard enough.'

I found nothing about Scudamore, save a broken nose, that suggested the rude, outdoor life he had led as a boy. His auburn hair hangs in lank array from a centre-parting and his face is gaunt and pale, as though all its colour has passed down the drain of a sauna.

It's the eyes that count. Brown, shading towards amber, they are deep-set and melancholy and when he grows tired or thoughtful – which was to become more and more frequent as the weeks passed and he hunted down winners – the left eye tends to close, the right to go big and round as a coin.

The effect of this asymmetry is transfixing, almost mystical and, together with those lank centre-parted bangs, it lends a Gallic air to his features. Sir Peter Escudamor IV, maker of the spurs-crest, off on the Crusades? Not likely. More a street-wise, fine-boned French pop star. 'Yes,' his mother, a wit, once said, humming as she took aboard a new notion of her son. 'Sort of a Sasha Distel, lighter-skinned though. And in need of a meal.'

Whatever his roots, Scudamore's looks are surely distinctive. And yet, until he had begun to move towards his century of winners, his had not been a household face. This lack of public acclaim bothers him, but not very much. He is a genuinely modest man. 'There's no side to Peter,' the man behind the bar at The Black Horse Inn once told me. 'You wouldn't know whether he rode a horse or pushed a wheel-barrow.'

'People wouldn't know me if I didn't have my name printed on the door of my car,' Peter said with a little smile. 'A gateman stopped me at Newbury the other day and wondered who I was and where was my jockey's pass. I started to tell him I was Peter Scudamore, champion jockey, and then I thought, well it's not worth the hassle.' He laughed and eased the car to the south out of Stow. 'Fair enough, why should he recognise me? When people meet me, they're actually surprised I don't have black hair. Jump jockeys should have curly black hair. Like John Francome.'

Peter, Francome's friend and successor, was on his way to his fourth consecutive riding title. His dominance over his colleagues in the winter game was more overwhelming than that of Francome or Stan Mellor or even the great Fred Winter in their days. Scudamore had 100 winners. His nearest rival, Richard Dunwoody, had 40.

We plunged through the morning mists of the Cotswolds, down an archway of noble beeches, through lovely golden villages, past the dry stone walls and the rolling pasture land. There were sheep here and there but the land was fenced mostly for horses. Scudamore drives a Peugeot 405, fast. The car is on loan from a car-hire firm who, in return, put their name alongside his on the doors and a mobile telephone at his elbow, which is standard equipment for the jump jockey.

The car phone is listed in *Directory of the Turf*, one of the sport's many annual bibles, and all through the trip to Fakenham it would flutter into life with calls made to and from trainers, owners, jockeys, friends and his secretary, whom at the moment he was trying to raise at home base.

'Morning. Thank you. Very kind of you. Any messages?' His voice was loud, for reception fades in and out in the Cotswolds, and its loudness took the form of command. 'Will you ring Ian Matthews for me? The trainer. Newmarket. He's got a horse in the last today at Fakenham – horse called See You There – and I see he hasn't got a jockey for it. Ask if he needs one?' Scudamore, in his insatiable appetite for winners, was trawling for spare rides.

I remembered what he had said when I first met him a few weeks earlier. He had said, 'I've got to go for every winner I can get and yet, at the same time, I can't take bad risks with horses I don't know.' He had said, according to my notes: 'The more you win, the more you have to win. It's a drug.' Then, as though cracking it out of a fortune-cookie, he had added: 'The purpose of life is to reach perfection. Every day you must strive for perfection.' He had delivered the homily deadpan, without irony and, from that moment onwards, I knew: here is a serious, obsessed man.

As he drove, Scudamore held the steering wheel lightly, as though it were reins in his hands. My attention was drawn to his wrists and his fingers, all unadorned: perhaps in his dangerous game, I thought, bracelets and rings are a peril to wear if you fall from a horse. The wrists and hands looked bony, almost frail, as luminous as porcelain. I remembered when we first met how his handshake had been gentle, as though he had nothing to prove. That had taken place late in October, at Uttoxeter, while he was looking for his 50th winner.

I had seen the white worm of a scar on his left forearm. The scar was the legacy of a fall taken in the spring of 1983 when he came down hard at Southwell, fracturing the forearm. It had been a bad, famous fall. At the time, five weeks before the end of the season, Scudamore was 20 winners ahead of John Francome, his nearest rival in the jockeys' table. But the injury put him out for the season. Francome drew level and, in a memorable act of sportsmanship, immediately stopped riding. The jockeys shared the title.

I had watched in the Uttoxeter weighing-room on that occasion of our first meeting, as Scudamore slapped a velcro-and-leather support round the forearm and hand: a gauntlet. It made him appear gladiatorial: Scu might have been one of his own forebears, preparing for the joust or a spot of falconry or, more to his contemporary liking, strapping on cricket pads to go to the crease.

Scudamore, statistically, has suffered fewer than his share of injuries: fractures to the skull, arm, leg, hand, fingers, wrists, a dislocated collarbone and numberless concussions, lacerations, strains, sprains and bruises.

The skull fracture deprived him of a crack at the title in the 1981–82 season; a year ago at Wolverhampton, he fell face-up on the far side of a fence and watched a horse land hoof-first on his body protector. That harrowing – 'How I Beat Death' – experience was food-and-drink for both the pop Press and the qualities. The estimable Jonathan Powell, then of *The Sunday People*, dined on it. He quoted the hapless jockey, Ronnie Beggan, who had ridden over Scudamore:

'I heard him groan as the hooves whacked into his ribs and the hind legs caught him with both barrels on his legs. I thought it was curtains. I can't tell you how relieved I was to see him alive in the ambulance-room.' To which, two paragraphs later, Scudamore responded as he was expected to: 'I was crippled, white with shock and the sweat was pouring from me. But it could have been worse . . . a few inches higher . . . and I could have been out for six months or for good.'

Scudamore has been stretchered off more tracks than he cares to recall. Injury, like dieting and money, is a question foremost in the minds of the laymen. 'I don't mind talking about injuries,' he lied. 'I just don't see any *good* in talking about injuries.' To do so tempts fate and the recent fate of three of his friends was fresh in his memory.

In the first fortnight of the season, the popular jockey Paul Croucher had died in a flaming car crash on a country road near Lambourn. Hardly a fortnight later Vivian Kennedy, a colleague attached to Charlie Brooks's yard, fell at a freak angle – a 30,000-1 chance, the Jockey Club doctor said at the inquest – at Huntingdon race course. He died while still in a coma. Then, in October, Jessica Charles-Jones – Peter used to ride with her jockey husband, Gareth, at David Nicholson's – broke her back in a fall at Southwell. She'll never walk again.

Fate had touched his father, too. It had marked Michael, blinding him in one eye, halting his career on exactly 500 winners, when on the same track that Peter had been trod on, Wolverhampton, he fell and was trampled by the field of follow-ing horses. There is no romance in injury and to his young son Michael had said: 'Keep one leg on each side of the horse and your head off the floor.' The sense of false valour nonetheless lingered in the young Peter for years – until that Southwell fall – and now he knows the difference between fearlessness and bravery.

'Terry Biddlecombe used to talk about how he broke every bone in his body, ticking them off from top to bottom,' said Scudamore. 'I'm not so macho. It's my determination *not* to break every bone in my body.' Scudamore meant no censure of Biddlecombe, the cavalier rider who was leaving the scene when Peter arrived. It was only that Biddlecombe chose to dwell on matters that were better left unsaid.

I told a Biddlecombe story. I said I remembered once inter-viewing the big, blond farmer's boy in the public steam bath in Gloucester. In those days Biddlecombe had made the steam bath his Press room; you joined him with a towel round your midriff, self-conscious, and came away pink, a couple of pounds lighter and with a wet, useless notebook in your hands.

All the jockey's raw quotes had sunk into the steam-softened pages.

Scudamore chuckled. There was, he admitted, something endearing about Biddlecombe. Where, I wondered, was old Terry now? Somewhere in Australia, said Scudamore. Trying to train horses. That was all he knew of the not long-ago champion. How old would Terry be now, I wondered, forty, forty-five? Scudamore shrugged and a truth rose unbidden: fame fades fast.

The phone fluttered. It was his secretary. Ian Matthews was sorry but he already had a jockey for Fakenham. Scudamore's fingers tapped thoughtfully on the wheel. 'Could you have a look at the card for tomorrow at Ascot?' he asked. 'I've got three rides. See if you can find me something else worth ringing up for. If nothing stands out, don't bother.'

'There is one called Mamora Bay,' she replied, 'which is one of Mrs Pitman's. I don't know –' Scudamore cut in. 'No,' he said. 'She'll have a jockey for that. That's fine then. Thank you, Caroline.'

The phone went again. '*Hallo*. Hallo, Charlie. How's the head?' It was Charlie Brooks, a young bachelor trainer, for whom Scudamore rode as first retained jockey. 'Thank you. Very kind of you. I've spoken to Pipey. He doesn't yet know if Out of the Gloom's going to be running. Give him a ring.' The person referred to as 'Pipey' was Scudamore's other regular trainer, Martin Pipe.

Thank you. Very kind of you. Scudamore was to use those two dry, clattering sentences over and over that day, express them without feeling, whenever he was congratulated on reaching his 100. They were brief replies, formal little calling cards he would distribute to well-wishers. He had worked it out beforehand. It seemed a simple, courteous – and unencumbering – response to being flung into fame. He explained: 'It's hard to say much and I don't want to sound rude. I *am* thankful. I *am* pleased with the record. But I'm trying desperately not to let it affect me. I don't want to get knocked out of the groove of race riding.'

Scudamore was in the groove. He was in his twelfth season and already had won 921 hurdle and steeplechase races – plus a few uncounted dozen in Norway, France, Belgium, Holland, Germany and such places. What is more, he had won the jockeys' championship four different times, that is to say won more races than any other jump rider in a season.

But still, lurking, was there something to prove that he preferred not to admit? At 30, he had yet to win steeplechasing's two major titles, the Cheltenham Gold Cup and the Grand National: the Double, the Ashes of National Hunt racing. Both these races had been won by his father, one of the most fearless of jockeys – until he came down at Wolverhampton. Did it niggle at him?

'No,' he said, and at least for the moment the matter was closed.

A jockey's car is his office and, as Scudamore spoke with his secretary, I glanced at the morning papers which were folded on the windscreen shelf. The front pages were full of his feat the previous day. 'Scudamore's Century,' cried *The Sporting Life*, 'Dedication is the Key to the Fastest Ton.' The paper pointed out, as did every other in the land, that when Peter rode a horse called Fu's Lady past the post in the Boston Pit Handicap, a Chase run over two miles and four furlongs at Haydock Park, he clocked up the fastest 100 National Hunt winners in history.

It beat the mark set on February 8, 1978 by Jonjo O'Neill, who went on to establish a seasonal record of 149. 'Everybody said it was a record which would never be broken,' the generous O'Neill was quoted as saying. 'Now Scu has done 100 before Christmas I just hope he keeps on riding winners, even though my record looks a goner.'

The praise went on. A target figure of 200 was mentioned but, offering 4-1 and 3-1 respectively, the bookmakers Hills and Ladbrokes seemed doubtful. Sir Gordon Richards's flat-race record of 249 winners, accomplished in 1946, was also cited. What struck me as most fascinating of all the accounts was a half-page box that appeared on the back page of *The Sporting Life*.

It carried the names of all of Scudamore's winners that season, with the dates, places, the horses' starting odds, their trainers and the prize money they earned for each win. Race followers are devout statisticians, especially about money, and such a detailed breakdown offered food for thought. As Peter did his morning phoning, I settled in to pursue it, toying first with the names of the horses.

Rahib, the first winner of the season. Obviously, he had Arab connections.

Hi-Hannah. She had already won twice this season. My daughter, Hannah, would fancy that mare.

My Cup of Tea. He'd won four-five-*six* times. He no doubt was the punter's cup of tea.

Celtic Shot. He was already famous. He'd won the Champion Hurdle last year at Cheltenham.

Beau Ranger. I already knew a bit about Beau Ranger too. He was owned, in part, by a friend, Peter White, the Somerset Cricket Committeeman who had made such a spirited attempt to keep Viv Richards on the books.

Strands of Gold. He'd fallen at Becher's last season with Peter. Still, he'd won a big one this term, the £29,544 Hennessy Cognac Gold Cup at Newbury.

Sabin du Loir . . . Sondrio . . . Bonanza Boy . . . Fu's Lady . . . Gazing out the car window, the names, like Isak Dinesen's herd of buffalo, came out of the morning mist, one by one, created before my eyes. What, I asked Scudamore during a lull in his phoning, was the meaning of 'Fu's Lady'?

'A pair of jeans,' he replied. 'The name's pronounced "F-U", like in the jeans. She's owned by the man who makes them. He owns Bonanza Boy as well – more jeans.'

I resumed my reading. Scudamore's mounts' total prize money, £264,098.15, was a good guide to an estimate of what he himself earned by riding the winners. At minimum, a jockey gets 7.5 per cent of their 'Penalty Value' which, determined by a complicated set of factors, is roughly the same as the winning money: say, if Scudamore got the minimum, about £19,000. What was more, I knew that Scudamore, like all professional jump jockeys, was paid a fee of £56.70, including VAT, for each of his rides. So far this season he had had 283 rides which put another £18,395 in his pocket. Therefore, his total track earnings to date in 1988–89 were just over £37,000. It didn't seem much for a man at the top of his sport. Steve Cauthen, after all, came away with more than that when he won the Derby a couple of years back on Reference Point.

The chart also showed that seventy-seven per cent of Peter's winners were the favourites or joint-favourites in their races. This meant, of course, that twenty-three per cent *weren't* favoured. Was this good or bad? Did it mean Scudamore failed to deliver the goods about one time in four? Or that he sprang an upset one time in four? Would a horse be a 'favourite' without him on its back? The permutations seemed endless. I glanced over at the jockey, the phone trapped under his chin. Just how good was this man?

One thing was certain. This season Scudamore was having mixed success with the two trainers who retained him as their top jockey. Brooks, who had taken over from Fred Winter at Lambourn, saddled only twelve of Peter's winners. On the other hand Pipe trained *seventy-five*. Fu's Lady, not surprisingly, was from Pipe's yard and after her historic victory *The Racing Post* spoke with the wizard from Somerset. 'Scu is so dedicated it's unbelievable,' said Pipe. 'Last night we all went out for a meal – and it was good, too. But he just sat beside us, smoking a cigar, and didn't eat a thing.'

When Scudamore got off the phone I asked him about Fu's Lady's record-breaking win at Haydock. 'I'm glad it's over,' he said. 'People were beginning to create pressure which wasn't there and it was getting to me. Take yesterday. I'd done my 99th in the third race and I was in a hurry to get out for the next. It's a long walk from the weighing-room to the paddock at Haydock and this press photographer stopped me and said, "May I ask you a question?" and I said, "Well, sure," and he said "When you win this race, will you –?" and I said, "Just go away."'

Scudamore shook his head. 'Can you believe it? "When you win this race." *When*. As though it was a certainty I'd win the race.'

Fu's Lady had been the even-money favourite largely because, two weeks earlier, Peter had breezed her home to a 10-length victory at Huntingdon. It had been his first ride on the 6-year-old mare and at Haydock, far the greater challenge, he had been by no means certain she would repeat her victory.

'Cantering down to post I suddenly got nervous,' he recounted. 'Haydock takes a lot of jumping and at Huntingdon the fences are small.' He had walked the mare forward to 'show' her the first fence, a common practice in British and Irish jump racing but one unique to the rest of the world. 'I can't honestly say it does any good but I wanted her to look at the fence. I wanted her to look at *all* the fences, which might sound stupid and obvious, but I wanted to impress on her that with big fences she'd have to adopt a slightly different style of jumping.'

Scu told me how he elected to start her down the middle of the course, to give her 'more fence' to look at, and then, not for the last time that season, he talked me through a race, fence by fence. 'She brushes through the top of the first, which is all very economical,' he said and gave a vanishing smile. 'But it adds a bit to the danger. So, we're through the first, then the big ditch okay, and Peter Hobbs starts coming upsides but I had the pace to dictate the race and I pushed her on coming off the bend.'

Scudamore was engrossed in the race, thumbs softly, properly along the steering wheel. 'Coming off a bend,' he broke off to explain, 'with a fence close to it, you always get a lot of fallers. I find it an interesting technical problem. You're tending to slow down, you see, and you're trying to regain your rhythm, and the bend is changing that rhythm and then there's the fence.

'Anyway, round the bend, change of scenery. She's going well, meeting everything on the right stride pattern – until we get to the final open ditch. She meets it wrong. This is the crunch. Some horses, the majority of horses, panic at this point. They want the decision made for them. But she's a horse with an instinct to get out of trouble. So I give her a loose rein. She's over – ah – she's learning to do things herself. Then the second last and we treated it with great respect, because I saw a horse fall there, and then over the last and we're going as fast as we can for the line.' The horse won by six lengths.

Scudamore smiled. 'Made all,' he said, meaning his horse had led all the way. The term was to become the call sign for a Pipe winner in 1988–89.

Peter was pleased but he kept the historic win in perspective. Fu's Lady century-setter, he said, hadn't been anything like the best ride he had had on a horse all season. The best, at least so far, probably had been a second-place finish on Beau Ranger, his possible Gold Cup ride, in the A. F. Budge Chase in December at Cheltenham. 'We responded to each other,' he said simply. 'He really tried for me. Pure guts.'

Scudamore for a moment reflected on Beau Ranger's superb but unheralded performance that day. It brought to his mind a sketch, or more accurately the words written *under* a sketch, he had once seen in the home of an American racehorse owner. The words demonstrated, in Peter's view, that people often don't know class when they see it.

The picture was by Sir Alfred Munnings, the outspoken former president of the Royal Academy and great painter of racecourse scenes early in this century. It showed a single, splendid horse standing against a rural landscape. 'The autumn start at Newmarket,' Sir Alfred had written in a letter beneath the picture. 'Too good for the ordinary ass to appreciate.' He was referring not to the quality of his work but to the common man's lack of feeling for horses.

I'd soon enough be exposed as an ordinary ass, I thought, and having just read a paragraph in *The Racing Post*, I reminded Peter that Fu's Lady's win might not hold up as his historic 100th winner. She could become only his 99th if the Jockey Club, racing's ruling body, took away a win he achieved in October at Cheltenham. The horse, Norman Invader, had not passed a drugs test after the race.

This brought up a topic which would not fade away. As the season progressed and Pipe himself moved towards winners' records of his own, critics would become harsh with the Somerset trainer. He would be accused, anonymously and without evidence, of dabbling in drugs, steroids, even blood-doping horses. It would be whispered that he was putting down hopeless horses at 'Mr Potter's', a Somerset slaughter-house.

'Rubbish,' said Scudamore, granting that in the case of Norman Invader an illegal drug might well have been found in the urine. Such illegal substances, such as caffeine, sometimes appear in horse feed because the suppliers fail properly to wash out their containers. 'It's the difference between Lynford Christie and Ben Johnson,' he said, citing the recent Olympics drugs controversy. 'It's the difference between ginseng tea and steroids.'

The phone fluttered. 'Hallo!' he barked. 'Speaking. Hallo, Ben. Thanks. Kind of you.' It was Ben de Haan, who is second jockey to Scudamore under Brooks. De Haan wondered whether Scudamore or he would be riding Brooks's horse, All Jeff, the next day at Ascot. If it was to be Scudamore, who had first call, de Haan wanted to ride another horse at Nottingham.

The call illustrated the awkward, if rewarding, position Scudamore found himself in during the 1988–89 season. As top jockey to both Brooks and Pipe, he sometimes found himself in a cleft stick: whether or not to turn down one trainer's probable winner to satisfy an unpromising commitment to the other? This led him to moments of nagging, uncharacteristic indecision.

'Where are you, Ben? At Charlie's?' said Scudamore. 'I'll ring Martin. I'll ring you back as soon as I know if Out of the Gloom is going to run. Which I doubt. He's got bad legs.' Scudamore then tapped out Pipe's office number in Somerset while, at the same time, shifting down and steering the Peugeot through a roundabout. The jockey looked happy, in command of the moment. 'Martin? . . .'

The Brooks–Pipe situation was clearly a potential problem, but it would not arise the next day. Scudamore's first choice for the Ascot race, Out of the Gloom, trained by Pipe, would not be running. Pipe said the ground was too hard. 'Right, that's all I wanted to know. I've got to let Ben de Haan know so I'll ring you back in a second.' Once again, Lambourn was dialled. 'Hallo, Charlie? I can ride All Jeff, if it's okay. I've spoken to Ben. Thanks. Cheers.'

Peter, in deference to my tape recorder, had turned off the radio many miles ago. Trainer and jockey were now discussing the prospects of the beautiful, if ageing, Sabin du Loir, the French-bred hurdler new to the Somerset yard. The 9-year-old was down to make his debut over fences the next day at Ascot but, from the thrust of the conversation, Pipe was doubtful. He reasserted his view that the ground would be too hard. Scudamore was disappointed.

'We can't leave him in, in the hope that it rains?' asked the jockey, fond of the horse, fond of its chances. 'I just – I don't know. Ascot is a different type of ground. And they *do* forecast rain down there . . . Oh, they're not expecting any rain. Well, then you can't do anything about it. Yeah, yeah that's fine. Cheers.' He rang off. For a moment, phone poised, Scudamore appeared to be trying to think of a number, any number, to ring. Then he clamped it away.

Scudamore's non-stop mobile phoning astonishes even his most experienced colleagues – 'I've never known a telephone to go that much,' says his friend, the jockey Simon Sherwood, 'he's on it every minute' – and his search for winners over Christmas now appeared to be reaching a frenzy. It was a drug. Scudamore was hooked. He admitted it. 'The more you win, the more you want to win,' he said. 'It hurts me not to win.'

We skirted Oxford and drove across the flattening Midlands. Scudamore, his voice just short of a shout, continued to receive and make phone calls. There must have been a fast dozen during which Scudamore exhibited his gift for simultaneously changing gear, steering, dialling and thanking people who phoned in to congratulate him. An owner called in and wondered, in passing, if his horse might try a novices' race next time out. Peter advised him, with velvet courtesy, that the horse had won a steeplechase the previous year and was no longer a novice.

He got a call from the Sheffield United midfielder Martin Dickinson, with whom Scu had struck up a friendship when both men were being treated for injuries at Lilleshalls. 'I just don't know,' he said at the end of the conversation. 'You can read the Form Book as well as I can.' Scudamore is mindful of the Jockey Club's view of jockeys tipping the public.

Scudamore took a call from a Greek-Cypriot in London. 'Hello, Steve,' boomed Peter. He grinned and lifted his eyes with a mock show of despair: this fellow might rabbit on forever. 'Thank you. Very kind of you. No, Steve. No! I don't want to go greyhound racing over Christmas. I've only got two days off and I want to spend it with my wife and my children and my parents. No . . . And a Happy Christmas to you. Cheers.' He rang off and laughed. 'That was Steve Chimonid. He makes my racing boots. We own a greyhound together.'

We stopped for petrol and, back on the road, Scudamore sucked on a small box of fruit juice. It was his first sustenance of the day. His mouth was dry. Jockeys' mouths are often dry. It's from the constant 'wasting', or the sweat-sapping saunas or, in the odd case, diuretics. Peter doesn't use the diuretics. Maybe, he thought, it was the champagne making him dry today.

He didn't look forward to Fakenham. He wasn't suffering from fatigue, he said, nor from emotional fallout after riding his 100th winner, nor even from the prospects of two indifferent rides. He simply didn't like Fakenham. It didn't give him the confidence. It didn't give him the arrogance he enjoyed when travelling towards a race course where tactical thinking and jockeyship might work.

'Fakenham's got no subtlety. Any idiot can ride Fakenham,' he said. 'Just go flat out. Also it gets slippery. And if there is anything a jockey hates, it's a slippery track. If I had a valid excuse, if I had fallen at Haydock, say, or my car had broken down, I might have rung ahead and quite happily given up the rides.'

Scudamore paused and grew sombre. 'But I couldn't, really. Be careful how you use this. A valet at Haydock told me yesterday about Chris Grant. He's a jockey up north. He's laid up with a broken leg. And his Missus has got cancer. She's gone through one set of treatments, chemo-therapy, or whatever . . .'

Scudamore explained how Grant's wife recently had postponed her second set of treatments to travel down to London to be with Chris when he received a Jockey of the Year Award. 'I thought of this,' he said, 'and I thought what Chris would have given to have my rides and I thought to myself: "who the hell are you, in this privileged position, to say you don't want to go to Fakenham?" '

The land was flat now, the fields covered in the wet, winter wreckage of beetroot. A sea mist hung over the landscape. We arrived at Fakenham at 11:25, fifteen minutes before the estimated time of arrival. Scudamore sat in his car, mobile phone turned off, and studied the racing press. He at last got out, heaved his bag from the boot and was approached by a fan. Would he sign an autograph book? The jockey, the toast of the racing world, swung aside the tools of his trade. He put his foot on the car bumper and signed the book, then another. He wrote in a spiky hand I would see many times through the season: 'Best Wishes. Peter Scudamore.'

The Shield of Love Divine

Scudamore wasn't always spelled that way. As the family name moves back through history it appears as Skidmore, Squidmor, Escudamore, de Scohies and at least thirty-eight other ways until finally, at the time of the Conquest, it comes to rest on a man named Ralf de Scudemer. Ralf, mentioned in the Domesday Book, came from Normandy to the borders of Wales, perhaps as early as 1058. He was a builder of castles and the founder of the English branch of the family.

Ralf flourished. So did his descendants. One line, the castle-builders, held, and still holds, land and grand houses in Herefordshire. These are Peter the jockey's forebears and cousins of which he knows little.

Peter's father, however, is marginally more steeped in family history. 'I once won a race and in the press they called me a Welshman,' he recounts. 'My father was furious. "We're English!," he shouted. "We built castles from Chepstow to Chester to keep the bloody Welsh out."'

Actually, the Scudamores didn't keep the bloody Welsh out too well. Way back, one of them married the daughter of Owen Glendower, the Welsh rebel (or patriot), who sought to divide the parts of the kingdom. But that's another story. In general, the descendants of the Herefordshire Scudamores glitter through English history. For example:

There was a Sir John Scudamore, Gentleman Usher to Henry VIII. There was his grandson, another Sir John, benefactor to the Bodleian Library at Oxford and *his* son, Sir James Scudamore, a soldier knighted for his bravery at Cadiz. The chivalrous Sir James Scudamore was the model for a character in Edmund

Spenser's epic Elizabethan poem *The Faerie Queene*, completed around 1596. Sir James's suit of armour resides in the Metropolitan Museum of New York. His feet were small.

In following generations there were many Scudamores, most of them knighted, who were Members of Parliament, friends of the diarist John Evelyn and the poet John Milton and yet another Sir John, who was ambassador to France in 1635. Retiring to his Herefordshire farm, Sir John grafted the Scudamore Crab, now known as the Red Streak cider apple.

This line – of Scudamores, not apples – zig-zags down into the 20th century to Peter's grandfather, Geoffrey Scudamore, a Herefordshire farmer, point-to-point rider, up-country National Hunt jockey and, during World War II, radio operator and gunner with the RAF. His plane crashed into Germany where, suffering facial injuries, he was captured and held prisoner-of-war.

Of Peter's father, more later. But perhaps it is appropriate, if not superfluous, to report the reaction of Mary Scudamore, Peter's mother, on first seeing her new-born son on Friday, 13 June, 1958. 'I checked him over,' she says, 'and then I thought, "thank God, he's in one piece." '

Another branch of Ralf, the castle-builder's tree had rerooted deeper into England and, according to the *Upton Escudemor Charter of 1148*, was granted an entire village in Wiltshire. The charter reads, in part:

'To all his men French, English and Welsh and his friends, Robert Ewias sends greetings. Know you that I have given to Godfrey Escudamore and his heirs the whole village of Upton Escudamore for his homage and service and the finding of one white warhorse . . .'

One white warhorse. Such a horse, I learned later, would have been a Destrier, originally French, but now lost in the mists of antiquity. Traditionally, it was a big brute, a cross between a Shire and a heavy hunter, trained to bite and lash out and to turn to the right when bumping a rival while jousting. It was strong enough to carry a knight in full armour. It was given in homage to Ewias, the overlord, a castle-owner on the Welsh border.

The Wiltshire Scudamores have died out. But the village, now called Upton Scudamore, still exists. It is not far from my home in Somerset and it seemed a fine place to explore. To get there you turn off the A350 between Westbury and Warminster and climb a hill – hence the 'Upton' in the place-name – and there in the centre of the village is a little Norman church, with a Georgian tower. It is called St Mary the Virgin.

The church was locked. The warden, Richard Carpenter, a retired farmer up the road, held the key. He also held the key to the family history, a bundle of documents.

'With all this interest in tracing ancestors these days,' Carpenter said, pulling on a jacket for our walk to the church, 'we've had Scudamores come along from all over the place. Canada. Wales. Akron, Ohio. Only yesterday a school-teacher from Bristol, whose maiden-name was Scudamore, took away a load of family research.'

Carpenter added that Peter has never been in Upton Scudamore. Peter thinks he's right but they're both wrong. 'The family once went to Longleat to see the lions. Peter didn't like the lions so we went home,' explains Michael. 'On the way back, we saw the signpost to Upton Scudamore and drove up for a picnic. We've got a photograph of Peter with his sister, Nichola, sitting under the signpost.'

In the churchyard, Carpenter showed me a huge tomb, crumbling and in the clutches of ivy. Unmarked and undated. It had caught his imagination as a boy. He had lived in the village since 1918. 'We can't be certain whose bones, if anybody's, are in there,' he said. 'But my father always said they belonged to an early Scudamore.'

We entered the church. There was a Norman font and a Scudamore organ designed in the mid-19th century by the vicar. There was also a small chapel, known as the Scudamore Aisle. In it lay two stone effigies. They were worn with age, much damaged, and remarkably big. One had his right arm knocked off and the other's legs were lopped off at the shins. One is of Sir Godfrey Escudamore, recipient of the village under the charter of 1148. The other represents Sir Peter Escudamor, either I, II, III or IV. If it's IV, it's the man who in 1323 put the stirrup on his crest. The stirrup, indeed six of them, were later to appear on the Scudamore Coat of Arms: gold against a red field, with buckles and leathers.

In the stained-glass window is the family motto: *SCUTUM*

AMORIS DIVINI which in Latin sounds splendid: 'The Shield of Love Divine'. But what does it mean? Perhaps nothing. The *SCUTUM* is thought to be a pun on the family name but Peter's mother, like many mothers, has theories on family. 'The "Scu" in the name of "Scudamore" comes from the word "escutcheon", which means shield,' she explains, 'and the "amor" means, well, of course, "love".'

The tour of the church was coming to an end and Carpenter, looking up, pointed out the last bit of Scudamore lore. It was a banner, hanging from a rafter and bearing the 'Crusaders' Cross' in the colour of dried blood. Continuing to gaze up, he might have been thinking of some medieval Scudamore, off on the Crusades. Or perhaps, like me, he might have had those stirrups on his mind. At last he spoke. 'The roof leaks,' he said. 'Could you have a word with Peter? We're starting a fund for a new roof.'

Journey's End

Fakenham's race card bears a Victorian engraving which depicts a long-necked thoroughbred reaching towards a finishing post: a rocking-horse winner. The jockey, slumped forward, appears to have been pitched there from his backward seat and now he's hanging on for dear life. The amateurish but sporting image makes a fitting logo for Fakenham: owned by the West Norfolk Hunt, it lies in the depths of fox-hunting country.

Fakenham holds only six race meetings a year, the fewest of any of the forty-four National Hunt tracks in Britain, and its pretensions are accordingly modest. 'We're the shortest circuit in England, exactly one mile,' said Pat Firth, the long-serving clerk of the course. 'If we put on a good race, we wouldn't get any runners.'

They don't get many news people either. The facilities are sparse. In the cramped Press shed, an agency man expressed relief that Scudamore hadn't held off to hit his historic century here in deepest, darkest East Anglia. If he had there wouldn't have been enough phone lines to carry the news to the outside world.

Peter came through the gate, pausing to sign more autographs, a saddle at his hip, his long racing bag slung over his shoulder. It's a dirty white bag, a tourist agent's gift for last summer's trip to Barbados, and it is crammed with jockey gear. He carries, unless the valet's got them, four pairs of riding boots, two 'light' pairs, weighing only eight ounces the pair and two 'heavy' pairs, weighing one-and-a-half pounds. He carries a jock strap, no underwear, ladies' tights, two small foam-rubber instep pads for his boots, a whip, two pairs of riding gloves, a wash-bag with toilet articles, three pairs of goggles, his leather forearm support and, of course, the helmet. He also had his medical book, certifying his good health, a valid passport without which a jockey is not allowed to board a horse.

In the weighing-room the valet, John Buckingham, had Scu's kit ready and hanging on the peg above his head: the dark blue colours with grey hoops he would wear in his first ride. Scudamore pulled off his shirt and slapped the support round his forearm.

In the first race on the card, in which Scudamore didn't ride, there were thirteen runners. It was a selling handicap hurdle and, second time round, a narrowly-averted pileup confirmed his misgivings about the tightness and slippery nature of the track. The incident happened as the packed field swept through one of the sharpest bends in British racing, the 90-degree left-hander at the cresting top of the course. An inexperienced jockey, trying to make up ground on the bend, drove his mount into the heels of the horse in front. The offending horse hit the rail, slipped sideways and nearly brought down the field.

A gasp passed through the crowd; it might have been nasty: in the previous meeting a horse had slipped and fallen there, mercifully escaping injuries. The mishap today resulted in a stewards' inquiry and afterwards a courteous appeal in the weighing-room for future caution at that point on the track. The winner, a 4-year-old bay gelding called Tigers Pet, was auctioned for 3,500 gns, a goodly price for a seller at Fakenham.

Scudamore rode in the third race, a handicap hurdle, on the bay gelding Zagazig. He'd never been on the 5-year-old before but 'Spotlight', in *The Racing Post*, was bullish. 'Zagazig has not been disgraced since winning at Uttoxeter,' it said, in reference to an October race at the Staffordshire track, 'and the booking of Peter Scudamore suggests a return to form is anticipated.' He was second favourite to the front-running chestnut colt, Old Eros, who according to the paper's expert, 'is in his element round a tight track like this.'

In the parade ring, the Newmarket trainer Neville Callaghan's instructions to Scudamore were fairly explicit. 'Give him a bit of light early on,' said Callaghan. 'He doesn't jump all that well.' Scudamore, swinging wide, gave him too much light. Old Eros, as expected, went to the front, avoiding the heavy traffic at the top turn, but began to falter three fences from home and fell at the next. Zagazig attacked late and came third, two lengths behind the winner, Kadan, another tight-course specialist.

The fourth race, the one involving only three horses, was a novices' chase. Scudamore quickly changed into the yellow silks and emerald green cap of the owner-trainer, Paul Kelleway of Newmarket, and moved towards him and the stable lass in the parade ring. However, when he saw another man, an official, talking earnestly with the two, Scudamore moved away.

It was an image I would see struck many times by many jockeys through the season. Peter stood, arms folded, the very picture of the outcast, the liveried hired-hand waiting to be called into conference. It appeared an excessively courteous, humiliating gesture to me, but Peter later explained: He had stood back because he had not wanted to interrupt a little ceremony. The stable lass was being presented with £25 for the best-turned out horse.

Scu had ridden the gelding, Majestic Ring, into a second-place finish nine days earlier at Huntingdon. The horse had shown little heart then and he showed little more at Fakenham and trailed in second place throughout. 'The horse was a bit timid,' said Scudamore afterwards, tearing off his forearm support, unbuckling his body protector, tugging off his racing boots. 'He jumped carefully, *too* carefully. It cost me the whole way round.'

Scudamore scavenged a dried-out sausage, his first solid fare of the day, from a barren tray of food laid out for the jockeys. He shrugged. 'Another day another dollar,' he said. It was the knock-on-wood sort of remark I was to hear from many jockeys upon the safe completion of a day's work.

The drive to London was dark and rainy. We passed Royston, in Hertfordshire, which prompted a conversation about Willie Stephenson who had trained Oxo, the horse on which Peter's father had won the 1959 Grand National. Peter, after completing his A-levels, had got his first riding – or at least riding-out – job with Stephenson and he looked back on the experience with mixed feelings.

'I learned a lot from Willie Stephenson. I thought a lot of him,' said Scudamore, and he chuckled. 'But I don't think Willie thought a lot of me. He said I'd never make a jockey. He said I couldn't ride that well. He said I was too big. He thought I'd make a fine estate agent.' There was an edge to Peter's voice and, after a while, he added quietly, privately: 'Willie Stephenson. Another stimulus.'

Peter called home, spoke to his wife, Marilyn, and the angels, Thomas, aged 5, and Michael, 4. He called ahead to a London friend, Alfie Buller, a Northern Irish property developer. Buller, in fact, was more than a friend. He was another, more positive, stimulus in Scudamore's life. He had a small family bloodstock business in Ulster and it was he who planted the idea of a similar venture in Scudamore's mind. 'Peter, that's what you've got to do.' Scudamore had done it. Together with his father, a family friend called Ted Prail, acting as financial director, and Paul Webber, the bloodstock agent, the company was formed the previous May: Peter Scudamore Bloodstock, Ltd.

More immediately, Buller keeps a flat with a sauna in the West End. Peter would spend the night there, as he often does before riding at Home County tracks. He would take his first meal of the day: almost certainly it would be steamed Dover sole, with spinach and a glass of white wine at Silks, a restaurant round the corner from St James's. With a 10 stone weight to make the next day, he'd then have a good sweat in the sauna. It would take an hour to shed the two or three pounds.

Scudamore, however, couldn't dismiss today's racing from his mind. It gnawed at him. He became preoccupied with the third race, the one he lost on Zagazig. 'I could possibly have won that race, you know,' he said. 'I'm not saying I *should* have won it, but I *could* have won it. I made a mistake. I gave him too much to do. I had him too far back four flights from home and he doesn't have the flat-out speed. I couldn't quicken him up.'

We approached the spreading glow of London. 'I'll tell you what did me good, more than anything, today,' he said. 'I'd sat in the car park, reading all those articles praising me, saying what a good boy I am, and I was beginning to believe it. And then I went out and rode a horse and got beat. I made a mistake. I was brought back to earth and I'll be a better jockey for it.'

Nothing

'I hate horse-racing. I think it's a waste of time,' said Father Mark Jabale, who was headmaster at Belmont Abbey when Scudamore attended the Catholic public school near his home in Herefordshire. 'But I'll always look at the papers and if Peter is racing I'll try to watch it on television. We think the world of Peter.'

Father Mark remembers Peter as a student of average academic gifts who, through sheer determination, achieved his A-levels in Medieval History and British Constitution. 'Whatever he set his mind to do he did, quietly and doggedly, regardless of the impossibility of the task,' recalls the jockey's former headmaster. 'He was a little chap, slightly built compared to some of the enormous Welsh boys, and yet he was a fearless tackler and he made the Rugby first XV. Wing-forward, I believe.'

Where, I wondered, did Peter get such fierce determination? 'I don't know,' said Father Mark. 'I really don't and I've often wondered myself. I've known Peter since he was fourteen and a great deal of it comes from the hero-worship he had for his father, Michael, a *very* special man. The way he spoke of him during the evening chats we had it was obvious he worshipped the ground that he trod on. Peter would never, *never* have dreamt of defying his father, doing anything that might conceivably displease him.'

A Catholic, through his mother, Scudamore became deeply religious at school. 'There was one particular priest, Father David Bird, who is now out in Peru,' the former headmaster continued. 'He had a group that called themselves "Nothing".

Nothing

That was their name, "Nothing", chosen I suppose in a self-deprecating way, and they had discussions on religion, theology, morals and ethics and rounded it off with a Mass. Peter was very religious about attending those "Nothing" meetings.'

Father Mark married Peter and Marilyn on May 29, 1983 and baptised their first son, Thomas. 'I couldn't baptise Michael,' he concluded. 'I was out in Peru at the time he was born.'

The Monk

Sheikh Hamdan bin Rashid al Maktoum, the Finance Minister of Dubai, is fond of swift horses and may his string increase. He bred Nashwan, a long-striding colt, who in a few months' time would win the Derby and capture the hearts of a nation. He also bought, for 100,000 gns, a strong, raw-boned yearling at the 1983 Ballsbridge Sales.

Even sheikhs make mistakes. The horse, which he named Rahib, was a flop on the flat. True to his name – it means 'the monk' in Arabic – he appeared to prefer meditation to battle. As a two-year-old and a three-year-old, the compact bay colt won none of his ten races. 'He was a big, beautiful thing but he just couldn't run. Very backward horse,' Peter Walwyn, his first trainer, told me and added, 'What's all your interest in Rahib? If you're writing a book about Scudamore, it must be a very long book.'

Rahib is a riches to rags story: one of the many well-bred, expensive horses with Arab names who fail as flat racers and, passing from hand to hopeful hand, stable to stable, finish their careers chasing National Hunt pin-money round the gaff courses of England and Wales. In the context of Scudamore's glittering season, he played a brief but bright part. Rahib, despite Peter Walwyn's lack of interest, seemed a proper horse to pursue.

Consider first Rahib's blood: not only was he one of the most expensive horses bought at that Ballsbridge sale, probably among the top 5 per cent, but he was by Final Straw, a super miler, who came second in the 2,000 Guineas. His dam, Head First, while nothing special, was thought worth the stab: dozens of Rahibs, after all, are worth one Nashwan.

The young colt was not only backward, as Walwyn suggested, he appeared to be going backwards over those first two seasons on the flat: in *Timeform* his 'rating' on speed deteriorated from 74 (moderate) to 67 (could do considerably better). He might one day make a modest mark as a stayer but he'd be no speed merchant. The sheikh lost interest in what in the catalogues was now called his 'big, rangy, quite attractive colt with plenty of scope.' Rahib was duly off-loaded at the Newmarket autumn sales of 1983.

In the lexicon of horse-racing, 'plenty of scope' is a sanguine expression, full of all kinds of promise, blinding speed not being one of them. At Newmarket he fetched 4,600 gns – 4.6 per cent of his original cost – and was cast down among the lowly 'plating class' flat runners. He continued to fail. In January 1986 at Huntingdon the Newmarket trainer, Derek Weeden, put him over hurdles for the first time. He was pulled up three out. 'He was a big, leggy horse,' recalled Weeden. 'He looked like he had the potential. What he wanted was time to make a chaser and his owner didn't have the time.'

Rahib, by now a gelding and less a monk than a mendicant, was once again put up for sale. This time it was at the Ascot December Sales in 1986. The bidding stopped at 625 gns, little more than what he would have commanded as dog-meat. The buyer, a small farmer-trainer from Leominster, Herefordshire didn't much like the look of the animal and he certainly didn't like the *Timeform* report: 'little to no ability.' What the farmer, John Price, did like was the pedigree. 'I once had a horse out of Head First,' he said later. 'He won a race.' So off went Rahib to the Welsh borders and yet another new yard. It held only two other horses.

How the mighty had fallen. The Final Straw dynasty – if that's the word for it – had petered out in a thin line of indifferent fillies and colts. Final Straw himself was gone. 'He now stands in Italy where, I'm told, he's thought to be the best stallion in the country,' says Tony Morris, the bloodstock expert. 'Which, I'm afraid, doesn't say much for the stallions in Italy.'

From his abysmal fall, Rahib finally rose – part of the way. In February 1987, now trained by Price, he won a race, a modest selling handicap hurdle at Stratford. Duly, he went on the market once again. 'I should have bought him back in,' recalls

Price, echoing laments down the ages. Instead, Dai Burchell, the trainer, got him for 2,600 gns, 'put him away for a few weeks' and then at Southwell, with his son, 'Little Dai' up, 'ran him second to one of Martin Pipe's horses which we could never have beaten anyway.' Finally, the fine hand of destiny had touched the gelding's withers.

Burchell liked the horse but, lacking an equestrian swimming pool, he saw problems ahead. 'I've only got fifteen, eighteen horses and if he broke down, well, I can't afford to be carrying an invalid,' recalled the affable Welshman. Rahib suffered from chronic leg trouble. 'What I mean is his tendons would always be firm, never puffy,' said Burchell, 'but red-hot.'

About those red-hot tendons, none in the yard worried more than Dianne Jones, his stable lass. 'Both his front legs were bad and we were always afraid he'd break down,' she later recalled. 'I used to hose his legs for hours. He'd love it. Then he would want to play. I'd give him a drink out of the hose-pipe and he'd snatch it out of my hand and squirt me back. Rahib was a great character.' To stable lasses, employed to handle the loving side of the business, horses are invariably 'great characters'.

They are also great eaters, and over this costly issue Burchell was in many minds: rest him or run him, sell him or keep him? The Welshman, a sorcerer who had taken his steel-plant redundancy money and put it into a training yard, is nothing if not resourceful: he attempted all four. He rested the horse, then chose a suitable race, a selling hurdle on soft-to-good ground, at Uttoxeter in April. Having thus planned to rest, run and sell the horse, he wanted to keep him. He was prepared to bid up to 2,500 gns to buy Rahib back.

However, there was another man at Uttoxeter that day, an elderly civil engineer from Lichfield named Jim Ashley, who in his day had owned four race horses but never a winner. He was prepared to go to 4,000 gns for a good-looking horse. He brought along a friend, Ted Barlow, a retired trainer who runs a local dairy farm, and was prepared to put his friend's horse out to grass.

Ashley and Barlow were keen on a couple of the horses that day. Ashley, apart from being a successful businessman, is four-square and charming, a grandfather with a flair for recalling all the cut and thrust of a race. 'It was a funny old race, this one of Rahib's. It was dominated by this old dodge-pot, starting and stopping, going out ahead by ten lengths and then coming back to the field,' Ashley later retold. 'Anyway, Rahib, a real honest horse, was always in the hunt and, about fifth from last, coming up the hill, he took it up and really started *galloping* . . . He won by six.'

Rahib had found a fan and, when Burchell dropped out of the bidding, an owner for 2,600 gns as well. 'We thought he had nice bone-structure and a kind face,' said Ashley. 'A good horse, nothing exceptional. Besides, my wife liked him, so I turned to her and said, "well, here we are, we wanted a horse and we've got one." '

Pipe, it came to pass, also had a horse running that day at Uttoxeter. He also had a subaltern in attendance and Ashley, discontented with local trainers, decided he'd put his with Pipe. The Somerset sorcerer was phoned and he accepted Rahib to the fifth yard of his little career. He was boxed up straightaway, and driven down to start yet another new life, this time in Somerset.

Burchell was regretful. 'I should have bought him back in,' he said.

Buck

Buck stuffs the damp towels into the drier, sets them tumbling, and returns to the weighing-room where on a big wooden table he unties his bundles of clean laundry. They contain socks, tee-shirts, jock straps, tights, britches, waterproof britches, gloves, mufflers, more towels. He holds up a pair of ragged underpants, once black, with yellow stripes across the bottom. 'Those belong to Allen Webb,' he says. 'He'll wear them until they fall off. He's worn them for years.'

Superstition is not a normal affliction among jockeys, Buck points out, although Brendan Powell and some of the other Irish boys pin St Christopher medals under their colours. Jamie Osborne wears Union Jack socks. 'The most superstitious jockey I've ever looked after was Graham Thorner,' he says, talking of the former champion rider, winner of the 1972 Grand National. 'He wouldn't ride in anything new. If he had a new saddle or a new pair of boots he'd find somebody else to ride in them first.'

Buck goes about his business. He unstraps bundles of boots, naming the owners of each pair as he slaps them onto two piles: one for the jockeys who will ride here at Kempton today, the second for those riding elsewhere whom he'll see at a later meeting. 'I know the boots. I clean them every day,' he says. 'Richard Dunwoody, he's here. Mark Pitman, he's at Towcester. Steve Smith Eccles, Towcester. There's Scu's. Peter Hobbs, a very long-legged bloke . . .'

The piles mount up. Buck pauses with a left boot in his hands. 'See that?' He lays it on the table and indicates a white smudge along the calf. 'Hywel's been hitting the rails. He gave me a

John Buckingham – valet supreme

bollocking when I couldn't get it off, but I can't get it off.' Buck smiles. 'He wasn't moaning, really.'

Buck is John Buckingham, the jockeys' 'val-et' – never say 'vallay' in racing – who with his brother Tom, at the moment at Towcester, looks after the riders on the tracks in the south of England. He travels from race meeting to race meeting in a red BMW, the back seat pulled out. In it, packed neatly, is the gear for about forty jockeys, spare boots and spare saddles, leather weight cloths and a boondoggle of breast-plates.

'I'd like to carry saddles for all of the boys, but I can't. I haven't got the room,' he says, now hanging Peter Scudamore's boots on the first hook above the bench along the wall. 'I'd like to have a less expensive car, too. But the BMW gives me peace of mind. When I set out from home at 6 o'clock in the morning, I know I'll get where I'm going. If my car broke down there would be no racing. Full stop.'

Scudamore is first in line of jockeys today because Smith Eccles, the one who usually occupies the pride of place, is injured and not racing. Buckingham determines the pecking-order, basing it on a blend of experience and achievement: Smith Eccles ('he's been in the game longest') and Scudamore are followed by Hywel Davies, Richard Rowe, Simon Sherwood and Dunwoody.

'Some of the young jockeys might come in the weighing-room and not like where I put them,' says Buckingham, moving down the row of hooks. 'They don't say anything but I can tell. And there is nothing they can do about it.'

Buckingham is the tough, compassionate, consummate valet. He rules his weighing-room, much as a chef rules his kitchen, although the term 'nanny' might be better employed. 'You have to look after them. Some of them have no idea of how to look after themselves,' he says and shakes his head. 'They take off their clothes and chuck them all over the place and expect me to pick it all up. Have a look-in after the last race. You'll see. Britches, boots, tights, under-shorts . . .'

The weighing-room suffers constant chaos, he says, but at no time quite like that between races, especially when there is a full field of jockeys. 'There is nothing worse than having seventeen saddles chucked on the table and you've got to find the one at the bottom for the next race,' he explains. 'Girths, pads, chamois hanging off. Then they start taking their colours off the wall. We've got to help sort out the saddles, get the boys dressed and get their weights ready – in a matter of seconds.

'Scu will sometimes come in, chuck his saddle on the table,' Buckingham goes on and his calm suggests the order he imposes on the weighing-room. 'I've got to get him ready for the scales, say 11 stone, and he's gone out and the Clerk of the Scales sends him back. 10 stone 13. Scu gives me a bollocking. Quite right, too.'

At times the weighing-room gets so clogged up with jockeys rushing about getting ready for the next race, Buckingham continues, that either he or his apprentice, Andy Townsend, goes out for help from the Clerk of the Scales. 'We tell him we're swamped and we need an "all-weigh",' says Buckingham. 'Usually they give it to us.' An 'all-weigh' is when the Clerk of the Scales exercises his right to demand that all riders, rather than the winning two and another randomly chosen, check their weights after a race. It slows down the flow of riders coming back to fling down saddles and seek out new silks and thus gives the valets a chance to get back on top of the job.

Buckingham hangs out the jockeys' socks, underpants, tights, all round the room, and then folds and rolls the large silk mufflers, tucking them neatly into the boots. 'I always put them in the left boot,' he says. 'My brother puts them in the right.' He folds one that Smith Eccles insists on getting: it is tatty and yellow with age.

The room is quiet, save for the slap-slap of his apprentice, Townsend, applying saddle soap to the piles of leather weight cloths. The cloths range from one pound to four pounds in weight, each with four leather pockets, one at the corner of each flap. Sheets of grey lead, about the thickness of cardboard, are piled near the scales; they will be slipped into the pockets to make up the handicap weights. 'If you wanted to load up poor Dessie,' says Townsend, talking of the great Desert Orchid, 'you'd put four pounds in each corner.'

One day Townsend will take over from Buckingham but, only 48, the master is still youthful and fit enough, though a good bit fleshier than he was on the day he and a horse named Foinavon left their prints in steeplechase history. Seldom does a day go by, says Buck, folding another white silk muffler into a triangle, without someone asking about the 1967 Grand National. I ask.

'A lot of people say how lucky I was and I tell them we all need a bit of luck in this world. I saw my chance and I took it.' There is a trace of bitterness in Buckingham's voice. 'And you've got to give Foinavon a lot of credit. He'd already galloped 3½ miles when we got to the pile-up.'

Buckingham has started his story in the middle. Perhaps, after twenty-two years, the race remains so embedded in his mind that the listener is expected to recall all the forerunning details. I had remembered the pile-up on television but, before seeing Buckingham, I'd needed to read up on the rest. It was one of the most chaotic Grand Nationals in history, due to a 'pile-up unprecedented in modern-day racing', as *A Race Apart: A History of the Grand National*, put it.

Foinavon had been the classic no-hoper. He had run dead-last the previous month in the Cheltenham Gold Cup and went off, with a dozen others, dead-last again in the betting at Aintree. He was 100-1. The odds looked about right from the outset, and Foinavon was settled in some thirty lengths behind as the leading pack crashed over Becher's Brook the last time round.

The next fence, the twenty-third, is the smallest on the course. It seemed to present no problems as the field thundered down on it. Suddenly, a loose horse swung across the front of the fence. A horse came down, then another. Soon, Balaclava set in.

'Incredible,' recalls Buckingham. 'Here I was galloping into a wall of horses. They were turning around, coming back at me, upside down in the fence. I weaved my way through in a canter and Foinavon sort of showjumped over the fence.' They won by fifteen lengths. Buck got paid no more than the £15 riding fee and the mandatory ten per cent of the owner's prize, which amounted to £1,763. As well as a silver cup, of course, which stands on a corner cupboard at his home in Chipping Warden, Oxfordshire.

Financially, he is doing better as a valet than he did as a jockey. He bills the jockeys through Weatherbys, the family business that administers much of racing, charging them £6.50 for one ride, £11.50 for two, £14.70 for three, £18 for four in a day. 'It's a nice enough living,' he says, 'but I'm not getting rich.' The job also has its over-riding satisfactions, he admitted, folding another muffler.

'It's being near to the boys,' he concludes. 'Imagine, in the next two hours, I'm going to have forty lads in here. Jockeys. I'll be talking to them and dressing them one minute and I'll be in the ambulance room trying to comfort them the next. They like me to be there. I can get off their boots. I can get off their clothes without cutting them off. It's a hard old game.'

From Riches to Rags
and Some of the Way Back Again

Nearly six months before our wintry car-ride to Fakenham, the 1988–89 National Hunt season had opened on 30 July, with an afternoon meeting at Newton Abbot and the racing public was buzzing . . . with talk about flat racing. It was mid-season and Pat Eddery had already kicked home 110 winners and on that afternoon, a Saturday, the northern horse Apache was fancied in the Chesterfield Cup at Glorious Goodwood.

Indeed, for weeks to come the jumpers, the poor cousins in the family of racing, would barely get a look-in. Even in the racing press that day, stories of the traditional curtain-raiser were driven to the inside pages. There are nevertheless those who love Newton Abbot, the shabby old race course down on the near side of nowhere; not least the jockeys who bring their families and girlfriends along to the seaside. It would be convenient. Jump racing over the next fortnight would be centred in Devon: Newton Abbot and, about twenty minutes away, Devon and Exeter.

In the close season, fifty-six days, he had ridden one day (and one winner) in Belgium. The family had spent a fortnight under blistering sun in Barbados, Peter playing a passable game of tennis and walking up and down, up and down, the beach. 'Peter's so *restless*,' recalled Marilyn. 'He can never sit down.' Back home, Scudamore's diary shows a good measure of domesticity:

July 5. *Sports Day, St Catherine's School, Chipping Camden.* The boys go to the local Catholic school. There were no Dads'

Rejected by the owner of Nashwan and Unfuwain, Rahib became the apple of Mr Ashley's eye and – eventually – a winner.

competitions that day but Tom, then 5, won the sack race and his team won the Cup. The boys have ponies, Flea and Tiggy. 'Daddy tells us how to keep our back straight,' reports Tom. 'He teaches us the names of the parts of the horses and how to hold the reins properly and he puts my legs in the right place.' Michael, 4, has little to add. He prefers to speak with his fists.

July 16. *Richard's Wedding.* West Tip, on which Richard Dunwoody won the Grand National in 1986, and Charter Party, which he rode to victory in the 1988 Cheltenham Gold Cup, were each led into the reception. Indeed, like all jockeys' lives, Dunwoody's touches racing at all points. His agent, Robert Kington, is Marilyn Scudamore's brother. His wife, Carol, is secretary to Michael Robinson, the Wantage trainer, and his father, George Dunwoody, was once a jockey and trainer in Northern Ireland. 'Peter and Marilyn gave us a silver tea spoon for a wedding present,' recalls Dunwoody. 'It had a horse on it.' Richard and Carol have a dog named Jonjo.

The week after the wedding the Scudamores, boys and all, had taken a house in the Devon countryside. Marilyn took the boys to the beach but for Peter the holidays were over. He wasn't saying a whole lot about his prospects for 1988–89. Certainly he wasn't letting his mind dwell on thoughts of a spectacular season. He'd done that a year ago, counted his chickens with Hywel Davies and Graham McCourt. They had reckoned, chiefly because of Pipe's strong yard of horses and some good ones with Charlie Brooks, that a Scudamore record-breaking season was 'on'.

What record? There was only one record: Jonjo's mark of 149 winners.

Those chickens, those 149 winners, were never to hatch. In midseason, just about on target, Scudamore had been called up for laying waste the young rider Bruce Dowling in a race, given a twenty-one-day vacation by the Jockey Club and finished the term with 129 winners. The Dowling incident, if not an example of brutal assault, illustrated a ruthless, some say almost psychotic, streak in the champion. I put the incident to him and, in recalling it, he preferred to see it as an example of the jump jockey's axiom: it's safer to be tougher.

'It was a novice hurdle with twenty-seven runners round Newbury and I had to find somewhere where I didn't get any trouble,' he explained. 'So I went down the inner and I found myself a nice run but when I swung off the bend he came up on my inside. If it had been Steve Smith Eccles or Richard Dunwoody they'd have shouted, "Scu, a bit of light" and I'd have said, "Yes" or "No", and if I said "No" and they kept coming they'd have got put out through the wing and have had to accept it.

'It was a shock suddenly seeing Bruce there and, with the cross-fence coming up and no running rail, somebody could have got killed. It was no use saying "Excuse me, I'd rather you didn't go there," so I positively threatened him.' The riders clashed. Dowling's horse fell at the next fence. The Jockey Club found both riders guilty of causing interference by reckless riding and suspended each for three weeks. 'In the weighing-room he said he was sorry and I accepted it,' Scudamore concluded.

Anyway, out of action, Peter's 129 winners had still been enough for another jockeys' championship title but well short of Jonjo's record. This season, he decided, would be pursued under mega-control: one race at a time.

In Devon, Scudamore kept fit by running along the back

country lanes. He never, even at the heights of summer indul-
gence, allows himself to get seriously overweight. Yet now he
had a half-stone to shed. 'The strange thing about running
round these lanes,' he said, 'is that while it's good for the weight
and the heart and the lungs it doesn't get you fit for race-riding,
nor does riding work.' Only one thing gets you fit for race-riding:
race-riding.

Also, and due partly to the running, he could pick up the
jockey's sure warning that his shape was still wrong: his racing
boots were tight at the tops of the calves. This tell-tale tightness
was not the fault of the boots. They were already nicely worn-in:
it is a measure of Scudamore's meticulous foresight that he'll
start breaking-in new boots and saddles near the end of the
previous season, when his body is still as tough as teak.

Peter was commuting daily from Newton Abbot to Pipe's
yard, forty-five minutes up the M5. Pipe, equally meticulous,
eager for an early-season strike of winners while other trainers
had hardly progressed beyond roadwork, had prepared sixteen
horses for the forthcoming hard-ground or, to put it more gently,
'top-of-the-ground' weeks of the season.

Pipe's programme caused Scudamore no conflict in commitment. 'When you're ready Charlie, give me a call,' he had said to
his Lambourn trainer but Charlie didn't give him a call. Charlie
was bringing on his horses slowly. 'Fred Winter taught me that
no horse likes hard ground,' was his inherited view, 'although
some of them stand up to it better than others.' Other inheri-
tances from the legendary Fred were the owners. 'If an owner
came to me and said, "I've got ten horses for you and I'd like
them ready for August," I'd say, "marvellous," ' said Brooks.

A top-of-the-ground horse, chiefly, is one with the long,
rhythmic reach to its stride, a horse, as Pipe will say, 'that
doesn't waste time in the air.' In contrast, a soft-ground horse
will probably move with more upright, concussive, digging
action suited to the softer ground of mid-season. 'Anyway,
that's the accepted theory,' Pipe will say with a wily little shrug.
Accepted theories, feels the former Taunton bookmaker, are
first to be tested and proven.

Scudamore finds Pipe's sceptical view of racing dogma re-
freshing and in July trainer and jockey worked together. They
bumped up and down the Pond House Farm gallops in a Range

Rover, watching the actions of horses ridden by the stable staff. What had all this gait-study meant? I later asked Pipe. 'I honestly don't know,' he replied slowly, going through the files in his mind. 'But it must have meant something.'

One horse that didn't waste time in the air and liked running on top-of-the-ground was Jim Ashley's Rahib. The gelding had now been with Pipe for just over a year, and although he had spent a considerable part of that time turned out to grass in Staffordshire on account of those all-too-fallible legs, he had also tasted some success. He would never receive the adulation of the racing public like Sheikh Hamdan's Nashwan, but under Pipe's tutelage – indeed only three weeks after joining him and running for Ashley for the first time – he had won a two miles five furlong hurdle race at Ludlow, chopping 25.5 seconds off the course record in the process.

'Rahib won a race for me,' recalled Ashley and, nearly a year later, he could see you through it, flight by flight. 'It didn't matter that he set a course record. You're so excited, you're so elated. The feeling never repeats itself.'

He injured himself later in a fall at Devon, but now he was fit again after ten months at home nibbling apples, taking carrots from the flat, open hands of his owner's small grand-children. The job now was to restore Rahib's confidence over small obstacles, then bigger ones.

'The first biggish fence he jumped in July,' Scu later recalled. 'He was reluctant, stiff, careful – *atrocious*. Alongside other horses, it was rather like you jumping upsides Ed Moses.'

The next session with the hesitant horse: magic. 'Rahib put his act together remarkably quickly,' said Scudamore. 'But then, horses never fail to astound me.' Pipe studied the list of early declarations. His form man pondered the form books. The going would be, without doubt, 'good to firm': the exact same ground the horse enjoyed when setting that speed record at Ludlow. Rahib was entered in the Dimplex Tango Handicap Chase, the 2:15 at Newton Abbot: first race 1988–89 meeting.

On the day of the race, the animal was checked, double-checked by the vet in the yard. His blood-picture was spot-on and his weight right for the distance: 1,032 lbs, a full 13.2 lbs trimmer than he was at Ludlow. With two other runners, Rahib was loaded into the horsebox. 'Everything's A-1,' said Pipe and he added a sentence we were so often to hear through the season. 'We're quietly confident.'

All of Devonshire, including the beaches and caravan sites, appeared to empty for the meeting. The race course, as on all such occasions, was crowded. A brass band tootled away near the paddock. Racegoers, passing through the gates, got fresh carnations when they plunked coins into the Injured Jockeys' Fund buckets. Bookmakers, guided by no recent form, save the odd summer flat race, arrived at uncertain odds. Rahib was made 10-11 favourite.

In the weighing-room, the jockeys slung down their bags. A camaraderie exists among jump jockeys, probably deeper than in any other sport, partly due to its residual amateurism, partly to its modest earning potential but mostly due to the dangers they share. The gang was there, or at least most of it: Steve Smith Eccles, Simon Sherwood, Brendan Powell, Paul Croucher, Hywel Davies, Lorna Vincent, Penny Ffitch-Heyes. The valet John Buckingham was hanging the colours for the first race over the bench place of each jockey. Among the missing was Dunwoody, a regular rider in the South West. He would phone down for results as he drove to the evening meeting at Market Rasen.

The women jockeys, banished to their own weighing-room up a rickety flight of stairs, came down for their bits of lead and to try out their weights on the weighing-room scales. They took no notice of the naked men round them. They ignored the obscenely decorated T-shirt, a tattered talisman, worn season after season by Steve Smith Eccles.

Scudamore is always amused by the presence of women in the British weighing-room. Here we are in the Age of Feminism, he feels, and yet for a man to wander into *their* changing-room would be ill-mannered. 'You ought to see it in Belgium,' said Hywel, pulling off his street shoes. 'I have,' said Scudamore. 'You ought to see it in Norway.'

On their minds, unspoken, loomed the prospect of forty-three weeks of riding ahead. There would be the mud and the snow and the cold, the awful white cold that stiffens your fingers and, after a sauna, lightens your head and sears like a poker down through your lungs as you ride. There would be the falls and the tongue-biting moments with owners. There would be the Mondays at Southwell.

Oddly enough, Scudamore, the champion, did not relish the prospect of the season. He was overwhelmed by it. Every year he was struck by the same feeling. 'Before the first race, you just sit there and want to get the season through and over with,' he said. 'It's like a big mountain of stone out there and all you've got is a chisel to chip it away.'

On the other hand, there would be the rhythms of riding a winner and the thrill of the run to the post, that drug that Scudamore would speak of later. Yet now it seemed to Scudamore, who's been at the game a dozen years, that the richest rewards in a season were to be found away from the track. 'I think the two loveliest moments come when you're schooling a horse and it jumps well, really well, and you think it will win,' he said. 'And then you go back down for your cup of coffee.'

Scudamore also thought about his horses. Would Celtic Shot be ready for the Champion Hurdle? What about Beau Ranger? What about this big fellow called Chatam? Would Strands of Gold, a bit of a day-dreamer, land on his feet over Becher's this time? 'You think about these horses,' he said, '– and they never work out as you think.'

Above their heads, the racing from Goodwood was on television. It lay there like wallpaper. The riders mostly ignored it. Flat racing isn't their game. Jump jockeys may occasionally work on a flat horse for the yard that engages them or, watching a race on the box, they may make a mental note of a horse that could come their way as a hurdler. Otherwise, and surprisingly, the two kinds of jockeys feel little in common.

'They're little shiny rats and I hate them,' John Francome once said in jest of the flat jockeys but, in truth, the two kinds of riders are basically cut from different bolts of cloth: nub-silk and sack-cloth. I was put in mind again of Brough Scott's differentiation between jockey and horseman.

Scudamore picked up the contrast. 'They ride with much more finesse than the jumping boys,' he said, 'but the only thing we envy about them is the money they make and the safe conditions they work under.' Peter nonetheless feels an affinity with Pat Eddery, champion on the flip-side of the sport. In a way, they come from the same jockeys' school. Eddery was an apprentice as a flat rider to the late Frenchie Nicholson while Scudamore, in his formative years, was with Frenchie's son, David Nicholson.

'Whenever I watch Pat Eddery, I remember David telling me that his father always used to say to his flat jockeys: "you've got nothing to sell but your style,"' said Peter, 'and Eddery has style, whatever crap people say about him bouncing round in the saddle. That's only at the finish and he finishes like Piggott.' Piggott, to the boy Scudamore, was the greatest of idols.

Then, of course, there is the likeable Ray Cochrane. He was once one of them. He was a jump jockey. The cheeky Smith Eccles later summed up the issue in this way: 'Ray's one of the nicest chaps you'd ever wish to meet. He understands racing a little bit better than the others on the flat. He's jumped.'

The topic of money was raised. The jockeys had got a pay rise: up 5 per cent to £56.70 a ride. They discussed a new regulation: the compulsory use of a body protector. The riders were to be penalised, in effect, for wearing the protector: the Jockey Club was making no allowance for the twelve ounces that it added to their racing weights. This was serious, especially at the outset of the season, especially at Newton Abbot which has no sauna.

Suddenly it was race time. 'One piece,' wished someone to no one and everyone, spinning his whip as he rose. 'One piece.' The jockeys filed out of the weighing-rooms looking small, pristeen – their white britches loose round their bottoms. 'One piece . . . One piece . . .'

The Clerk of the Scales, Charles Stebbings, weighed-in the jockeys for the first race: two riders came in overweight, one by two pounds. For Scudamore 10 st 12 lbs was no sweat. In the paddock, Pipe gave his instructions, his call words that would ring down through the season: 'Be handy. Get him jumping. Make all.'

Peter, as usual, took his time settling down his horse and, as usual, he was last man down to the start. He circled, dropped his head and prayed. Scudamore is devout and he speaks of his religion with none of the born-again fervour of the American sportsman. 'I'm devout,' is the way he puts it, 'but not as devout as I should be.

'Down at the start of a race I'm probably closer to God than at any other point in my life. That day at Newton Abbot I didn't pray that Rahib might win. I didn't pray for a record season because God's not worried about the 2:10 at Newton Abbot or, for that matter, horse-racing. I prayed we'd all get round the course in one piece.'

They broke. The 1988–89 National Hunt season was under way. Its opening two minutes looked bad for the champion. Rahib wasn't handy. He wasn't jumping. He certainly wasn't making all. His owner, Jim Ashley, was in the stands and many months later he could still give a fair account of the race, spieling it off with the enthusiasm of a North Country Peter O'Sullevan.

'He joomped out real slow,' said Ashley in his rich, Black Country accent, 'and he was making no headway at all until he began to rally. Second from last he was in with a squeak. Going over the last, Scoody all of a sudden set him alight and he powered past them all and he snatched it on the line.'

Rahib won by a short head from Celtic Crackle, which was ridden by the jockey who had weighed-in two pounds too heavy. The excessive baggage – in theory, one pound avoirdupois is worth a length in distance – may have cost the other rider the race. 'Was this the first race lost through the Jockey Club not allowing a pound for the new compulsory back protector?' speculated Steve Taylor in *The Sporting Life*. Who knows? In different circumstances Scudamore may have judged his race differently.

At the end of the race Scudamore was sore in the back and the thighs, and then, suddenly alert to Rahib's discomfort, he pulled up and quickly dismounted. If it had been Peter's first race of the season, it was Rahib's last. Those front tendons were warm and sore. Once more he was sent north to pasture. Still only 6, he would be back late in the 1989–90 season.

The champion jockey did not win on either of his two other mounts that day. Still, nobody else scored a double at Newton Abbot nor at Market Rasen that evening. One race into the new term and Scudamore had taken his place at the top of the class. What's more, it was a Saturday victory. 'The best day to win on is Saturday,' he said afterwards. 'Because you've always got Sunday to think about it.'

*   *   *

On Monday, again at Newton Abbot, Scudamore was subject to a not uncommon trial in the life of a jump jockey: the stewards' inquiry. It came after he finished seventh on a Pipe horse, My Cup of Tea, third favourite in a hurdle race. He weighed out and was called into the stewards' room, together with Pipe. 'The stewards were sitting down at a table and we had to stand up in front of them,' Scudamore said, describing the ritual hearing, 'and right away I felt like a naughty boy. At those inquiries, you're presumed guilty until you prove yourself innocent.'

Why, he and Pipe were asked, was My Cup of Tea so 'tenderly ridden'? The implication being, of course, that the horse was 'hooked up', that is, not allowed to run at his best. Scudamore explained that the horse was pulling and 'diving at the hurdles', and by the back straight was out of the race. 'My Cup of Tea is a bit frightening to ride,' he said afterwards, 'and there comes a time in a race when your chance is gone, that you try to get home in one piece.'

The explanation was 'recorded', accepted but not beyond doubt. Scudamore felt angry, humiliated over the decision. He felt the stewards may have been influenced by the widely-held notion that all of Pipe's horses make all of the running and when one doesn't there is something amiss. In fact, most frequently, My Cup of Tea's race plan has been to 'drop in' and come on late in the race. 'The stewards,' Peter said, 'were perfectly entitled to call us in with that result but, equally, we were perfectly entitled to expect them to know the horse. Surely, that's their job.'

Scudamore would like better-informed stewards but, unlike many jockeys, does not favour a panel of circuit professionals. 'I've seen it in Australia,' he said, 'and I'm against it.' He feels that professional stewards, watching races from day to day, might grow to bear grudges against particular jockeys. 'Some jockeys,' he says, 'would be marked out to be got at before they did anything wrong.'

But back to the matter of winning. 'It's always good to get off the mark first ball,' Scudamore said of that first win, at Newton Abbot, and to retain the cricketing metaphor, he quickly played himself in. A fortnight later, he was in full flow and on 11 August, he raised his total of winners to 11 by hitting a 'four', again at Newton Abbot. Perhaps oddly, only once all season would he win four races in a day and, less oddly, he'd remember the disaster that nearly happened. It took place in the third race, a low-grade Novices' Hurdle with £950 to the winner.

Scudamore rode Hi-Hannah, a three-year-old filly. She was the favourite – 8-13 – and a Pipe horse and Scudamore leapt out into the lead. In his dust trailed Boca Chimes who swerved and fell at the first flight, bringing down another horse, Omyword. The two horses milled about, uncaught, as the field circled the racecourse. Over the last flight, eighty yards from the post, Scudamore glanced back. He was well clear and, as the video-tape shows, blissfully unaware of what was coming straight at him.

It was the two loose horses. A loose horse is unpredictable. Once its rider is unseated, it will usually gallop on with the other horses or, at best, run out at the first curve. It may turn round and bolt back towards the stables. *Two* of them, a ton-and-one-half, coming at you in a fast, swirling gallop is a serious matter. Especially so when you're not looking. Peter finally glanced up. There was only one way to swerve, away from the rail. He did and only by a split-second, a dozen yards, did he miss the collision. 'She's a sharp little filly,' he said, 'and it was easy to manoeuvre around them.'

Jimmy Frost, a local jockey, took the incident less lightly. Frost, who would have a famous encounter with a loose horse later in the season in the Grand National, criticised the race-course. By its nature, and with the River Teign running beside it, Newton Abbot has no escapes through gaps in the rails for loose horses.

Frost suggested that British courses, like those in New Zealand, might provide mounted stewards to round up such dread-noughts. It fell on deaf Jockey Club ears. Scudamore wasn't surprised. 'It's an interesting proposition, maybe impractical, but it might save a life,' he said. 'Why don't they look into it? Because New Zealand did it first?'

(The matter was to rise and sink again when in May the luckless Neale Doughty was bowled over and knocked out of racing for six months by an oncoming horse at Sedgefield.)

Scudamore had not stayed for the 4:40 race that afternoon but he was aware of the field. A horse called Arbitrage was running and the name caused him to reflect briefly back to January when, at Newbury, he was fined £300 for pulling the horse up. He was accused of not making sufficient effort. The charge, he felt, was nonsense. But it still rankled and as he left the Newton Abbot weighing-room he stopped to pass along a small joke with Paul Croucher, who would ride Arbitrage that day. 'Give him a good ride,' said Scudamore, 'but don't win by too far.'

Those were the last words he would ever say to the young jockey. The next morning Scudamore was awakened at home by a telephone call from Simon Sherwood. Croucher had been killed in the early hours of the morning in a car crash on the road out of Lambourn.

The tragedy of Croucher's death devastated racing. It cast a pall over Lambourn, the heart-land of National Hunt training, and robbed the new season of its innocence. Still, the races came and went and the winners kept going in for Scudamore.

On 24 August, it was time for Charlie Brooks to have his first runner – the 11-year-old former point-to-pointer Chalk Pit. Brooks had now formally taken over from Fred Winter, who was too ill after a fall ever to be Master of Uplands, in Lambourn, again. Chalk Pit ran in a novices' chase at Devon and Exeter and Peter helped get the young trainer off the mark 'first ball'. It was the career first National Hunt victory for both Chalk Pit and Charlie.

A glow of pleasure settled over Uplands. There could hardly have been a more marvellous start to the season. It lasted just five days. The young Irish man Vivian Kennedy, attached to the yard as its 'conditional jockey' took a horrific fall at Huntingdon. In hospital later he was declared 'brain dead' and his life-support machine was switched off.

Kennedy was one of the nicest and most gifted young men in the game, known even to some people outside it through a radio programme that veteran commentator Lord Oaksey had made about him. His death was a terrible and unwanted reminder of the dangers of the sport. At the end of this bitter-sweet month, Peter had ridden twenty-two winners.

Uplands

It was another accident, this one off the racetrack, that put Charlie Brooks into the position of being one of Peter Scudamore's principal employers.

Anybody in Lambourn will tell you how to find Uplands, Fred Winter's place. You take the road towards the gallops, turn down a lane of oak trees, and there it is, up on the left. You're greeted by a labrador, a going-away gift from John Francome to the guv'nor. A terrier appears, tail quivering, and starts a game of fetching a stick when you throw it. A mare, led by a lad, clatters over the cobblestones with that slow, slumping stride that belies all her power. The lad says, 'morning'. The greeting is more a nod than a word.

Uplands should be no different from any yard where they train race horses but when you visit there for the first time, as I did in the middle of October, you sense a sadness hanging over the place.

Fred Winter is somewhere in the house, ill. I never met the stricken man, sixty-three years old, nor did I see him ride. Yet the legend suffuses the yard. On the office walls are framed photographs: Winter, the jockey, astride Kilmore, winner of the 1962 Grand National; astride Mandarin, who the same year took the Cheltenham Gold Cup; Winter, the trainer, with Jay Trump and Anglo, winners of the National in 1965 and 1966. A charcoal portrait of the stern man, eyes radiant through wrinkles, looks out over the desk.

At the desk, now running the yard, sat Winter's former assistant, an Old Etonian named Charlie Brooks. Brooks has been responsible effectively for the training of horses at Uplands

51

The young master of Uplands, Charlie Brooks, with his most famous charge, Celtic Shot.

since Winter suffered head injuries two years ago in a fall. Brooks spoke of the accident that flung him, seemingly unprepared, into one of the most lime-lit jobs in the sport.

It happened early in September, 1987. 'We'd been at Stratford that day,' Brooks recalled. 'We'd had our first runner of the season and he was on brilliant form, considering we'd just had a horse beaten which perhaps should have won. Considering, too –' and he smiled, 'that I rode a horse which ran appallingly badly. I remember driving home, wishing the guv'nor was on such good form all of the time, and next thing the phone's going in the morning. "There's been an accident. Better get back here as soon as possible." Mr Winter was in a coma . . . To be honest, I've never been able to discuss the horses with him from that day onwards.'

Winter left Brooks a string of horses and a legacy of self-reliance. 'He was a marvellous man for giving you a bit of rope to hang yourself,' said Brooks. 'When he went on holiday in the middle of the season he wouldn't leave instructions. He'd say he didn't know what the ground was going to be like, or the opposition, so consult with the head lad and get on with it. Once, on the day he got back, we had three winners and one beaten by a head.'

Brooks is tougher than his boyish looks might suggest. He was a footballer at Eton, a fair goalkeeper, and he likes to tell the story that on leaving school he was turned down in the same week by Watford and Winter. 'I was too short for a keeper,' he said, 'and too tall for a jockey.'

He rode as an amateur, though, and had a dozen winners under rules in the 1985–86 season. He was then the assistant to Winter, having worked up from stable lad and now, at 25, he dutifully wears his uniform, the trilby, with a touch of unease at the races. He prefers, he says, working with the horses in the yard, or on the gallops. It is no easy job, whatever one's background, to follow Fred Winter. What's more, as though a gentle reminder of his obligations, Brooks can look one field away and see a thatched barn in the legendary Fulke Walwyn's yard.

'This idea of living up to a reputation doesn't worry me at all,' he said, and he looked like he meant it, 'not in the slightest. I'm not going to achieve the same things as Mr Winter achieved but maybe I will in some areas he didn't. The only pressure I'm feeling is that the horses do well enough not to be taken away.'

At the end of the season, no horses had been taken away, but right now it was in the middle of October and although Scudamore was moving along like a train, approaching his 50th winner, he had ridden only three for Brooks. They were all on the same horse: the 11-year-old gelding called Chalk Pit. 'Mr Winter would tell you everything if you asked him, but otherwise he would never tell you anything. That's why he was a good teacher. He gave one responsibility. It was up to you to observe him, and learn, and I suppose the basic thing I learnt was that every horse needs a different amount of work. For example, if you've got a nervous horse, inclined to do too much work, you'll soon burn him up if you send him out with twenty other horses.

'Chalk Pit was a very, very nervous, wired-up horse and he'd get over-excited when other horses were around. He'd lose his concentration. So he had to be schooled by himself,' said his trainer. 'What's interesting is that someone like Peter, who is basically so wired-up and unrelaxed himself, could get the horse to relax. But he did. No rushing, no crashing about, as soon as he sat on him. If I was a horse, honestly I'd like to be ridden by Peter.' And the horse seemed to agree.

What other qualities did Peter bring?

'He's strong. He can really pick up a tiring horse. Another thing I like about him is that he doesn't use his stick much. He never knocks a horse about. This season there's not one horse that'd come back with a weal mark on it. Not *one* horse. To be honest with you, a lot of this business about jockeys getting criticised about using the stick too much . . . to me, it's the trainers who ought to get criticised, not the jockeys. I can say give the horse one crack, maybe two, no more. Then where Peter is especially good is that when he gets down off a horse he'll tell you exactly what he thinks and how it's doing.'

At the beginning of the season, a contract was signed with Scudamore. Its conditions were similar to those David Nicholson devised and offered Scu years ago, similar to those the champion jockey had previously agreed with Winter at Uplands. If perhaps unique among jockeys, the contract is decidedly *laissez-faire*, placing the burden of winning squarely on Scudamore.

The champion, regardless of the time he spends in the yard, gets no retainer whatever, no salary, no work-riding or schooling fees. 'It's in Peter's interest to spend time with the horses,' said Brooks with a smile. 'Otherwise, it would be like saying I'll drive your car in the Grand Prix but I won't come round and get the thing fixed beforehand.'

In return, the contract doesn't tie him down. 'Mr Winter's contracts with Peter never stipulated that he must ride a horse when requested to do so,' said Brooks, 'and my contract with Peter says exactly the same thing. It deals only with the percentages of winnings that Peter gets from the owners.'

Peter's percentages of winnings, to be sure, exceed the mandatory, if approximate, 7.5 per cent for first place and about 2 per cent for second. Still, his is no lazy man's contract: his income, which would climb to well above £80,000 before this season was out, depends hugely on riding winners. 'I don't know any other jockey who's got quite the same contract,' said Scudamore, now thinking ahead to the first big races on the National Hunt calendar. 'But that's the way I like to work.'

Under his care, Brooks had forty-five horses. Among them was the stable star, Celtic Shot, winner of the 1988 Champion Hurdle at Cheltenham. Peter's first major Festival winner, Celtic Shot had been on holiday through the summer, at pasture at the home of his owner, David Horton, near Stratford-upon-Avon. Scudamore found the 7-year-old had matured, relaxed with his rest. He was fond of the horse and its owner but had mixed feelings as he began to work with the champion.

'He's too precious, because of what he has done and, with a horse like that, you're always a little worried that something might go wrong,' he said, thinking of the 7-year-old gelding striking himself, damaging a tendon, even falling and breaking a leg or a shoulder. 'It spoils the pleasure of riding him. It's always a relief to get off.'

Brooks, a realist, had recently taken a crucial decision. He had begun to 'fax' his proposed race entries to Martin Pipe, putting an asterisk beside the horses he particularly wanted Scudamore to ride. This step was taken to avoid conflicts between the two trainers in the use of Scudamore as a jockey. If their plans were known far enough in advance, went the theory, other suitable races might be found at another date for the horses.

Does Martin fax back? 'No,' laughed Brooks. 'He hasn't got a fax machine big enough to hold all his entries.' More seriously, he cited examples when Pipe had passed over races to accommodate his own plans.

'It hasn't always worked out but, to be honest with you, if I hadn't been flexible,' said the young trainer, 'I'd have forced Peter into a position whereby he would have had to say "sorry" but he couldn't ride for me any longer. I understand this. Peter doesn't want to ride one horse at Uttoxeter when he could ride four likely winners at Ludlow and if an owner insists on my using Peter, that's my problem, not Peter's. The thing is, everybody's determined it can't work. Apart from the three of us.'

Brooks has training in the blood. His father was a trainer, and in Winter and now Scudamore, he has been able to draw upon the experience of two of the all-time greats of the winter game. But still – and you feel they would both heartily approve of this – he remains very much his own man.

Faint Hearts

Through September and into October, Peter was mostly riding lesser-known horses on lesser-known courses. The racing Press, now in the dying days of the flat season, set Scudamore a target: 'Scu closes in on the fastest 50 in history.'

Scudamore was wary of the target. He considered such a small milestone to be synthetic, a Press concoction to coax readers back to a diet of National Hunt racing, which in part, at least, was true. For all that, the challenge to Scudamore was piquant: the great John Francome, the king before him, had reached his record half-century on 10 November, 1984. It was on 20 October, with twenty days in hand to catch Francome, that I joined Scudamore at the pretty little Uttoxeter race course in Staffordshire.

Peter then had 48 winners. I stayed with him from Thursday through Saturday and in that time he had no winners in three rides at Uttoxeter, none in two at haughty Newbury and one in three at seedy Stratford-upon-Avon although, in the 1:40, a novices' chase, his horse looked a winner until it fell at the last. 'I counted my chickens too soon,' he said. The next day the headline over my story in *The Sunday Times* read: 'Scudamore: a forty-niner still chasing the nugget.'

Scu may not have ridden any winners, but my observation of him had been far from fruitless.

The incident that remained vividly in my mind was Scudamore, not riding, but sizing up a horse he saw for the first time in his life. It was at Uttoxeter. The race was a novices' hurdle over two miles and the form of the horse, previously a flat racer, was poor: P-P-0, meaning pulled-up, pulled-up and nowhere. 'What

I didn't want to find in the paddock,' he said later, 'was something standing on its hind legs, breathing fire.'

The horse he found was not breathing fire. He was a small 5-year-old chestnut bay gelding, leggy and a bit weedy, but compact. I don't dislike your confirmation, thought Scudamore, but do you like jumping? The animal held its head high and was looking at things outside the paddock. He was unsure of himself. I'm going to have to find you a bit of hope, thought Scudamore, build up your confidence.

The trainer wasn't there. The stable lass, holding the horse, said he pulled hard, took a strong grip. She need not have spoken. The Australian nose-band, a strip of orange down the front of his face, meant to keep the bit high in his mouth, told it all. He's the kind of horse who'll try to go faster than I want him to go, thought Scudamore, he'll get flat, if I don't watch it, and hit the hurdles hard. I'm going to have to kid that horse. He gave him a slap on the neck: you're a stronger character, little fellow, than you think you are.

In the race, delayed for about a minute by the skittish horse, Peter nursed him round, kept him away from the other runners. The tape dropped and by pure will and by pushing and shoving in the saddle Peter moved into second place three fences from home. At that point, Peter played his one card. He hit him lightly on the shoulder. 'That showed up everything,' Peter said later. 'Instead of making him go faster, that little slap made him realise, "I'm trying my best and it hurts. I can't do it." He gave up.'

Scudamore has given plenty of thought to this kind of horse. A timid horse will carry his head high. When you put him under pressure he'll throw his head back and try to get out of it. 'On the other hand,' Scudamore said, 'a horse that carries its head low will usually, not always but usually, jump well because he knows where he's going. My father pointed this out to me years ago.'

If you show a whip to a horse and he looks at it, don't bother using it. The horse won't take it. On the run to the finish line, Peter said, don't lift your stick too high. It will unbalance the horse. He had worked this out as a young jockey, written it down in a notebook.

Unfortunately, during those first three days together, from

Uttoxeter to Stratford, he had not been able to make much use of the whip tip. The winners weren't coming. He was growing frustrated and whether the record concerned him or not, pressure was building. Things were becoming, as his wife had said over the phone: 'harrowing'.

Peter was no stranger to pressure, not after all these years in the saddle, but the search for winners was getting to him. He had said something to me in his car – it was dusk, August 12, I remember, on the A38 west of Derby – that struck me as a cry of poetical panic. 'Why was I riding today at Uttoxeter? I could have been at Taunton,' he said. 'Why am I going to Newbury? I could be at Ludlow.'

Scudamore rode his next big winner for Brooks. It was on the Monday, 24 October, after I left him at Stratford when, aboard a handsome gelding named Wolfhangar, Peter won the Garfunkel Novices' Chase at Fakenham. He won it after surviving another stewards' inquiry – barging, this time – to beat Francome's fastest-50 record by sixteen days.

Otherwise, there was a passing moment of anxiety at Uplands. What Scudamore had feared had happened. Celtic Shot was hurt while he schooled him. It was not noticed at the time but the next morning he was found to have knocked his check ligament, the short ligament behind the knee. The horse had probably struck into himself with the other hoof, causing a minor, commonplace injury but one that required rest. There would be plenty of time, plenty of races before March, when he defended his Champion Hurdle title at Cheltenham.

Beau Ranger

It is 26 June, 1981, the day of the Ballsbridge Tattersall Derby Sale in Dublin. The foremost sale of National Hunt horses in the British Isles, it lists 257 animals in its catalogue this year. Lot no. 196 is a three-year-old chestnut gelding. He wears a big blaze and three white socks, one of them dribbling like spilled milk down a foreleg.

His pedigree is good, perhaps very good, but unproven. By Beau Chapeau, a useful Irish flat racer and hurdler, now dead, lot no. 196 is the 'first produce' of Sand Martin, a promising brood mare, in a marriage arranged by a breeder named Con Brosnan, from County Cork. Brosnan is unburdened by fancy notions of genetic engineering, either arcane or scientific. He goes straight in, so to speak, and when his Sand Martin broke down there was nothing to do but to breed from her.

'Beau Chapeau was a good hoss, standing maybe thirty miles down the road, and I liked him,' he explains simply. 'So when she met with an accident I had her covered.' It cost him 400 punts in stud fees.

The result of this union, a 'tidy little hoss' in Brosnan's view, now comes into the Dublin sales ring. He is given the swift eye by Ted Walsh, the polymath of Irish racing: owner, buyer, commentator and top amateur jockey. The horse looks athletic enough, thinks Walsh, but he may be a bit 'shallow through', which in short means he might not stand up to the punishing strain of jump racing. He also looks smallish at just under 16 hands high. What is more, in Walsh's opinion, he may be slightly too 'straight in front', that is, his forelegs are not shaped to absorb shock and he may lack the shoulder room to reach out.

'I've got a bit of a soft spot for Beau Chapeau horses,' Walsh says afterwards, 'but this one wasn't quite right. I thought he might just win a bumper and go on to win a couple of hurdle races. But he didn't strike me as a three-mile chaser. He wasn't going to carry 12-stone round Cheltenham and win.'

This judgement is not wholly shared by Patrick Hogan, a beef farmer and small-scale horse dealer in from Tipperary. Hogan – not to be confused with *the* Pat Hogan, the Limerick man – was to admit that his bullish judgement may have been impaired by frustration. 'I'd come to Dublin to buy a horse for my cousin and, to tell you the truth, I was near the end of my tether,' he says later. 'Then I saw this honest little horse being led round . . .'

Hogan watches him. Hogan glances for the hundredth time at the pedigree in the catalogue. He sets much store by the dam. Sand Martin may have had no noticeable track record, either on the level or over sticks, but her paternal half-brother is Rag Trade, who in 1976 set Irish eyes asmiling when he narrowly beat Red Rum in the Grand National. Their sire, crucially, was Menelek. The name Menelek rings with awe round Irish breeding circles.

Indeed, the record of the venerated stallion, who died at the age of 22 in 1979, goes some way in explaining how fine jumping blood differs from fine flat-racing blood: winner of only one goodish race, the Warren Stakes at Goodwood in 1960, Menelek was chiefly a 'stayer', which is to say, what he lacked in pure turn of foot, he more than made up in the stamina and athleticism required of National Hunt horses. He also possessed the gift of passing his virtues to his off-spring.

Lot no. 196 moves well round the ring. Hogan is surprised at what little interest he arouses but, after all, it is late in the day and the trade has gone sluggish. 'Nobody much liked him,' he says much later, 'and I could tell by the auctioneer that, believe it or not, I was the only customer for him.'

Brosnan hopes the bidding for his horse will reach five to six thousand guineas – horses, like fine antiques, are still knocked down in guineas. Such hopes soon expire. Hogan gets the gelding for 2,800 gns. 'I couldn't have bought *anything* for the same money that day,' he was later to recall. 'I was fond of the horse when I bought him but I was actually more fond of him when I got him home.'

Home to Beau Ranger – Hogan's cousin so names him, 'for no particular reason' – is one of six white-washed boxes at a neat little yard near the village of Toomevara in Tipperary. He is backed by a nearby farmer, schooled and the following spring taken to Limerick Junction where he is ridden in his first race. It is a 'bumper'.

The bumper is a two-mile flat race for young horses, a showplace for future hurdlers and steeplechasers which is popular in Ireland. Beau Ranger wins his race easily and returns to Toomevara where a week later two groups of buyers visit from England. The first is the trainer David Gandolfo. He is not overly impressed by Beau Ranger. He looks like a greyhound, the trainer thinks, he'll never jump fences. Gandolfo returns home to Oxfordshire.

Meanwhile, the Taunton car dealer Peter White, together with the Somerset trainer John Thorne, are on a trip through Ireland, in search of a suitable National Hunt horse. They visit their pal, the irrepressible former seminarian Barney Curley, gambler, horse dealer and punter's friend, at his home at Mullingar. There they see Forgive 'N' Forget, who is to win the 1985 Cheltenham Gold Cup. The price is 40,000 gns. Too dear.

The Somerset pair move on to Hogan's place, following a tip from a friend of Thorne's daughter's. It is there they see Beau Ranger. White, while immediately excited by the looks of the horse, is alert to his trainer's reaction. 'I hadn't been into horses very long,' he says later, 'and John had won all these cattle awards. He liked the horse. He was struck by his conformation and all his heart room. He thought he could fill out a bit with a good summer.'

It is the horse's forelegs that draw Thorne's lingering attention. He runs his practised fingers down the cannon bones, greasy with ointment, and finds them warm. Hogan explains: only eight days before, Beau Ranger has entered his first race, the bumper, and won it. Therefore, the sore shins. Thorne concludes that the shins are not serious. All the young horse needs is a long rest.

'We went back to Mr Hogan's farmhouse and sat there chatting for a couple of hours,' recalls White, a former Somerset County Cricket Club committeeman and an accomplished chatter himself. 'My God, the Irish don't half open the whiskey and gin bottles. And haul out the sandwiches. Tremendous fun. I told them we had seen six or seven horses on our trip, which was true, and that we would be in touch in a week's time.'

White and Thorne spend the night in a nearby hotel and, on the way to the airport the following day, have lunch with Ted Walsh, who asks if they've found a horse. 'We quite like Beau Chapeau's gelding,' says White. 'The one at Patrick Hogan's.'

'He runs today in a bumper at Limerick,' says Walsh.

'What? You're joking,' says Thorne. 'We saw him last night and he's got shin trouble.'

'He runs today at Limerick.'

White and Thorne fly back to Bristol and that evening White's phone rings at home in Taunton. It is Thorne. The horse has won his bumper race in Limerick and White has ten minutes to decide if he wants to buy him. White checks with an uncle, for the White Bros enterprise is a family syndicate, and buys Beau Ranger for £19,614. The odd figure is a conversion from Irish punts.

Thus, on 29 May, 1982, Beau Ranger's career as hurdler and steeplechaser can be said to begin. Over the next seven seasons he will be trained in two yards in England. He will suffer jaundice and a puzzling back injury, those dreaded enemies of promise, and yet run in exactly fifty races by the end of the 1988 calendar year. In that time, his strike rate will be enviable: eighteen wins (in two bumper, two hurdle, and fourteen chases), three seconds, and six thirds for a total win-place prize money of £121,682.

Beau Ranger would, despite Ted Walsh's misgivings back in the Dublin sales ring, get round Cheltenham, carrying 10 stone 2 lbs to win the 1987 Mackeson Gold Cup Handicap Chase. He would get round with 12 stone and Peter Scudamore on his back, moreover, to finish third in the 1988 Cheltenham Gold Cup. By November, Beau Ranger is quoted as second favourite, 12-1, behind the great grey, Desert Orchid, 6-1 for the 1989 Gold Cup on 16 March.

Scudamore is uncertain. He feels, at that point in time, that Bonanza Boy may be the better Gold Cup candidate but, thinking of the chestnut gelding, now rising 11 years old and carrying a bit of a belly, he smiles with affection. His mind returns to the ride they shared in the A. F. Budge Chase at Cheltenham.

'We didn't have a chance at the top of the hill,' he recalls. 'But he was jumping *really* well and the run we got on the inside of Pegwell Bay, the way he got himself just in front after the last. Pure guts. Pegwell Bay came back and beat us. But we'd responded to each other. Beau Ranger's a good little horse. He's got all the heart in the world.'

The Somerset Sorcerer

A bony foreleg of a horse stands on the floor of Martin Pipe's office. It looks like some kind of Winged Victory, abstract and intricate, perhaps set down there as a source of inspiration. It is not. It is a Christmas present from Pipe's wife, Carol, and from time to time her trainer husband will gaze at it to refresh his memory on the mechanics of the race horse.

Pipe is superstitious. 'He won't let any of the owners have green in their colours, not the new owners anyway,' says the cockney Chester Barnes, the former international table tennis star and Pipe's all-round p.a. and factotum. 'He hates green. He's superstitious, too, about boxes. When we've had a winner, he wants the next horse to be saddled in the same box. If we have a loser, we saddle it in a different box. He's funny that way, he is.'

Those whims apart, a clue to the success of the otherwise pragmatic Pipe can be found in a glance down the huge board that is tilted across his desk each morning at Pond House Farm, near Wellington, under the Blackdown Hills of Somerset. On it are hooks and tabs, red, yellow, green and blue, colours once used at his father's bookmaking shops in the West Country.

'The colour-system helps me be quick and correct,' said Pipe when I went to see him. 'When you're accepting bets and taking telephone calls, you're in real trouble if somebody wants to put down £50 and you get it all wrong. It's the same with training horses. You're dead if you're not quick and correct.'

He'd certainly been quick and correct so far through the season. It was January 4, 1989, a chill winter morning. Steam rose from the coffee cups. Pipe had had no winners – no runners

Martin Pipe on the gallops at Nicholashayne.

— the previous day but already he had saddled 106 winners from 253 runners. Pipe's statistics, for the record, were worthy of note: 42 per cent of his runners had been winners, with 72 of 185 (39 per cent) of them hurdlers and 34 of 62 (55 per cent) chasers. Clearly, and with the schooling gifts of Scudamore, he was learning the chasing game; heretofore Pipe, to the pleasure of his derisive critics, had been thought chiefly a hurdler-trainer.

Pipe was wearing his checked cap: already he'd been out on a tour of some, if not all, of the hundred and ten horse boxes in his yard. He had read *The Sporting Life*. It was crisply folded on the desk, reminding me of Chester Barnes's remark about the guv'nor. 'Look at the way he folds his *Sporting Life*. Always the same way, as neat as a knife. He goes bonkers if you fold it any other way.'

He had spoken with his laboratory technician, Katie Redgate, who was running blood tests on the horses that were scheduled to go on the following day: Avionne, with Jonothan Lower, at Nottingham; Honest Word and Gloss, maiden hurdlers, with Scudamore at Lingfield.

Pipe bestrode the world of jump racing like a Colossus. His nearest rival in the wins column was Josh Gifford, far back on 35, and as for percentage of winners, well, no one with serious intentions on British tracks was within a shout of the Somerset trainer. Only the Irishman Jim Bolger, with one winner from one runner (100 per cent), and flat-trainer Barry Hills, three winners from four (75 per cent), had better records among the top 125 trainers.

What is more, Pipe's 106 winners were achieved with 52 different horses in a yard which, right now, contained 103. 'At least I *think* it's 103 horses,' he said, shrugging. 'They're always coming and going. I suspect we've got the biggest turnover of any National Hunt yard.'

Pipe glanced over up at Scudamore who was leaning over the guv'nor's shoulder, his leather puffa-style jacket still on, and peering at the colour-board. 'Scu,' said the trainer, 'what do you think, today? Chatam?' He indicated a yellow tab, the colour signifying that the 5-year-old hurdler, a former French flat racer, still needed some bringing on before running this season. 'Chatam,' said Scudamore. It would be a French day for schooling: Chatam, Voyage Sans Retour, the chaser Rusch de Farges.

Peter gets down there early, probably earlier than necessary, as though to soak up and contribute to the electric atmosphere that hums round the yard. I glanced over at Pipe. He has returned to the coloured tabs and, with the conviction of Kasparov over a chess board, he suddenly moved one to another column.

'What I think, frankly, about Martin Pipe,' Peter had said on the way down, 'is that what he does is so simple that to do it correctly is difficult. To do something better than somebody else in this sport, I can tell you, takes a touch of genius.'

'Secondly, Peter continued, 'he knows horses. He knows their *capabilities* which some trainers don't. He knows how to place them. In other words, he knows a goose from a swan and he'll make sure he doesn't enter a goose in a swan race. What I mean is, he won't go to Ascot or Cheltenham to socialise. He'll only go there to win.

'Thirdly,' Scudamore concluded, 'the blood-testing. He tests his horses scrupulously for virus and, as he puts it, they've got to be "spot-on" or they don't run.'

Pipe listens closely to his retained jockey and, unlike some trainers, is not afraid to admit it. 'I think all my horses are brilliant,' said the trainer. 'But unfortunately they're not. If Scu thinks they're rubbish, he says they're rubbish, and it's up to me to find a way to tell the owner. We don't sell our owners dreams. There's no use living in cloud-cuckoo-land.'

His voice was faint, surprisingly shy for someone that you might expect to be a tough guy. It was shot through with humility, too, as befits a successful man who seeks more success. 'At school, I never dreamed of training horses,' he said. 'When hands went up for careers, I was the only boy who wanted to be a bookmaker.'

Martin Charles Pipe, aged 43, is not the prototypical, Establishment racehorse trainer. The only child of David Pipe, the high-profile West Country bookmaker, Martin went to Queen's College, Taunton, a Methodist school not particularly partial to horse-racing and the twilit world of professional gambling. Remembered at college as a quiet, modest boy, an average scholar, best in maths, and a good cricketer whose father paid him a shilling a run, he made little impact at Queen's. In all, as one former master put it: 'Martin didn't seem like a boy headed for the limelight.'

Martin nonetheless entered his father's business, sweeping out the shop, handling the football pools, later managing a Pipe emporium at Butlin's holiday camp in Minehead. He trained the odd racing greyhound. He rode out for his uncle, Ken Pipe, a local permit holder. He began point-to-point riding and then, gingerly, National Hunt races. 'I didn't make much of a jockey,' he admitted, 'and even now I can only just about stay on a horse.'

It was coming off one, a horse called Lorac – his wife's name spelled backward – that put him out of amateur National Hunt riding with a broken thigh in 1973. It left Martin with a slight limp, a preference for getting round the yard on a bicycle rather than on foot and, best of all, an ambition to train racehorses.

By now, his Dad had sold up the thirty-five Pipe betting shops – keeping one in the centre of Taunton – and in 1972 purchased Pond Farm, 73 acres plus derelict farm buildings, for £40,000 at auction: a bargain buy, even then. Pipe the elder was to build it slowly into a 300-acre establishment. Martin soon took out a permit and moved uncertainly into horses, mostly point-to-pointers and sore-legged hurdlers.

'We didn't have the clientele to buy the expensive horses,' he explained, always acknowledging his father's role in the enterprise. 'We were just trying to get success, so we got the cheaper horses, the hurdlers off the flat, for £500 to £1,000.' As a permit holder, he saddled his first winner, aptly called Hit Parade, aptly at Taunton, in the 1974–75 season. He's never looked back. The progression of winners, despite the odd hiccough, continued apace:

1974–75	1	1982–83	23
1975–76	5	1983–84	32
1976–77	5	1984–85	51
1977–78	2	1985–86	79
1978–79	6	1986–87	106
1979–80	12	1987–88	129
1980–81	14	1988–89	106 (to that date)
1981–82	20	Total	591

His winners were all hurdlers in those early days. Pipe's great leaps upwards came in 1985–86 and the following season. They came with good reason. In January 1985 he enrolled in the Racing Industry Course at the Worcester College of Agriculture, a two-week course specialising in the conformation and feeding of the racehorse. He won the Best Student Award and the respect, approaching awe, of the principal, Hedley Dodds. I once met Dodds during a race meeting at Worcester.

'Martin wasn't interested in just the traditional thinking about the horse,' Dodds recalled at the time. 'He had an open mind. He wanted to learn new ideas, blood-testing and that, and I remember how he recorded every ounce of the different feeds we gave to the horses. His interest in detail was remarkable. He wanted to learn the horse from the head to the hoof.'

While at the college, Pipe found an old text book to which he still often refers. 'The most important passage in the book,' Pipe recalls, 'is one that says, "The horse's body must never be asked to do what it has not been prepared for." '

The veteran Dennis Dummett, Pipe's head lad, came in. He spoke quietly with the boss. He wore a plum-purple black eye. 'Dennis has been with me since I started. He's an important part of the team,' said Pipe and smiled. 'See that black eye, I gave him that. He fed a horse that got beat.'

Dummett merely grinned as his guv'nor told the true story behind the injury: 'We had a collision didn't we? We're speedy round the yard and Dennis was running in one direction and I was bicycling in the other. We hit head-on. It was on the day of the 100th winner.'

That had been a memorable day, December 29 at Taunton, when the chaser Mareth Line won handsomely, ridden by Scudamore. The Mareth Line win shattered, by nearly ten weeks, the quickest century mark in National Hunt history, set in March 1983 by Michael Dickinson, the magician of his day.

Praise for the Somerset record-buster had been grudging. The trainer David Elsworth, Pipe's harshest critic, passed along half-a-loaf of homage. 'Martin deserves a lot of credit,' he said, 'for his energy-rate more than anything else.' Mrs Monica Dickinson, Michael's mother, was equally stingy. 'In some ways you have to say that he has improved some horses,' she said. 'I think that if horses from small yards went to Henry Cecil, Michael Stoute or Luca Cumani they would be entitled to improve.'

At Taunton, Pipe said that talk of a double century was silly but there was already such talk among bookmakers: he was quoted at 8-1 to break the 200 mark: 'It's all down to my staff, the "team", and my training facilities.'

It can be argued that the most valuable team member, apart from Scudamore, is the inconspicuous figure of Roy Hawkins, the form expert. Hawkins can often be found in the single Pipe betting shop in the centre of Taunton, or in his house down the lane, a place stuffed with all manner of statistical data, all at his finger-tips. 'Roy studies the opposition,' said Pipe. 'That's all he does. He's got his nose in the book all day.' This is nothing new, since for years Hawkins worked in the Pipe bookmaking shops.

Bookmaking. Bookmaking. The word rings like a clanged anvil round the yard. 'Yes,' Carol had said earlier in the kitchen. 'Most important. I think the bookmaker's side of Martin's life also has taught him to be realistic about the chances of horses. If a horse has been 50-1, 50-1, 50-1 all its life, what chance had it got of winning at Cheltenham?' It is Pipe's cool, bookmaker's approach to National Hunt racing, once the clubbable reserve of the gentleman trainer, that has encouraged suspicions of him and his methods.

Pipe has been accused, amongst other things, of luring horses from other trainers. This charge he denies, never so comprehensively as he did to Michael Seely, the respected racing correspondent of *The Times*. 'I've never approached anyone else's owners in my life,' he told Seely. 'All the horses I train have been offered to me. This talk is very upsetting and disappointing. And I certainly wouldn't train horses for nothing as reported. It costs far too much money.'

How much? I later asked the Taunton car dealer, Peter White, who in a family syndicate owns Beau Ranger. He showed me Beau Ranger's invoice for December, the month just gone.

Training Fees	£442.68
Blacksmith	£51.00
Transport to Kempton	£65.60
Vets: for Insurance	£25.00
Vitamins	£10.00
Clipping	£8.00
Blood Tests	£24.00
VAT	£93.94
Total	£720.22

I later showed the invoice to another trainer. He said he thought Pipe's charge for clipping was a bit cheeky, since he himself did it for free, but the other entries, especially the training fees, he found remarkably reasonable.

Pipe – due largely to the high turnover of horses in his yard –

is also accused of peddling his failed or broken down runners to a certain Mr Potter's. The grimly named Mr Potter's is a famous – or infamous – abattoir in Avon where busted racehorses and unwanted ponies suffer the bullet. Yet, try as they might, no newspaper has been able to build a case of wanton slaughter against the Somerset trainer.

Further, he is accused of dabbling in drugs and blood-doping. True, the hurdler Norman Invader tested positive after his victory on October 5 at Cheltenham and was later mandatorially disqualified by the Jockey Club. Pipe was, by turns, weary, hurt and angered by all the innuendo which had been skilfully and carefully put about in the tabloid press.

'No comment,' said Pipe, but his defence was to be forceful and feasible, the one Scudamore had explained to me on that early car ride down to Fakenham: that the detected drug was not knowingly administered. It had been present in the feed before it even reached Pond House Farm. The problem is not at all uncommon in equestrian yards.

As for the blood-doping, that old Finnish device of boosting an athlete's energy by introducing oxygen-rich blood to his system, there is no evidence whatever that Pipe has tampered with his horses. The tacit suggestion arises from the fact that the yard's modern scientific equipment includes that laboratory for monitoring a horse's blood which was set up in 1987 by the veterinary haemotologist Barry Allen, of the Animal Health Trust at Newmarket, a world authority on such matters.

'It was costing me a fortune to send out my horses' blood for testing,' said Pipe, 'so I decided it was quicker and cheaper to do it myself.' The result, the only trainer's on-site lab in Britain except for the one at Guy Harwood's flat-racing yard in West Sussex, is comprised of three major pieces of equipment: one for measuring the red cells, another for the white cells and a third for the haemoglobin, the oxygen-carrying pigment in the red cells. 'We get the results of the haemoglobin within two and a half minutes,' said Pipe. 'The others take a little longer. Two and a half hours.

'All this measurement won't tell you if a horse will win,' Pipe added, 'but it will tell you if it has no chance.'

Allen later spoke of his visits to Pipe. 'I've worked on the gallops at Martin's and taking blood samples off the horses after exercise,' he explained. 'Some of them come up to the magic blood-count figure and go on to win. Some of them don't and they seem to tire. I think, therefore, that at least theoretically blood-doping would be beneficial to some horses.'

Theoretically, he emphasised, was the operative word. 'It would take something like a three-year research project at some major institution to learn how to do it,' he added. 'It could be done. But Martin Pipe couldn't do it.'

What Pipe does with his blood-testing, he says, is to take much of the 'guesswork out of training. On occasions, we've tested a horse in the morning, loaded it up and taken it to the racecourse and then withdrawn it at the track because the blood reading wasn't right. It's got to be spot-on or the horse doesn't run.'

In addition to the lab facilities, Pipe has an indoor swimming pool which, as he puts it, 'gives the horses a weightless gallop', a solarium which eases back problems such as those suffered by Beau Ranger, who probably spends more time under the heat lamps than any other horse and, finally, a strange-looking 'Force Plate', a platform attached to a computer. 'It tells me the horse's weight and how it is being distributed,' explained Pipe, 'which you can't see with the naked eye.'

The telephone rang. It was Hawkins, with early views on the races next day at Lingfield. Scudamore was sunk into his *Racing Post*. I went outside and was given a tour of the yard by Dad, David Pipe, the ingenious odd-job man round the place. It was he, for instance, who put together the wood-chipper for the all-weather gallops. He felt that traditional, hard-edged wood-chips bed badly on the gallops. 'So,' he said, smiling, 'we don't cut 'em, we mash 'em.' He laid down the covered canter which he called 'the best in England.' He devised its raker-roller-sprayer which looks like something out of a Heath Robinson cartoon. 'If you want something done,' his daughter-in-law Carol had said, 'just tell Dad he can't do it.'

In his Range Rover, Pipe must be the fastest driver in Somerset. We sped over to the gallops, an uphill, all-weather, six furlong run along the Devonshire border. Chatam, the horse that most concerned Pipe and Scudamore, was galloped twice up the stretch, over three hurdles, Peter aboard, another horse alongside. He travelled sluggishly and Pipe felt, more than Peter, that he hung slightly to the left.

Chatam would need more work but neither trainer nor jockey was unduly concerned as we returned to the farmhouse. 'You can't force a horse to work,' said Peter. 'You sometimes find a horse that's a lazy worker at home but full of life on the race track. I was talking to Walter Swinburn once and he was saying that the Aga Khan's horses always work lazily at home. I found that hard to believe. It must be the way they're brought up.'

A bigger concern, at least for the moment, was the going. Chatam wanted it soft. Would it be too hard to run the gelding in ten days' time in the IR£50,000 Ladbroke race at Leopardstown in Ireland? What were Chatam's longer-range plans, I wondered. Indeed, what plans did Pipe have for the Cheltenham Festival in March, for Liverpool in April?

'It looks like Chatam, if he's good enough, in the Champion Hurdle, and we've got Beau Ranger in the Gold Cup,' he said. 'Then, of course, Strands of Gold, if he can stay on his feet, in the Grand National.' In the fickle world of horse racing, even in the pragmatic Pipe's little corner of it, none of these projections proved to be true.

Under the Whip

In November, with the approach of the Mackeson Gold Cup Handicap Chase, Scudamore made his own luck and rode it. He was at Plumpton on the 7th of the month when the jockey Luke Harvey was hurt in a fall and, alert to a spare ride, he car-phoned Captain Tim Forster, the trainer. Would the captain like him to ride Luke's mount, Fiddlers Three, the next day at Devon and Exeter?

The captain would, Peter did, and the horse won. Forster, with his first jockey, Carl Llewellyn, out with a broken arm and Harvey still crocked, then turned to Scudamore to ride Pegwell Bay, his entry in the Mackeson, the first major handicap chase of the jumping season which was being run that Saturday at Cheltenham.

Pegwell Bay was a powerful 7-year-old and Llewellyn, his usual partner, gave Peter a tip. 'He'll like Cheltenham, he likes left-handed courses,' said the young Llewellyn, 'but the horse is a brute. You won't hold him. You're better off sitting up there fairly handy.' Scudamore took aboard the advice but on race day, in the paddock, Captain Forster's instructions were 180 degrees in the opposite direction. 'Drop him in about sixth or seventh,' said Forster who felt the ground was too fast.

In these circumstances, I later asked Scudamore, who do you listen to: jockey or trainer? 'Trainer,' he said. 'If you don't follow instructions and get beat you're an idiot. If you do follow instructions and get beat you've at least done as you're told.' Or, thirdly, I wondered: if you break the instructions and win? 'It depends on the trainer,' said Scudamore. 'I've won under those conditions and trainers have told me they'll never put me up again.'

Carl Llewellyn's misfortune was Scudamore's good luck when he picked up the ride on Pegwell Bay.

In the event, it didn't much matter. As soon as the tape went up, Pegwell Bay, pulling hard, pressed to get his white face out front. 'After three or four fences I was more or less in second but running too free,' Scudamore recounted. He was also being forced out by Gee Armytage, whose horse was jumping out to the right. 'I was getting a bit cross with Gee so I had to go past her at the water jump. And as soon as I did the horse settled well. He sort of dictated the race. I had a lot of horse underneath me when I straightened up the hill and over the last two fences I just sat on him.'

Pegwell Bay won by ten lengths. Captain Forster paid tribute to modern technology, the car phone. Llewellyn, arm in plaster, shook Scu's hand. The champion had been round the game too long to offer much sympathy. 'It's happened to me before, bringing on a horse only to miss out at the end,' he said. 'It was my turn to be fortunate.' Like all of Napoleon's great generals, he had been lucky. He had now won 66 races.

Nov. 13. Entry in Scudamore's diary. 'Father Paddy rang to say "well done".' And Simon Sherwood rang to say 'Well done. Another win. Yawn. Yawn."' And Pegwell Bay's owner rang with thanks and congratulations.

Scudamore was on a roll, euphoric, and six days later his enthusiasm was unbounded when Sabin du Loir, after sweeping fifteen lengths clear, coasted home by a dozen to win the Racecall Ascot Hurdle at Ascot. He jumped so nicely, so willingly, that Peter began to think of the horse as a steeplechaser.

Meanwhile, back at Uplands, Celtic Shot was back at work, his ligament sound, ready for his comeback. He made it in the obscurity of midweek at Leicester, 21 November, in the Thorpe Satchville Hurdle.

That day, Scudamore rode a nicely-judged race: he kept Celtic Shot off the pace until the final flight and then, with insouciance, swept home by four lengths. On the Corals' chart, the defender climbed to second place – 6-1, with Kribensis at 5-1 – in early betting on the Champion Hurdle. 'The ride went perfectly,' Scudamore told the Press. 'I was delighted with him.'

Peter was being economical with the truth, following an age-old convention in racing, whereby the jockey does not wish to prejudice his position with an owner by being uncomplimentary about the horse. He was, in fact, less than delighted before, during and after the race. 'It was a terrible sort of race to have to ride,' he said. 'Here he is, the Champion Hurdler. The strong favourite. Nothing all that good to beat. You can't *win* that sort of race. You can only lose it. And we did. He just wasn't electric. I was satisfied, but not overjoyed.'

Two of his top-liners – Sabin du Loir and Celtic Shot – had now got off the mark for the season, nonetheless, and two days later, in a chill fog that reduced visibility to two fences at Haydock, a third important horse tucked his first win under his girth. Beau Ranger, with slabs of lead on his back – all told Peter would ride at 11 st 13 lbs – was entered by Pipe in the

Edward Hanmer Memorial Chase. He'd won it the previous year and, walking out now, he looked shiny and well in the paddock.

'Beau Ranger looked almost too well,' the magazine *Update International* said later, and went on to point out: 'It was interesting to hear Martin Pipe confide that Beau Ranger's blood had been four spots better than when he had won the Mackeson in 1987, yet another indication of the detail to which the trainer goes to discover the precise fitness of his team.'

Four spots better? Was Pipe, unchallenged, mind-boggling the Press with veterinarian lab-speak? Even experts at Bristol's Langford School of Veterinary Science didn't know what he was talking about. Later, I asked Pipe himself. 'No comment,' he said, in one of his stone-walling moods.

Anyway, it was a formidable field, including Smart Tar, Tickite Boo and Durham Edition. Beau Ranger, foot-perfect, making all and jumping like a stag, saw them off to win the respected chase by six lengths. Scudamore now had three fine candidates for the Gold Cup which, although four months away, was forcing its way into his mind: Beau Ranger, Bonanza Boy and Strands of Gold.

Still, the job at hand was to win races day-by-day. A Haydock harvest of five winners in two days, November 23 and 24, raised Scudamore's grand total to 81 for the season. It seemed nothing could stop him, save the unspeakable, and that evening I got Peter on his car phone.

'Two winners,' he said and then a tiny air of disgust clouded his voice, 'and a two-day holiday.'

The winners were Enemy Action, the promising young hurdler from Pipe's yard, and Run and Skip, the veteran front-running chaser trained by John Spearing, which lifted Scudamore's total of wins for the season to 81. The 'two-day holiday' was the Jockey Club's punishment for 'improper use of the whip' in urging Run and Skip past the post. The stewards found seven weal marks on the nearside and one on the offside of the animal.

The Jockey Club rule at the time stipulated that one weal, any weal, found on a horse must result in a jockey being stood down and, faced by the evidence, Scudamore made no appeal. He nonetheless found the punishment unjust. 'I hit many horses as hard as I hit Run and Skip,' he claimed later, 'but they don't mark.'

Scudamore also objected to the Jockey Club guidelines whereby stewards were obliged to inquire into, if not convict after, any jockey seen to hit a horse ten times from the second last fence or hurdle. The weal again was the smoking pistol. 'Some stewards observe it, some don't,' said Peter. 'We jockeys don't know where we stand.'

At Newbury, two days later, Richard Dunwoody was nailed for two days on another wrinkle of the rule: 'unreasonable force and frequency' in the use of the whip. He fought back. 'On the flat, the (ten hit) guidelines work all right because the horses are running for you,' said the Ulsterman. 'But a lot of jumpers need a smack otherwise they turn round and laugh at you.' He raised the ten-hit law and said that at some tracks, Folkestone for one, the second last was nearly a half-mile from home.

If both jockeys ignored the central question – when does hurting a horse become unacceptable? – they did so not only through their zealous will to win. They, like all their brethren, jump and flat, must ride on the cleft stick of Jockey Club rules: face penalty if you don't get the very best possible placing out of your mount while, on the other hand, face penalty if you hurt the animal in doing so.

It's a difficult balance to strike – if that's the word – and the jockeys sought clarification with the Jockey Club. The two groups met. Scudamore, as joint-president (with flat rider Paul Cook) of the Jockeys' Association of Great Britain, argued that the weal didn't automatically mean that a whip had been excessively used on a horse. Other factors should be considered: thin-skinned horses, light-skinned horses, horses that had recently been clipped, he said, and even dew in the air could contribute to marking. Haydock, for example, had been heavy with dew.

'Peter put the case eloquently,' recalled Michael J. Caulfield, who recalls being 'blooded' as the Association's secretary that day. 'The Jockey Club is terrified of bad publicity,' he said after only weeks in the job, 'which is understandable because you've got to promote the sport. At the same time, you've got to allay the public's fears if the public have the wrong idea. They aren't always right.'

The Jockey Club listened. They pondered. Weeks passed. 'If you asked them to buy a cup of coffee,' cracked Caulfield near the end of the season, 'they'll first form a sub-committee to discuss the issue. The Jockey Club doesn't do anything in a rush, unless the public tells them to, like they did after the Grand National.' Caulfield was referring to the clamour over and the resulting changes to Becher's Brook following the deaths of two horses after the 1989 National.

Scudamore, nevertheless, was satisfied that something would eventually be done. After the Haydock suspension, however, and through the rest of the season, he was to use his un-marking 'felt' whip. 'It has its drawbacks on wet days,' explains Scudamore. 'It leaves a mark and it gets heavy. But that doesn't matter if it saves me two days of riding.'

Weals were removed from the law, the ten-hit guideline left in and a crime of swinging a whip from above the shoulder introduced.

Misuse of the whip, together with Becher's Brook in the Grand National, is the most emotive National Hunt issue in the eyes of an increasingly sensitive and vociferous racing public. The Jockey Club is keenly aware of this. It is also the most imprecise and least-understood rule. A whip stings. It's meant to. Yet properly used, perhaps only 'shown' to a horse, it is no unduly cruel tool. The skilled jockey uses it to guide his mount, retain its balance and to tell it when to take off and shovel on the coal.

There are rules where on the body a horse can be legally hit. 'Save in exceptional circumstances, such as a horse attempting to savage another or a jockey,' writes John Hislop in his *The Proper and Improper Use of the Whip in Race Riding*, a copy of which is issued to each licensed jockey, 'a horse should never be hit anywhere other than behind the hip-bone or down the shoulder.' With this, no respectable jockey would disagree.

Innocent by his own lights, if not the Jockey Club's, what most upset Scudamore was his loss of a winning ride during his 'two-day holiday'. Still, his winners came apace and he finished the month on 88, the highlight of the final week being victory in the Hennessy Gold Cup at Newbury.

Strands of Gold was Peter's ride that afternoon. The big 9-year-old, once under the guidance of Jimmy Fitzgerald in

Yorkshire, had flourished over the past months in Somerset. He had run three times for Pipe: a clumsy performance in a chase the previous Boxing Day at Wetherby, the agonising fall at Becher's when in the lead and travelling strongly second time round in the National and a promising third behind Desert Orchid and Kildimo in the Whitbread.

Through the late summer and autumn, Strands had been paddling up and down Pipe's swimming pool, his Fountain of Youth, and been coaxed back to confidence over tiny fences by Scudamore. Was he ready for the Hennessy, all 3 miles, 2 furlongs and 82 yards of it? Would he be the first horse since Diamond Edge in 1981 to win the gruelling race on his first outing of the season. Pipe privately thought not. 'I'm worried,' he said to Scudamore, legging him up in the paddock. 'I'm afraid he's a bit short of work.'

'Nonsense,' said Scudamore, well-enough placed to know. 'He's done as much work as Beau Ranger. And look at what Beau Ranger did at Haydock.' Pipe and Scudamore feed off one another's opinions and Peter's confidence cheered up both trainer and rider. 'People get Martin wrong,' Scudamore said later. 'They think his horses are super-fit first time and that's not always true. Many improve for their runs.'

Strands of Gold didn't need much improving that day. It was Scudamore who had the sweat: nearly two hours of it in the Newbury sauna to make the minimum 10 stone weight before the race but, once off, they stayed handy. He and the compact gelding – his dam, Sweet Fanny, was so small she finished up pulling a trap – saved their heart for the end and finishing strongly won by six lengths. Immediately, Strands was made 16-1 favourite for the Grand National.

It was a flattering bookmakers' endorsement but it would be prudent to recall what Scudamore had thought, four months earlier, as he sat in the Newton Abbot weighing-room and considered the season. 'You think about these horses,' he had said, 'and, you know, they never work out as you think.'

The Duke

A bronze sculpture, depicting a horse and jockey clearing a hurdle, stands on top of the television set in David Nicholson's sitting room at Condicote, not far from Peter's place in the Cotswolds. The horse is Broadsword, the rider Scudamore, and the race they are winning is the 1980 Finale Hurdle at Chepstow. 'It's a very good reproduction,' said Nicholson. 'It's as I used to see Peter when he was riding for me.'

In jump racing, the names Nicholson and Scudamore will always be linked. David, known as 'The Duke', and Peter's father Michael were fellow jockeys in the fifties and Peter, aged 4, was a pageboy at Nicholson's wedding. Willie Stevenson was Nicholson's uncle, what's more, and when Peter reluctantly took that job with an estate agent in Stow-on-the-Wold he kept his hand in with horses by riding out for the Duke.

Nicholson remembered the young rider well. 'He might have been a bit crash-bang-wallop to begin with and he wanted a bit of steadying, a bit of rhythm and polish. But he was keen, *God* he was keen,' he recalled early in the 1988–89 season. 'And he was a natural horseman who'd been up through the Pony Club and done a bit of point-to-pointing. I was looking for somebody because Jeff King, my retained jockey, was getting towards the end of his career. So I asked Peter to become my assistant trainer.'

Peter came to Condicote in 1978, was soon Nicholson's stable jockey, became champion jockey under the Duke and, at the end of the 1986–87 season, left to take up the top jockey's post at Fred Winter's Lambourn stable. Nicholson was, perhaps still is, wounded by the move. Equally, Scudamore felt his future lay with Winter in succession to the great John Francome. It was, he felt, an opportunity he could not turn down.

Whatever the merits of the case, each man retains respect for the other. In the evenings they sometimes talk shop on the phone and, early in November, Nicholson called on Peter to ride a horse for him when his stable jockey, Richard Dunwoody, was injured. The Duke now gave a slow, thoughtful and measured view of his Cotswold neighbour. 'Going racing with Peter was always a pleasure because one was always discussing things,' he said. 'I'll never forget going to Ascot about five or six years ago when he was riding Very Promising for me against Buck House in the H. & T. Walker Gold Cup.

'We got into the car, he drove, and we discussed tactics for about five minutes and very little else was said the whole way to Ascot,' Nicholson continued. 'I could see he was concentrating on one thing: winning the race. Everything was going through his mind. I've never seen such concentration, and for so long a time.' Scudamore, pacing his horse beautifully, duly beat the great Buck House. 'It was,' said the Duke, 'the best race I've seen in my life.'

Nicholson thought for a moment. 'I don't think and I've been round racing for forty years – that I've seen anybody with as much dedication and will to win as Peter has got. I suppose Stan Mellor was the nearest thing to it.' The Duke smiled. 'Peter may not be the best ball player in the world, or the best natural sportsman, but by Christ, you try to beat him. He'll fight to the bitter end.' The Duke laughed outright, thinking of, then sharing the outrageous prospect of Scudamore intentionally losing a race. 'Stop a horse,' he mused, 'I don't think Peter would know *how* to stop a horse.'

On video, Nicholson replayed races that Scudamore had ridden for him. In each, he pointed out how stylishly low in the seat Peter was riding, how he was *squeezing* the horse forward, always with *rrrrhythm*. 'He doesn't ride like that any more. He's too high above a horse through a race,' said Nicholson and he paused, gestured at the stature of his bronze boy on Broadsword.

'I don't want to appear to be knocking, especially after what happened between Peter and me,' he said carefully. 'And I'm not saying he's riding better or worse. Only I don't think he rides as stylishly now as he did when he was riding for me.'

Peter, whatever his style, rode that winner for Nicholson. It was on Springholm, the 5-6 favourite, in the Winterbourne Handicap Chase on November 9 at Newbury. It was Scudamore's 62nd win of the season.

Written in Red

On December 17, the day after our long journey by car to Fakenham, Scudamore was riding at Ascot. He got there in good time and handed the Declarations Clerk his necessary credential: his Medical Record Book. On the opening page appears Peter's previous medical history. He is allergic to penicillin and, at the age of eight, got his first of a series of anti-tetanus injections. He suffers from no notable illness, eye conditions nor skeletal deformity.

The clerk was interested only in the last entry in the following pages full of 'Recordable Accidents'. It was written in blue, dated 23.1.88, and read simply: 'fit to ride'. This clearance was entered just below a notation, in red, that on the same day Peter had suffered a 'bruised hip' at Kempton Park.

Red, in short, means a jockey must stop riding until a Racecourse Medical Officer's signature, in blue, passes him fit. Peter's medical book is sprinkled with blues and reds, from bruises to a broken tibia, from sprains to a head injury with bleeding from the right ear that he suffered in 1981 at Taunton. Today, after the fourth race, another entry was to be written in red.

Strands of Gold had a crashing fall. The strong gelding, winner of the Hennessy Cognac Gold Cup in November at Newbury, was favoured to win the SGB Handicap Chase when he ran straight into the third fence. 'He sometimes misses one out,' Scudamore told the Press afterwards, 'just the way he did when he fell at Becher's in the National.'

This time Peter was flung like a rag doll into the air and onto the turf. He lay there in a prudent bundle and, finally unfolding,

85

Not the fall from Strands of Gold, but still Ascot. This time it's Memberson and Brendan Powell on the deck, and Peter's attempt to avoid them will lead to him parting company with On The Twist.

answered the first-aider who was manning the jump. What day was it? Saturday. Where are we? Ascot. What horse were you riding? Strands of Gold, the bugger.

Under the unwritten Jockey Club rule, 'if you hit the deck, you have to be seen', Scudamore was taken, limping to the 'Jockeys' Hospital' near the weighing-room. He was seen by Dr Norman Gordon, one of the three medical officers assigned that day to Ascot. Dr Gordon examined the jockey, wrote 'twisted neck, knee' in red in his medical book and, accordingly, Scudamore was forbidden to ride Mou-Dafa later that day.

Dr Gordon, a veteran of fifteen years on the job, considers Scudamore a skilled faller: not only is he properly rolled up in a ball, with his head and arms tucked in – 'If you stick out an arm,' says the doctor 'it gets broken, simple as that.' – but he has the sense to stay down until he knows he's fit to get up. 'Young riders often get up too quickly,' adds the doctor.

Gordon makes a distinction between hurdling and chasing

falls. Hurdle falls are worse. 'If a jockey comes down over a hurdle he usually gets hurt,' he says. 'That's because a hurdling horse, when it falls, usually gets tripped and it dives. The jockey is catapulted straight down at 45 degrees or less and that's bad news.' The remark brought to mind Viv Kennedy, killed earlier in the year in a sharp-angled hurdling fall.

'Also,' the doctor went on, 'hurdling, the horses are travelling faster, there are more of them round the faller and perhaps the horses are a bit younger and not so experienced. Hurdle falls worry me.'

Steeplechase falls, while more spectacular, are less dangerous because of the trajectory of the horse's jump. 'For lack of a better term, the steeplechase horse has a purer fall,' explained Dr Gordon. 'He doesn't find his feet on the other side and by that time the jockey is aware of what's happening. He'll be kicked out of his irons and, with more time in the air, he rolled up in a ball. Also,' the doctor concluded, 'the steeplechase jockey is less likely to get kicked or landed upon because the horses are more widely spread out.'

Speaking of distinctions, I wondered if there was a difference between flat and jump jockey falls. 'Yes,' he said. 'The mechanics are different, for a start. When a flat jockey hits the ground, he usually hurts himself because he's travelling faster, he's riding shorter, the horses are bunched up and, besides, he's not used to falling. Also, he's only too keen to see the doctor.'

Dr Gordon smiled. 'The National Hunt jockey, on the other hand, is accustomed to falling and he's anxious *not* to see the doctor. He's a tougher breed. It's a different sport, isn't it?'

As Scudamore left the Ascot racecourse early that afternoon, a certain little Cypriot-Londoner carried his bag to the car park. Paper signs were plastered on the windscreen: 'Congratulations. 100 Winners.' Scudamore grinned, took them off and climbed stiffly into the car. He was okay. He said he would be fit to ride the next day at Towcester.

Driving back to the Cotswolds, he discussed his fall from Strands of Gold. 'He's a natural jumper. He's as good a jumper as I ride,' he said, 'and, unlike some horses, he's got a natural instinct to survive. So I trusted him and going down the first fences I tried to relax him. Switch him off. Conserve his energy.'

Strands of Gold had jumped the first two fences well. 'About seven strides from the next, he lost his concentration and I knew we were going to get it wrong,' Scudamore continued. 'I elected to look for the longer stride and he agreed with me. Then, at the last moment, he said, "no" and put his feet down, straight into the fence.'

He drove on, twisting his shoulders rather than his neck as he looked out the window. 'Maybe I should have growled and slapped him on the shoulder but you can't do that, not when you're trying to relax a horse.' Scudamore shifted gears, pulled out and overtook a car in the slow lane. 'If I hadn't relaxed him, if I hadn't trusted him, he probably wouldn't have fallen. But he wouldn't have won, either.'

The Song Remains the Same

Dec. 23: Entry in Scudamore's diary: Pheasant shooting, Grange Hill. The shoot, leased by his friend Raymond Mould, is on the land behind Peter's house which ironically he and another friend Nigel Twiston-Davies will shortly own together. The party, including trainers Nicky Henderson and Oliver Sherwood, both crack shots, bagged a hundred and fifty-six birds and one pigeon. David Nicholson got the pigeon with a lucky shot. Peter, not fond of blood sports, was among the 'one or two holes in the line', according to Mould's Game Book. 'I can't shoot straight and I'm not all that bothered,' says Peter, in a rare confession to a deficiency in a sport. 'I like eating pheasants. I don't like killing pheasants. I don't like killing anything.'

Christmas was like any other day, abstemious – Peter was given an orange-juice squeezer by Marilyn – and on Boxing Day he rode one of the most satisfying races of the season. On Sabin du Loir, a 9-year-old that had been trained by Michael Dickinson and David Murray Smith before joining the Pipe yard. His owner Brian Kilpatrick, who had forbidden Scu to use a whip on his pet, also opposed the horse going over fences. Peter nonetheless had prevailed on the steeplechase account and, having schooled the horse diligently, took him to Newton Abbot that day for his debut in the Mid Devon Novice Chase. 'Sabby,' the 1-2 favourite, flew round the course and won by thirty lengths.

Scudamore was now on 105 winners and with four more the following day, the Welsh Grand National meeting at Chepstow, he lifted it to 109, streets ahead of his nearest rival, Mark Dwyer, on 46. On that Chepstow day, December 27, Scudamore probably rode more high-octane horses to victory than he would on any day in the season. All, too, were trained by Pipe who, in passing, had another winner at Wolverhampton to lift his season's total to 99.

The Chepstow results: Enemy Action smashed his nearest rival, the useful Magnus Pym by twelve lengths in the Finale Junior Hurdle Race, Bonanza Boy opened the same space from Run and Skip in the Welsh National, Fu's Lady left Sirrah Jay fifteen lengths adrift in the Wiseacre Handicap Chase and, finally, Elegant Isle beat Wink Gulliver by twelve lengths in the Scout Novices' Chase. All horses, save Elegant Isle, were the favourites.

Scudamore was to close out the calendar year on 113 winners, an awesome figure, but all was not well back at Mucky Cottage. Marilyn was down with the 'flu. Thomas and Michael were off-colour and in desperation Scu phoned a friend in Hampshire. It was Fiona Moore, the former British international eventer who had worked with Peter and Marilyn, when Peter's wife kept the books at David Nicholson's yard. 'I was in the bath and all Peter could say was "Help! Help! Come quick",' she recalled later. 'So I went.' She was to stay with the Scudamores through the rest of the season.

The Complete Cobbler

A photograph of Princess Anne, on a racehorse, rests behind the counter. Her Royal Highness has just finished her race and, head low, stands high in her stirrups. 'See those boots,' the man behind the counter points out, speaking in an accent that betrays his childhood in Cyprus, his youth in the East End of London. 'I made those boots.'

He has given me his calling card. In a half-dozen different typefaces, it reads:

The Complete Cobbler
Specialist

In Horse Racing
And Riding Boots

Director: 28 Tottenham Street
Steve Winter   London, W1

Steve Winter? I had understood from Scudamore, on our trip to Fakenham, that the name of his bootmaker was Steve Chimonidee. The man says, 'It *is* Steve Chimonid. But in England nobody can pronounce "Chimonid". So I changed it to "Winter". My name means "Winter" in Greek.' He opens his hands and cocks his head with a grin.

Twenty-eight Tottenham Street lies around a few corners from the headquarters of the Jockey Club in Portman Square and across from a Mecca betting shop, which is a good thing for Steve; a punter and a Scudamore fan, he nips over to place bets and watch the races on closed circuit television. The Complete Cobbler is a cosy shop, a flight of stone steps up from the street, and rich with the smell of leather and boot polish. Ticketed shoes and handbags clutter the shelves.

Only a sharp eye, however, can pick out Steve's passion: the racing boot. In the window, dwarfed by other shoes, stands a wee 'riding out' boot of Michael Roberts, the South African flat rider. Steve made it: size 2½, the smallest among his jockeys. On the wall, in various stages of construction, hang three normal pairs he is making. Each is tagged to observe the social distinction, gentlemen-and-players, that is still present in the racing game. 'Mr P. Jones' and 'Mr N. Stevens' mark the boots of amateur jockeys while, beside them, the 'Dever' pair are for Peter Dever, the professional.

The beauty of the boots is beyond class, however, and Steve is proud of his work. Quality boots, he reckons, are a requisite of racing. 'If you walk out into the paddock and find a million-dollar horse and a jockey in tacky boots – well, it's simply not on,' he says. 'An owner likes his jockey to look as good as his animal.'

Steve is swarthy, aged forty-one. He was born in Larnaca, son of a Cypriot who joined the Royal Engineers in World War II. The family came to London when he was nine and settled in Camden Town, hardly equestrian country, yet Steve was keen to ride horses. At fourteen, he did some point-to-pointing in Essex. 'I was mad on the sport,' he recalls. 'But I couldn't keep it up. I couldn't afford a horse.' On leaving school, he took up shoemaking in Newmarket, among the jockeys. He then worked with weighing-room valets, making boots on the side, and in 1984 opened the shop.

The Complete Cobbler knocks up boots for about every important jockey on the English Turf. His clients include (on the flat) Pat Eddery, Steve Cauthen, Willie Carson, Greville Starkey and Walter Swinburn, and (over the sticks) Peter Scudamore, Steve Smith Eccles, Richard Dunwoody, Simon Sherwood, Mark Dwyer, Chris Grant, Phil Tuck and dozens of others. You name 'em, Steve shods 'em.

Princess Anne, too. Steve advances no Royal Bootmaker claim but hers certainly are his and, pouring me a 40-year-old brandy into a plastic cup, he explains. Steve made the boots for

Graham McCourt, a regular customer, but McCourt found them a bit short in the leg. They went into the spares bag of John Buckingham, the valet. There they remained until the Princess decided to take up racing. To find her a boot, Buckingham sat her down on a bench at Newbury.

The image is irresistible: Her Royal Highness, like some sort of Cinderella, trying on jockeys' boots. This one is too loose, this one too tight. This one too long. Graham McCourt's is just right: it is suitably short in the leg. Anne wears them to this day. 'What,' I wonder, 'is the Princess's size?'

Six-and-a-half. 'Which means her feet are size six,' explains Steve. 'All jockeys take a half size too big, even Princess Anne. The reason is that when they stand in the stirrups, the heel and toe press down and the big toe gets cramped. The big toe needs room.' Scudamore's boot is about normal, size seven-and-a-half.

I pick up a boot and heft it in my hand. It feels remarkably light. But, this, apparently, is nothing. An impish grin creeps across Steve's face. The lightest boot he makes is the 'cheater', he says, the boot used chiefly by flat jockeys. The top looks like a conventional racing boot but, turned over, the sole and heel are fabric or thin leather, much like a slipper. A pair of cheaters weighs about 4 oz, astonishingly light, but this is their purpose. 'What the jockeys do, when they're heavy, is weigh-in with cheaters,' explains Steve. 'And after the Clerk of the Scales passes them through they change in the weighing-room and ride in their regular boots.'

Steve acknowledges that the cheaters are illegal. Who uses them? 'Put it this way,' he says. 'If you want a pair of cheaters you can always find some in the weighing-rooms. That's all I can tell you.'

The Complete Cobbler pours another old brandy, raises a toast as though to seal the conspiracy. We will maybe go greyhound racing one day, he says, watch the bitch he owns together with Scudamore. Gina Emm is her name. She's a handy little thing. She's already won sixteen races. And certainly, we'll go jump racing. 'I'll be at Cheltenham for the Festival,' he says. 'I'll be at Liverpool for the Grand National. I always go to watch my boys at the big ones.'

Festival Fever

It is February 1, the final day for entering horses in the Cheltenham National Hunt Festival, and sixteen telephonists are gathered in the operations room at Weatherbys in Wellingborough, Northamptonshire. The lines – and fax machines to accommodate entries from Ireland and the United States – have been open since the previous afternoon. The room is especially feverish now, however, for the dozens of British trainers have waited until the last moment to commit their horses and entry fees.

The fever has swept up from Cheltenham itself where the night before the General Manager, Edward Gillespie, probably the best and certainly the most helpful race course official in the business, was phoning round to twenty trainers to gee them into getting their entries up to Weatherbys. 'Some of the top horses aren't even entered,' he reported, declining to name the negligent offenders. 'Some of the big races have only four nominations.'

Scudamore is at Hereford today, plunging to his 146th victory, and fretting over his failure to lay on a helicopter to thrash over to the last race at Windsor where, as luck would have it, Pipe's horse Might Move wins with Jonothan Lower. The chopper, even if available, would have cost him £700.

Of the approaching Cheltenham Festival he professes calm. 'I'll let Martin and Charlie deal with the realities,' he says, 'and I'll do the dreaming.' In fact, the Festival, looming even larger than his run for the 150, is taking shape as a nightmare. Scu's banker, Pipe's banker, everyone at Nicholashayne's banker, is dead.

Rusch de Farges, another of Martin Pipe's French imports and a 'chaser who grew in stature throughout the year, quoted at one time as low as 12-1 for the Tote Cheltenham Gold Cup, although in the end he didn't run at the Festival.

Scudamore won't talk about it. In what he and Pipe will look back on as the tragedy of the season, the promising Out of the Gloom died five days ago, pitched over with a burst blood vessel while being hosed in the yard. It happened on January 27, less than a week after the dark 8-year-old gelding's stunning 12-length victory in the Premier Long Distance Hurdle at Haydock.

Scudamore and Pipe, thrilled by the performance, were earmarking the horse for the Stayers' Hurdle at Cheltenham, three miles and just over a furlong. Now their best hope for the Festival is dead.

Anyway, at 9:30 that morning, Miss Gale Harrison, Martin Pipe's secretary, comes on from Pond Farm, Nicholashayne. This is the first season Weatherbys has accepted entries over the telephone and the procedures are precise, cryptic and foolproof. Miss Harrison is first asked only her 'Pin' or security number. The telephonist taps it onto a screen. Miss Harrison's name comes up. What is your name? She says it. It tallies. Pipe's secretary is then asked what Festival race she wants to enter and she replies by number: for example, 01561 for the Champion

Hurdle or 01582 for the Gold Cup, which she knows from her Racing Calendar.

Tap-tap. The race name is confirmed. So it goes on, each animal and its trainer and owner and, importantly, its age also doubly confirmed. 'If anything doesn't tally-up,' explains Michael Goacher, manager of Weatherbys' entry operations department, 'it gets passed over to our four trouble-shooters on the "help desk".'

Everything Miss Harrison says does tally-up, of course, for Pipe is too exact to commit such organisational blunders. Still, she has plenty to concentrate on as her boss has made a gigantic list of entries to the Championship races. It is the biggest from a single trainer this year. It numbers 29 declarations for the nine races and reads thus:

TUESDAY, MARCH 14

The Waterford Crystal Champion Hurdle Challenge Trophy (Estimated total value £85,000) With £72,000 added to stakes for 4 yrs old and upwards. Weights: 4-y-o 11 st 6 lb; 5-y-o and up 12 st. Fillies and mares allowed 5 lb. About two miles. 43 entries. Fee per horse, first stage: £175.

Chatam
(The 1988 winner was Celtic Shot, trained by Fred Winter and ridden by Peter Scudamore)

Peter's dilemma here is deepening. 'I'm trying to keep every-body happy,' he says. 'I have to be polite. I can't tell people to get stuffed. If they both insist on my riding their horses, I'll be in trouble, won't I?' Still, he wants to ride a winner and, on this score, nobody is particularly bullish: Celtic Shot isn't firing, at least in Peter's view, and Chatam himself has just been thumped at Haydock. 'It isn't a problem,' he says, 'but could develop into a major problem.'

Scudamore's commitment will be to the title-holder.

The Arkle Challenge Trophy Steeplechase (Estimated total value £60,000) With £50,000 added to stake for 5 yrs old and upwards which, at the start of the current season, have not won a steeplechase. Weights: 5-y-o 11 st; 6-y-o and up 11 st 8 lb. Mares allowed 5 lb. About two miles. 34 entries. Fee per horse, first stage: £122.

My Cup of Tea
Sabin du Loir
(The 1988 winner was Danish Flight, trained by Jimmy Fitzgerald and ridden by Mark Dwyer)

The Waterford Crystal Stayers' Hurdle Race (Estimated total value £60,000) With £47,000 added to stakes for 4 yrs old and upwards. Weights: 4-y-o 11 st; 5-y-o and up 11 st 10 lb. Fillies and mares allowed 5 lb. Three miles and about one furlong. 46 entries. Fee per horse, first stage: £105.

Bonanza Boy
(The 1988 winner was Galmoy, ridden by Tommy Carmody and trained by John Mulhern of Ireland)

The Waterford Crystal Supreme Novices' Hurdle Race (Estimated total value £50,000) With £27,000 added to stakes for four yrs old and upwards which, at the start of the current season, have not won a hurdle race. Weights: 4-y-o 11 st; 5-y-o and up 11 st 8 lb. Fillies and mares allowed 5 lb. About two miles. 100 entries. Fee per horse, first stage: £87.

Honest Word
Jabrut
Patriote
Sayfar's Lad
Sondrio
Tel-Echo
Voyage Sans Retour
(The 1988 winner was Vagador, ridden by Mark Perrett and trained by Guy Harwood)

WEDNESDAY, MARCH 15

The Queen Mother Champion Steeplechase (Estimated total value £70,000) With £65,000 added to stakes for 5 yrs old and upwards. Weights: 5-y-o 11 st 6 lb; 6-y-o and up 12 st. Mares allowed 5 lb. About two miles. 18 entries. Fee per horse, first stage: £140.

Beau Ranger
Fu's Lady
Kescast
(The 1988 winner was Pearlyman, ridden by Tom Morgan and trained by John Edwards)

The Sun Alliance Novices' Chase (Estimated value £65,000) With £45,000 added to stakes for 5 yrs old and upwards which, at the start of the current season, have not won a steeplechase. Weights: 5-y-o 10 st 8 lb; 6-y-o and up 11 st 4 lb. Mares allowed 5 lb. About three miles. 62 entries. Fee per horse, first stage: £132.

Pharoah's Laen
(The 1988 winner was The West Awake, ridden by Simon Sherwood and trained by Oliver Sherwood)

The Sun Alliance Novices' Hurdle Race (Estimated total value £50,000) With £27,000 added to stakes for 4 yrs old and upwards which, at the start of the current season, have not won a hurdle race. Weights: 4-y-o 10 st 12 lb; 5-y-o and up 11 st 7 lb. Fillies and mares allowed 5 lb. About two miles and a half. 126 entries. Fee per horse, first stage: £87.

Pertemps Network
Rolling Ball
Sayfar's Lad
Tel-Echo
Voyage Sans Retour
(The 1988 winner was Rebel Song, ridden by Simon Sherwood and trained by Oliver Sherwood)

Peter, torn between Sayfar's Lad and Pertemps Network, watches films. 'There isn't much in it,' he concludes. Sayfar's has won over the two mile stretch, likely will go farther and is good on the soft ground that Cheltenham might present. On the other hand, Pertemps . . . No, there isn't much in it.

THURSDAY, MARCH 16

The Tote Cheltenham Cup Steeplechase (Estimated total value £110,000) With £100,000 added to stakes for 5 yrs old and upwards. Weights: 5-y-o 11 st 4 lb; 6-y-o and up 12 st. Mares allowed 5 lb. About three miles and two furlongs. 42 entries. Fee per horse, first stage: £175.

Beau Ranger
Bonanza Boy
Rusch de Farges
(The 1988 winner was Charter Party, ridden by Richard Dunwoody and trained by David Nicholson)

The Daily Express Triumph Hurdle Race (Estimated total value £55,000) With £35,000 added to stakes for 4 yrs old only. Weights: 11 st each. Fillies allowed 5 lb. About two miles. 78 entries. Fee per horse, first stage: £87.

Enemy Action
Honest Word
Jabrut
Kabartaylor
Liadett
Voyage Sans Retour
(The 1988 winner was Kribensis, ridden by Richard Dunwoody and trained by Michael Stoute)

When the deadline is reached at noon, the telephonists have taken more than 500 of the 549 total entries for the nine forthcoming Championship races. The work load seems staggering. 'It is,' says operations manager Goacher, 'but you ought to be here for the Easter Bank Holiday. We'll be taking declarations for twelve different jump meetings. It'll be a madhouse.'

Scudamore's other trainer, Charlie Brooks, has made eight entries in the Championship Races: Celtic Shot in the Champion Hurdle, Bajan Sunshine in the Stayers' Hurdle, Arden in the Supreme Novices' Hurdle, Another Schedule and Bruton Street in the Sun Alliance Steeplechase and Arden and Auction Law in the Sun Alliance Novices' Hurdle.

Beating Jonjo

The all-time jump record, 150 winners in a season, finally came up on 7 February, in a midweek meeting, at the modest little race course at Warwick. There was no need for a dawn dash to get there in time, for it is only about forty minutes up the road from Mucky Cottage, and that morning the Scudamore household seemed relaxed. It wasn't. Nerves were raw. The milestone was getting to them. 'Why are you in such a bad mood?' Peter asked Marilyn, over and over, as they prepared for the day.

'I'm not in a bad mood.'

'You are in a bad mood.'

'I'm *not* in a bad mood,' she snapped and, dressing the boys, realised not for the first time that season that any tetchiness on her part might be due to her feelings of guilt. She hadn't witnessed Scu's 100th winner at Haydock. She hadn't been at Fontwell when he drew level the day before with Jonjo's record of 149 winners, igniting the public and the Press.

Instead, Marilyn had taken the day off from her job to go hunting. She had gone hunting partly to keep her mind off his racing and – here was the nitty-gritty of the guilt – partly because you simply don't turn down the offer of a day out with the Heythrop.

It had been an exhilarating day out, too, until it began to drizzle late in the afternoon. She had been cantering out of a field onto a farm road when a post-and-rails appeared in front of her and three hedges in the distance. Her legs turned to jelly. She'd had enough. It was time to go home. Yet to recount her day, speak of her delicious fatigue, tell how she felt such a fool when she waved at a helicopter and said it was Scu – it all

Good trainers, good horses, good weather, good luck with injuries and a great deal of superb horsemanship bring Peter past Jonjo's record.

seemed so stupid. Her life seemed trivial that evening when her husband – 'Peter the King', as the *Daily Mail* was to put it – walked through the door.

Marilyn washed her hair. The season had been harrowing; that was the word she used. The spectre of an injury to her husband, a fall, loomed large before any race day, larger still before a big race day, and big race days seemed to be coming one after another. She thought that if Scu – like many another fan, she called him 'Scu' – was hurt riding, then at least he would be hurt doing something he loved.

'If he has a fall, if he has a *bad* fall and is badly injured or whatever, I think I could accept it,' she once thought aloud. 'But what worries me more is the car. If anything serious happened to him in a car accident, I would find it terribly difficult to cope with. It would be such a waste.'

Marilyn dried her hair. She would come along later, with a friend, to be at Scu's side at Warwick. She had arranged for friends to pick up the boys from school. She would return by four o'clock to take them to the dentist. Marilyn put on trousers and a bold-checked tweed jacket and welcomed her in-laws, Michael and Mary Scudamore, who had driven over from Herefordshire.

The world soon bore down on Scudamore. A photographer from the *Weekend Telegraph* magazine, preparing a preview of the Grand National – this headline turned out to be 'Peter the Great' – arrived and when he was finished Scudamore went into Cheltenham with a list of answers to questions put to him by his accountant. They dealt mostly with the nearby land, 390 acres, he was buying with his neighbour and friend, Twiston-Davies, and his new business venture, Peter Scudamore Bloodstock, which this season ran like a *leit-motif* through his life.

Scudamore had an agent now, too, but he was charmingly unaccustomed to fame. The previous weekend, prior to a meeting at Sandown, he had attended a dinner at a Heathrow hotel. He was being paid, he told me, £300 and *he didn't even have to speak*. 'That,' he said, 'was the first time I've ever been paid to eat.' Graham Gooch had been there, John Conteh, Nigel Mansell, James Hunt . . . and, although he had met some of them before, Scudamore remained puzzled by those he considered genuinely famous. He expected them to be different from the rest of us: physically larger, perhaps, glowing with nimbuses, certainly bright and engaging beyond measure.

'I overheard James Hunt talking to Mansell and all they talked about was motor racing. *Motor racing*,' Peter had recounted, perplexed. 'I don't know. Somehow, I didn't expect it. But the famous aren't always what you expect.'

Anyway on his return from his Cheltenham accountant, cars had accumulated in the drive while, in the garden, the family washing hung out in a warm breeze. A man's shirt lifted and waved its sleeve, as though in mute reminder that life went on at Mucky Cottage.

At 11:15, precisely as planned, we set out towards Warwick in Peter's father's car. Michael Scudamore drove, with his good eye on the tachometer: this is a new car, he explained, and I can't let the engine go over 3,000 revolutions per minute. Peter's mother sat in the passenger seat, anxious that her son might be injured, vaguely recalling him as a boy in his first point-to-point. Time passed so quickly, she thought, and for the moment she stayed silent lest she say something wrong. Peter, yawning and distracted, fidgeted in the back.

Michael, who knows his son's moods, was soon keeping the atmosphere light with conversation. He spoke of a horse, a half-brother of one of the dozen he keeps in Herefordshire for Peter Scudamore Bloodstock, of which he is a director. The horse, he said, won a race recently in Ireland. Peter didn't reply.

Michael mentioned the monstrous prices houses were fetching these days in the Cotswolds. He had been to America, he said, bringing me into the conversation, and ridden in a steeplechase at Saratoga Springs. That was before he got married. He drove slowly, a warm and generous man, watching the dashboard, his neck held rigid. His thinning hair looked the same hue as his son's, auburn, and you thought of the durable male genes in the family. *Scutum Amoris Divini.* 'The Shield of Love Divine.' Whatever that meant.

Mrs Scudamore told a story. It happened while Michael was courting her in Herefordshire. While hunting with Michael, she was thrown. 'I lay on the ground, moving my arms and legs, wondering if anything was broken. And do you know what Michael said to me?' she recounted. 'He said, "Now that you're down, could you get the gate?"' Michael chuckled. He had borne the anecdote many times. We talked about the weather: it was the mildest winter in memory. No one mentioned the race meeting at Warwick.

Peter said few words of any kind. He was annoyed. He was also annoyed at being annoyed. Why was his father driving so *bloody slowly*, he thought? It wasn't only because the car was new, with only 350 miles on the clock. It was because Father was becoming a slow driver. If he, Peter, was at the wheel he would arrive at the race course in good time. He would avoid any crowds that might prevent him from getting in the weighing-room an hour before the first race. My job, he thought, is to be thoroughly prepared to ride winners. Wouldn't I be a prat to turn up late?

Scudamore studied the form of the 1:30 in *The Sporting Life* and *The Racing Post*. His mount in that first race, the Ryton

Novices' Hurdle for 4-year-olds, was a chestnut colt named Anti Matter. My friend 'Spotlight' in the *Post* had picked him as the 9-4 favourite and had this to say about the colt's prospects:

'Anti Matter, beaten at odds-on when making his hurdles debut at Newton Abbot last month, looks worth another chance. Trained by Francois Boutin last year, when he won over 1m and narrowly failed to land a 1m 1f listed race at Maisons-Lafitte, Anti Matter ran as though in need of the race at Newton Abbot – despite his starting price of 2-1 on. Fourth to Landski, racing prominently until weakened going to the second last, he should know more this time.'

At Newton Abbot that day, the colt had been ridden by Martin Pipe's second jockey Jonothan Lower on ground as 'soft' as that forecast officially for Warwick. Scu himself had never ridden Anti Matter in a race but he remembered having schooled him once at Pipe's: a smallish horse, perhaps a bit short in front, he recalled, with a fairly good jump. He hadn't yet got his orders from Pipe but, absolutely central to the tactics, was the proven truth about the colt: Anti Matter had more speed than staying power.

Of the other fourteen starters, the major dangers, he felt, might lie in the two untried horses from France, Ling and Prince Valmy, both of whom had won there on the flat last autumn. They could finish anywhere but they were expensive and therefore quite likely useful. Their sires, respectively Far North and Mill Reef, were Nijinsky horses. Mill Reef won the Derby at a mile and a half and, as racing men know, a mile and a half horse can handily make the two mile trip over hurdles. I've got to keep an eye on them, he thought. I can't expect them to go off thirty lengths in front and come back.

Other than their having won, evidence from which to predict the French horses' performances was hard to find and Scudamore, always thorough in his preparation, sought other, proven horses that might give him a guide as to how the race might go. He wanted at least two – not one, but two or more, in case the one fell or ran below par – against which he might measure himself during the race. He saw that Steve Smith Eccles on Elegant Stranger and Dale McKeown on Realism, alone in the field, had been placed in novice hurdles. Elegant Stranger, from form, was a front runner. Realism was not.

The trainers of these two horses, as well as the French ones, were also to be taken into account. 'In a general sense, you get to know the traits of a John Edwards horse, say, or one trained by David Murray Smith,' Scudamore said later. 'But I'm not going to tell you what they are. You can't print it.'

Scudamore pondered in the back of the car. 'I was trying to predict the unpredictable,' he said later. 'You can either go in and wing it or you can have an educated guess. I prefer an educated guess.' He was constructing such a guess when his thoughts were disrupted by the faint thrash of a helicopter overhead. It was Martin Pipe and the faithful Chester Barnes, flying up from Somerset. The trainer's hovering presence deepened the urgency of the day.

Scudamore had resumed his planning when, out of the corner of his eye, he saw the red car of the jockey Brendan Powell overtake and streak from sight. It shook him. Was Brendan in a hurry? Was he in the first race?

Scudamore checked the papers. Brendan didn't ride until the 3 o'clock. He must have been speeding for some other reason. In fact, had Peter realised, it was reason enough to renew his anxiety: Brendan was beetling to Warwick to get his girlfriend, the jockey Lorna Vincent, there in time for the first race. Scudamore tried to sleep.

We arrived in good time. Warwick, with its shabby Edwardian grandstand, is one of the oldest racecourses in Britain, dating back to 1714. In the old days it was laid out on common land with a hill in the infield. 'I can remember being wheeled past in a pram and seeing sheep and cattle grazing on the Common Hill,' recalled Reg Harris, the head groundsman who has been there for thirty-three years. 'I can remember as a lad learning to sledge down the hill in the winter.'

Common Hill is still in sight, a huge and overgrown hump of earth dumped there during the dredging of a 'dead arm' of the nearby Grand Canal in the 1790s. The hill is a familiar and unfortunate landmark of the racecourse, blocking vision of the back straight from the stands. 'That's why we don't have any fences or hurdles out there,' said Harris. 'Nobody could see them if we did.'

For all this, Warwick is notable for the eccentric feats that have been achieved there. In 1847, on a course no longer in use, a horse called Chandler was said to have made a jump of 37 feet, from takeoff to landing, in a steeplechase race. In doing so, he cleared a brook and two fallen horses and riders. The leap seemed barely believable and, in fact, I later learned that *The Guinness Book of Records* fails to recognise it, preferring a jump of 8.4 metres (27 ft 6¾ inches), set in 1975 by a horse called 'Something' in South Africa.

Still, the might of Chandler, once a chandler's cart horse in Sutton Coldfield near Birmingham, is beyond dispute. An ugly creature, 'a fiddle-headed brute', according to his unimpressed breeder, Chandler went on to win the water-logged Grand National of 1848, a punishing race in which three horses were killed. His owner and rider collected £7,000 from the bookmakers, a staggering coup that in 1989 would have been worth about £200,000.

In the Chandler Suite, situated on the ground floor of the members' enclosure, there was no painting, nor even a plaque, in celebration of the horse. However, the site of the jump, Harris told me, is still there, beyond Common Hill and near the 2½ mile steeplechase starting gate. Later I went in search of it. Cog's Brook turned out to be a dirty, sluggish little brook lined with hawthorns and blackberry bushes. Yet, from bank to gravelly bank, the carry did indeed look prodigious. I found no marker to commemorate the jump but a more pressing Midlands emotion was aero-sprayed on a nearby cement shed: 'Wogs Out'.

Then on May 18, 1985 the retired jump champion John Francome took on Lester Piggott in a charity flat race over one mile and six furlongs. Piggott won, but not by much: three-quarters of a length. He rode a hurdler called The Liquidator which ironically was trained by Pipe. The race, which even in rain drew a record crowd of seven thousand, was the brainchild of the Clerk of the Course, the young Edward Gillespie, who, even as the Scudamore car drove into the car park, was cooking up a ceremony to honour Peter's 150th winner, if indeed it was to happen that day.

Peter was away from the car like a shot. The fans had yet to gather and he slipped untroubled into the weighing-room. There, above the bench John Buckingham had hung the colours of the owners, the brothers David and Terry Few from Taunton: vivid yellow, with a red disc on chest and back, red and yellow halved sleeves and a red cap. No green here to worry Pipe, and if Scudamore was seeking more omens the colours were promising: he had been wearing Few silks on January 18 at Ludlow when, riding Kings Rank, he equalled his best-ever season record of 132 winners, a mark he had set the previous year.

Scudamore wasn't seeking omens. Rather he was getting changed, ears kept open, seeking clues to his rival jockeys' frames of mind. 'I could tell, sitting there, that there were quite a few horses fancied in the race,' he said later. 'It's a general feeling I get. People were quiet, or asking how I was going to ride my race. Was I going to make it (the running)? Was I going to drop in a bit? When they're talking like this I know they feel they're in with a chance. It's when jockeys start laughing about the birds they pulled last night, you can be sure they don't care two hoots about the next race.'

Jockeys, I had been surprised to learn over weeks with Scudamore, will take time before a race to talk over their plans through the first few hurdles or fences of a race. They do it in the weighing-room, and again as they mill round the starting post. This by no means amounts to 'fixing' a race. It only underscores how dangerous they regard their game. But once the traffic clears over the opening obstacles, it's pretty much every man-and-horse for himself. The devil take the hindmost.

Scudamore, concluding his pre-race assessment of the weighing-room mood, decided that there would be nothing much out of the ordinary in the shape of the race. There would be a fairly steady pace over the first two hurdles.

The owners Few came from the stables, having enjoyed the privilege of seeing their horse and chatting briefly with Pipe, who said their fellow had travelled well from Somerset. Anti Matter's weight and blood the previous morning, he said, had tested spot on. Anti Matter? The name, drawn from the nomenclature of nuclear physics, seemed a curious choice for a racehorse and some weeks later I asked Alan Cooper, the agent of its first owner, the Greek shipbuilder Stavros Niarchos, about how it might have been arrived at.

'It is odd, isn't it?' said Cooper. 'But I wouldn't have any idea. Mr Niarchos's daughter names most of his horses.' Anti Matter's breeding is classical, its recent history touched by tragedy. He is by King's Lake out of Firyal, who in her turn was sired by

Nonoalco, winner of the 2,000 Guineas in 1974. Foaled in Ireland, trained in France, Anti Matter came up for sale early in November 1988 at Longchamps, near Paris. Pipe and Barnes, who frequently travel together to sales, were there. They studied the sales catalogue and, as Barnes later recalled, 'we saw about fifty horses that day.' They also saw the Yorkshire-man Martin Blackshaw, the former jockey who had set up as a flat trainer at Chantilly.

Blackshaw was keen on Anti Matter. He'd seen the neat little colt on the French flat and it looked a sound animal with a fair turn of foot. He recommended it to Pipe. So did Cooper, Niar-chos's agent. The Somerset trainer in his turn, took an instant liking to Anti Matter. It was his kind of horse: compact, strong and small. Small horses suffer less wear and tear on the legs. Best of all, the colt was sound: the fundamental thing to look for in a horse, feels Pipe, is soundness. If purchased at a reasonable price and raced in middling company, he reasoned, Anti Matter would be good value as a bread-and-butter winner. He got the colt for Fr.135,000 (about £12,500 at the time), a reasonable price.

Blackshaw, fluent in French, led Pipe to other horses. Pipe eventually bought six and offered the Yorkshireman payment for his advice. Blackshaw would take nothing, not even a drink, and now, at Warwick, as he saddled-up Anti Matter, Pipe thought of those Longchamp sales and of the helpful Yorkshire-man. On January 23, a week after Anti Matter first ran in England, Blackshaw was killed in a car crash on an icy road near Chantilly.

In the bookmakers' enclosure, Anti Matter opened 5-4 favourite. The bookies' chief concern was whether the other two French horses, Prince Valmy and Ling, running in their maiden race in Britain, were being brought along solely for the exercise. Their opening prices, 4-1 and 7-1 respectively, didn't support this notion, but a drift to 7-1 and 9-1 at the 'off' did. Gaelic Issue, at 8-1, closed third favourite between them. Anti Matter shor-tened to evens.

There was more for the alert jockey (and bookmaker, no doubt) to learn in the parade ring. Scu looked at the French horses, the neophytes, being led along by their stable lasses and decided they were not fully fit. They looked a bit burly, like athletes out of shape. They looked, he thought, as if they needed a race to improve their fitness, and this gave him hope. 'Still, you can't be sure,' he said later. 'Sometimes, if they're good horses, they'll overcome that poor fitness first time out.'

Scudamore met the Few brothers in the parade ring, chatted courteously with them, and listened to his trainer's instructions. 'He didn't get the trip last time,' said Pipe, referring to the front-running tactic he had tried with Anti Matter at Newton Abbot. 'Switch him off this time. Save his energy. Hold him up until about two out and then use his speed. Just try it.' Then, as always, he added, 'But use your own judgement.'

Pipe, as is his habit, thereupon meticulously checked the horse's tack: he pulled the girth up a hole, looked over the buckles on the bridle and, after giving his jockey a leg up, tightened the surcingle. On the horse, Scu straightaway took heart. 'He felt different from what I remembered,' he explained later. 'He has a nice big neck on him. Funny, and it depends on the horse, but at home when some of them are relaxed they feel small. Yet at a race, they'll get excited and bulk up.'

He cantered up past the stands, in vivid view of the proud Fews who, binoculars round their necks, stood high up on a members' enclosure gangway with Pipe and Barnes. Scudamore's yellow shirt with its bull's-eye red disc leapt out from the muted colours round him.

Down towards the start, Scudamore moved through rough, soft ground which Anti Matter didn't much fancy. Crikey, Scudamore thought briefly: is the going going to be softer than 'Soft', the official report? He put it out of his mind and, milling round the start, he asked the starter to give his girth a tug to check it for tightness. He prayed.

Warwick's hurdle track is sharp and shortish, in an angular oval, just over one mile six furlongs in length, with eight obstacles, two of them to be taken for a second time on the run-in. It travels left-handed round the outside of the steeplechase track. Scudamore, Graham McCourt on Big Finish, and Steve Smith Eccles on Elegant Stranger, lined up on the inside, beside the steeplechase dividing rail.

'Are you going to make it?' asked McCourt expecting Scudamore to go to the front as is not uncommon with a Pipe–Scudamore horse. Scudamore said no, he'd drop in behind the leaders.

'Eck, you go in front,' said Scudamore, moving behind Elegant Stranger's rump, watching McCourt line up on his own inside. He turned to McCourt. 'I'm not going in front, Graham,' he warned. 'But I'm going down the inner.' McCourt agreed to drop in behind him. Smith Eccles then asked Peter his intentions. 'Have you got my inner?' he said with the mock menace he commonly affects. 'Because if you do you'll be jumping fences, not hurdles.'

Smith Eccles meant jokingly, though with serious implications, that if Scudamore challenged him on the inside, he would drive him onto the chase course. 'No,' said Scudamore, not intimidated. 'I'm just going to track you.' Peter likes 'tracking', that is to follow behind, the veteran Smith Eccles. 'Eck knows what he's doing,' he explained later. 'He's not silly. If he's going well, he won't let me up there. If he's not going well, he *will* let me up there.'

'The horses are under starter's orders,' came the commentator's voice. It bore the lucid, metallic monotone that stirs the blood of the British racegoer. Pause. Then suddenly the gate, just a yellow elastic rope, snapped across the track. *'And they're off,'* resumed the commentator. *'They make their way towards the first. Ling and Woodknot are amongst the early leaders . . .'*

Anti Matter, hugging the rail, was giving Scu a handful. He began pulling as they swept towards the first flight. Scudamore gave him a pull to get him back on his hocks for the upward impulsion needed to clear the obstacle. The horse didn't respond. Instead, he lunged through the top of the hurdle and Scudamore muttered quietly – 'sod it' – and thought to himself: you should have let his head go.

'. . . as they jump the first flight, along with Enchanted Cross . . . Elegant Stranger, prominent on the inside, joins the three leaders as they run on towards the second . . .'

Scudamore settled his pulling young horse, let his head go into the second hurdle and the horse jumped it well. He was where he wanted to be. Barely thirty-five seconds into the race, unremarked and perhaps unremarkable. Scudamore had faced and fluently resolved a small dispute with his mount. A *modus operandi* had been established for the next three-and-a-half minutes of the race: Anti Matter, within reason, would be given his freedom.

The field of horses pounded past the finishing post, first time round, and bent to the left towards the third hurdle, some two furlongs away. Relax him, thought Scudamore as the horse moved away from the rail, save his energy.

'. . . and Ling on the outside is the leader over the third, from Elegant Stranger in second place. Turning now, with the leaders well grouped up together, Realism is showing up well. So too is Woodknot. Enchanted Cross is just behind the leaders and then comes Explosive Spirit. After this one, Rocquelle as they go up the hill . . .'

Anti Matter now lay about ninth, a half dozen lengths behind, and Pipe muttered to himself: good position, hold him up. Anti Matter met the third hurdle nicely but, on taking off, skewed to the right. Scudamore thought, Shit. I hate horses jumping off to the right on a left-handed track. It jumps me into the middle. It can kill me. Yet, there was no corrective. You can't pull a horse about when he's jumping.

'. . . Ling still with the advantage of about three or four lengths from Prince Valmy. Prince Valmy continuing to race wide on the outside, as they go out of sight from the stands . . .'

Suddenly, there was nothing to watch. In the stands, Dave Few took his binoculars down and smiled. 'Give me an earth-mover,' he said, bringing to bear the only expertise he could offer. 'Just give me an earth-mover. I'll shift that hill out of the way.'

Out of sight, Elegant Stranger, with Smith Eccles aboard, had kept to the inside rail as planned. But Smith Eccles was losing touch. 'My horse was sending out distress signals,' he said later. 'We were going nowhere.' Accordingly, the veteran jockey moved off the rail and looked over his left shoulder. 'Any time you're ready, Scu,' he shouted. No Scu. Smith then looked over his right shoulder. Ah, the bugger's gone to the outside, he realised. He's looking for the good ground.

Scudamore indeed had drifted farther and farther across to the outside of the track, pounded past Cog's Brook, where Chandler put in that thirty-seven-foot leap. In truth, however, Scudamore hadn't so much gone outside as been taken there by the resolutely right-jumping Anti Matter. Nonetheless he was pleased. The ground was better, not so cut up, and deep in his mind he was reassured of this by the rich green turf stretching on ahead.

'. . . as they begin to come into view again and on to the next flight of hurdles, which is the fourth. Still quite a long run until they get to it. And Ling is the leader by just two lengths from Prince Valmy. In third place, two lengths away again, comes Realism. And then Anti Matter, who's made headway. That's gone up into fourth place . . .'

The colt, full of fluency, began to go well. Scudamore hoped, with rising confidence, that nothing was moving up on the inside. He didn't look, however, for the rhythms were flowing too sweetly beneath him. Instead, his eyes were pinned straight ahead on the raised bottom of Tom Morgan riding Prince Valmy and, still farther ahead, on the emerald green colours of the front-runner: Bradley on Ling. We can't let Brad get out of touch, Scudamore thought with just a quiver of doubt in his horse. Maybe we're not good enough to hit the front.

Anti Matter continued to hang right but Scudamore felt the horse's easy, rising power between his legs. He let the colt accelerate, *to the outside*, round Morgan who held his line to let him pass. Kind of you Tom, thought Scudamore, you could have put me in trouble. He took the fourth, the first of a trio of flights down the back, without effort and, in the stands, Pipe thought: he's won. He nearly said as much to the Few brothers but held his tongue: Scu still had four hurdles to jump.

'They go to the middle flight on the far side and Ling is the leader. Anti Matter moving up on the outside and jumping very well there for Peter Scudamore, going up to take second place behind Ling.'

Five furlongs from home and it had become a two-horse race. Smith Eccles far behind on the blown-out Elegant Stranger, was riveted by the duel. 'I was cruising along,' he said later, 'just watching Scu. I was watching my mate making history.'

Scudamore now felt he could pick off Bradley and Ling at will but he resisted the temptation. Don't go whizzing by him, he thought, mindful of his instructions, mindful of his mount's inexperience, or you may land in a heap. He swung into the middle, took the third from last and, turning for home, drifted right again. In his experience, he reckoned: 'the ground is usually better up the outside at Warwick. Also, the way the horse was going right I'd have the rail to keep me straight. Everything was adding up in my favour to go right-handed.'

'. . . *Ling is the leader by about three-parts of a length from Anti Matter, who is going very easily in second place . . . In line for home, two flights of hurdles left to jump. The horse with the sheepskin noseband is Ling, who's made all the running. In the yellow and red colours, coming up very strongly is Anti Matter to challenge . . .'*

They both jumped the second from home cleanly. Don't go to the front too soon, Scudamore told himself. '. . . *Ling under pressure as they run between the last two. Just over a furlong left to go . . .'* In the stands, Peter's wife and his mother both turned away, heads to the wall. Okay, Scudamore shouted at himself, *go for him.*

The horse exploded forward. '*Peter Scudamore looks like he is going to set racing history today with his 150th winner of the season. And he's gone clear on Martin Pipe's Anti Matter. He's eight or ten lengths out in front. Anti Matter —*' and the commentator's voice was drowned out by the cheering.

Scudamore passed the post and lifted up out of the saddle. In the stands, Pipe and Barnes, without a word to the Few brothers, turned and shouldered themselves through the crowd and down the outdoor stairs towards the unsaddling enclosure.

The first jockey to get to Scudamore was Smith Eccles, who had finished dead last. 'Well done, kid,' he said for, at 33, Eck is the senior man on the circuit. Gracious and generous as his record was eclipsed, Jonjo O'Neill, now a trainer and with a runner in the last race, presented Scudamore with a trophy and a good-natured quip. 'Peter has yet to have a ride for me,' he said, 'I'll have to find him a bad novice chaser just to see how good he is.'

Champagne was poured, just a sip, round the weighing-room for there was more racing that day. Within the hour, Scudamore had notched his 151st winner on another Pipe horse, Pertemps Network, a promising hurdler that would shine through the season, and the racing press sought to put Peter's achievement into perspective. The 151 winners total, run up so early in the season, was commonly recognised to be astonishing, with no observer pegging it so high the following morning as Tony Stafford, racing editor of *The Daily Telegraph.*

'Coming, as it has, with more than three months of the season remaining, it vies with Bob Beaman's Mexico long-jump of

113

29 ft 2½ in. as entering the realms of improbability,' wrote Stafford, adding that Scudamore's winning total 'could indeed, by the end of the season, become the record that will never be broken.'

Scudamore, driving home with Marilyn, had other races, further targets in mind. There were, for example, still eight more winners to go to reach a career total of 1,000, something heretofore achieved only by Francome and Stan Mellor, and then there was tomorrow at Ascot. Champagne was poured at Mucky Cottage that evening and the boys, Thomas and Michael, tumbled round the sofas in the sitting-room. They were proud and relieved at the afternoon's results: the dentist had found nothing wrong with their teeth.

A Real Good Horse

'Great horses have a gait, a rhythm when they run, and you never feel you're going flat-out,' Scudamore said. 'Everything's in the right position and you've got all the time in the world. You can stand off or put in a short one.'

The champion jockey might have been talking about a handful of celebrated horses he's ridden: Corbiere, Burrough Hill Lad, Broadsword, perhaps Celtic Shot. He was talking about Sabin du Loir, the classy little French gelding, the horse with the proverbial bottom of a cook and the head of a king. 'He's a real good horse,' he added quietly. 'He may be as good as ever I've sat on.'

Scudamore, perhaps unknown to himself, had just shifted into top gear and overtaken another car on the motorway. It was in December and Sabin, a hurdler by trade, had made his debut as a chaser at Newton Abbot a winning one.

'With a good horse,' he said, 'a real good horse, you can feel his power when he goes past other horses – acceleration like a fast car. Yet, in a funny sort of way, time seems to slow down. You can see your stride, and you've always got a choice. When you're going badly, there's only one stride pattern there. Yes, Sabin's a good horse all right.'

Sabin du Loir – from one champion trainer to the next.

Peter Scudamore and toothy friend on the gallops at Uplands.

The all-conquering combination: Martin Pipe and Peter Scudamore
prepare to 'make all' again.

Two of the 'nearly' horses in Peter's record-breaking season. Chatam (*above*), after a very promising run in the Triumph Hurdle the year before, was regarded as a great prospect for the Champion, but when he eventually returned to the racecourse, he disappointed. Sabin du Loir (*below*) was more successful but still missed out at the Festival.

The junior Scudamores proudly display the Mackeson Gold Cup
after Pegwell Bay's victory at Cheltenham in November.

Jonjo O'Neill makes a presentation to Peter as his record of 149 winners in a season falls.

Connections can still hardly believe Scu's 'miracle' ride to win the
Racing Post Chase with Bonanza Boy at Kempton.

Bonanza Boy was a tiny mount for tackling Aintree's huge fences.

Desert Orchid, 1989 Gold Cup winner, returns with stable-lass
Janice Coyle and his owner Richard Burridge.

David Nicholson (*left*) and Fred Winter (*right*) two great
jockeys-turned-trainers with whom Peter was connected until the
days of Pipe and Brooks.

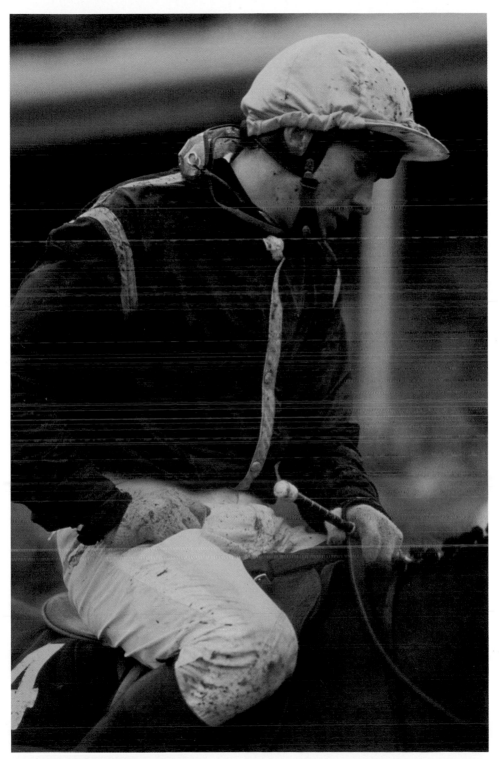
The ill-fated Enemy Action was to die later at Aintree.

As landmark after landmark was passed in an historic season, there were plenty of occasions to celebrate. Peter and Marilyn after the 150 (*above*) and Peter at Towcester (*below*).

February 14

Lost in a litter of milestones, the one Scudamore cherished most was the one he reached on February 14 at Newton Abbot, the benevolent track of his season. It was the 1,000th win of his career which stretched back to August 31, 1978 when, at nearby Devon and Exeter, he got off his career mark with a win on a horse named Rolyat.

'My other milestones seemed to be public,' he said afterwards. 'This one was private. This was the one I wanted most.' It stamped his credentials on National Hunt history: only Stan Mellor (1,035) and John Francome (1,138), had reached the 1,000 mark.

The horse, the third of his treble that day, all trained by Pipe, was a leggy 4-year-old filly named Avionne which he drove out to a three-length victory in the Hound Tor Novices' Selling Hurdle. He did it, with playful satisfaction, while the master was away: Pipe was on holiday, albeit phoning home regularly, in the Bahamas.

'Whenever Martin's away, we want to do well, just to pull his leg,' said Peter. 'His Dad, David, was in charge and he told me to drop her in a little bit, which is unusual for us.'

Although he was riding the well-backed 4-9 favourite, Scudamore's win had been thoroughly planned, yet it was imprecisely executed. It was in the fifth race of the day. 'I walked the course when I got there and the ground was very, very heavy,' he said, illustrating the fact that official reports – 'soft', in this case – are not always to be trusted.

'Although it's a tight track,' he said, 'I definitely decided that the ground was better out, off the inside.' He did his reckoning:

if I lose ten lengths taking the longer way wide, he thought, the going's got to be eleven lengths faster to win.

Scudamore then won the second and third races, respectively on Wingspan and Let Him By, and was on an emotional high. Confidence, even for a champion jockey, is a flighty commodity and now with the prospect of a hat-trick of winners he was brimming with it. Otherwise, when Avionne broke in the next race, he might not have cast aside his plan to go wide for the better ground.

'Getting away, I had the inside and I thought I'd cling to it, *right down the rail*,' he said, 'in the hope that I'd find a strip of ground that wasn't chopped up, that nobody else had gone down all day. Then, at about the stands turn, there was a lot of traffic problems in front of me and it seemed prudent to drift out a bit.'

Back on plan 'A', on the outer, he made up his ground quickly and by the time he was half-way round the 2 mile course, four hurdles from home, he was battling it out with his father's horse, Proud Soldier, ridden on the inside by Dai Tegg. 'I'm not sentimental, soft, about my father's horses,' the hard-nosed jockey continued, 'and in this case I thought, I've *got* to beat him. I'd look stupid otherwise because I could have ridden Proud Soldier myself.'

Tegg stuck to the inner, Scudamore to the outer, worrying if Avionne would stay on the soft ground. 'She did,' Peter concluded, 'and that was the deciding factor.' He took it up from the second last and won by three lengths. In the unsaddling enclosure, Michael Scudamore turned to David Pipe. 'We must be the best sires here today,' and once again the champagne was flowing. Peter had reached not only his 1,000 overall but his 158th win of the season.

Sondrio Meets the Captain

Sondrio has led a curious life. As an entire horse, that is to say one which has not been gelded, the Irish-bred colt seemed set for a promising life as a stallion. He had already won four flat races in Europe and the 1986 Hialeah Turf Cup, a Grade 1 race in Florida, when Geraldine and Jim Ryan bought him at private sale for well into six figures. They flew him home to County Kildare, booked 50 mares to be covered at Ir £3,000 a fling, and sent him along to the local stud.

There he fired blanks. His stabs at fatherhood failed. He was declared 100 per cent infertile. So, what do you do with such a fast, expensive horse, still only seven years old? How do you cut your losses? Well, you cut your horse. You castrate him and send him out to seek his fortune as a hurdler, perhaps a chaser one day. This the Ryans did and in the autumn of 1989, no longer sore in the loins, Sondrio appeared at Pipe's yard in Somerset.

At first, the gelding seemed to glory in the loss of his manhood. With Scudamore aboard, he won his first three outings. The maiden one was the Dinmore Novices' Hurdle, a well-chosen £680 run in November at Hereford, a sharpish right-handed track which he didn't much fancy. He won by ten lengths. He then won £1,518 against a stronger field in the Ashton Novices' Hurdle a fortnight later at Haydock, oval-shaped and running to the left. Best of all, he took home £2,427 in the Durham Rangers Novices' Hurdle in January at Ascot when, taken on round the final right-hand turn, he beat off the challenge to win at the line.

The Ryans were chuffed. Their loss-cutting operation

119

Sondrio: Radclyffe Academy, Class of '89.

appeared to be creeping along nicely. The recoup seemed at hand. Yet, on closer inspection, the notes of these races were coloured by doubt: 'mistakes . . . mistakes . . . mistakes.'

Sondrio was finally found out at Kempton Park on 25 February. This was a day that turned out to be memorable indeed for Scudamore, as we shall see, but Sondrio's hurdling performance gave no cause for celebration. Kempton is a right-handed track, decidedly so, and on his tour over the sticks Sondrio had kicked out more stumps than a petulant batsman and, worse, he swerved resolutely left at every flight.

Already, Fu's Lady, favoured to win a 2½ mile chase, had made a horlicks of a late fence and after admirably picking her up from the floor, Peter had pulled her up. So when Sondrio had blundered badly, finishing far back in seventh place, Scudamore was fed up. 'This is it,' he said. He was thinking of fewer than three weeks forward, when Sondrio was aiming to tackle Cheltenham's Supreme Novices' Hurdle. 'I'm writing him off for the Festival.'

Pipe didn't. Instead, he sent him off to Oxfordshire where a former Army officer runs a correction centre for delinquent horses. It was there, in the grounds of Lew house, that Sondrio met Capt. C. R. Radclyffe a fortnight before Cheltenham. In all of the British Isles, perhaps the world, Charles Radclyffe is the accepted genius at sorting out 'difficult' horses.

When I went to meet him, Radclyffe was waiting on the gravel drive in front of his 15th century Cotswold-stone farmhouse. A tall, handsome craggy-faced man, in his sixties, he's as straight as a ram-rod, but considerably more friendly. He turned out to be outgoing, discursive, aristocratic, endearingly vague and, most striking of all, a man with the bone-deep, instinctive feel for a horse.

In the war, Radclyffe was in the Royal Scots Greys, 'the last regiment to be mechanised', and afterwards he'd been an amateur rider. 'I rode a lot of point-to-point and under rules but with little success,' he said, as we crunched through the gravel towards the house. 'One of my few successes was beating Harry Llewellyn in a hunter chase at Cardiff.'

He laughed. 'Also, I must have been one of the very few people who rode in a hurdle race and fell off before I got to the first hurdle. Somewhere down in the West Country. Extraordinary horse, you never knew whether he was going to swerve to the right or left.'

We were now sitting in the drawing-room, the pleasant smell of a wood-burning fireplace round us. A picture of a pretty young woman, his daughter, rested in a silver frame on a side table. She was a film producer, Sarah Radclyffe. Among her credits were *My Beautiful Laundrette*, *Wish You Were Here* and *A World Apart*. He talked about her other films, the opening nights, her new projects, chuckling away. He was prouder of her than of the hurdlers and jumpers, all of them once his or handled by him, that hung in photographs on the wall.

'We have two sides to our horse business,' he explained. 'One, we buy two or three store yearlings every year which we break and sell to go chasing. I suppose Corbiere was one of my better ones. We had two others recently, Morley Street and Mole Board. Quite good hurdlers at the moment. Cheltenham horses this year.

'Anyhow, we also have horses to school, fifteen or so at a time, the difficult horses,' he went on. 'I'm a tremendous believer in the loose school where, of course, a horse jumps round by itself, without anybody on its back. He'll jump it correctly. I feel if you get a horse jumping correctly off its hocks, he'll probably jump a bit slowly at first, especially the hurdlers, but the Scudamores of this world will very soon quicken him up.'

The transition from flat runner to hurdler is the easiest and the most lasting, of course, because horses from the flat have nothing to *unlearn*, Radclyffe explained. 'On the other hand,' he continued, 'getting hurdlers to jump fences is another matter. They've gone on their forehand. Their heads are down and their weight's on their forelegs. I want to get them all, hurdlers and jumpers, *all of them* to sit back on their *hocks*.' A man of boundless enthusiasm, the captain's speech is peppered with italics.

Radclyffe makes no claims of founding the Loose-School system of training. He reeled off a string of forerunners: Jack Gittings, 'probably the finest nagsman in England in his day', and Harry Bonner, Reg Hobbs, Fred Rimell. 'There was a man who dealt in hunters near here, Stanley Barton. He had one,' he said. '*Marvellous*. In fact, I copied mine from Barton. I can't explain it easily. But it seems to work. We average 80 to 100 winners a year, races won with horses we've had at the school. It gives us tremendous interest to see how they do. On one Bank Holiday we once had eleven horses running on the same day.'

How'd they do?

'I can't remember,' said the captain.

I asked him what was the principal failing of a 'difficult' horse. Confidence, he thought, and then he expanded the notion. 'I think a lot depends on the modern owners,' he said. 'They don't want to win next week. They want to win tomorrow or, preferably, yesterday.'

He chuckled. 'We had two people last year, *terribly* nice, and they had just bought two 3-year-olds in Ireland, great big horses, 16.2 hands high. Completely untouched. They'd hardly seen man nor beast when they arrived here to be broken in and on the eighth day the owners arrived and said, "Do tell us, how are our horses jumping in the loose school?" "Good gracious," I said, "this will take two or three weeks. I'm still driving them in the long-reins." To which they replied, "*Long-reins*? Is that a good thing to be doing?"'

The captain popped to his feet. 'Anyway,' he said, 'come along and have a look.'

Radclyffe's loose school was out behind a stone barn. It looked shabby, jerry-built, no smarter than any old amateur's equestrian school down the road, and not very big: altogether about 13 metres wide, 40 metres long, open-sided, with head-high boarding all round and girders holding up a sheltering roof. The floor was a mixture of sand and ashes. An oval track, no more than four metres wide and maybe 80 metres in circumference, ran round the boarding. The inner rail was merely a two-rung fence, just high enough to keep in a horse.

With pride, Radclyffe showed his four improvised, thingamy-jig jumps. There were two on each long side of the oval. They were wooden poles, wrapped in foam rubber and held in place by tyre tape and stretching clear across the track. Brush and twigs were stuffed under the jumps. The track gave a feeling of narrowness, confinement: I would have hated to see ponies try to do it in pairs. Plainly, a horse might refuse but he could never run out.

'A horse can't go very far wrong in this loose school,' said Radclyffe. 'He's got to keep reasonably straight. With that rubber, we've more or less eliminated giving him a big knee and yet it's big enough that he damn well knows when he's hit it.' In the sand, parallel to and on each side of the jumps, lay unpainted take-off rails.

Now, the *pièce de résistance*. They were ropes and pulleys, weighted down with rusty scraps of farm machinery, with which Radclyffe could lift and lower the heights of the jumps. *Squeak-squeak*, down in the sand. 'If a horse has lost his confidence,' said Radclyffe, 'you can put the thing on the floor.' *Squeak-squeak-squeak*, and it goes to any height, up to your waist. 'In the end,' said Radclyffe, 'a horse so loves going round that you can't stop it. I'll show you in a minute.'

He called a lad and while the lad fetched a horse, the captain mentioned that he had put many horses right for Martin Pipe in the past. The first was Baron Blakeney, who won the Triumph Hurdle at Cheltenham in 1981 at 66-1. 'Modern trainers just don't have the time to loose-school a horse,' he said. 'Especially a difficult horse. We've had difficult horses here that we've had out on the hour, every hour.'

The captain treats newcomers much the same and when Sondrio arrived he got the standard, opening-day treatment: a bit of roadwork through Radclyffe's 500-acre farm, reached only after a walk down the busy A4095, with the captain driving on ahead, his headlamps blazing in midday to slow down the traffic. 'We're touching on Brize Norton aerodrome,' he said and chuckled. 'I reckon when a horse leaves here he's traffic-proof, cattle-proof, dog-proof and aeroplane-proof.'

He explained how horses, when they then come here to the covered school, are encouraged along, step-by-step. 'What happens is always the same,' he explained. 'We put a jump on the ground and a lad comes in with the horse. We keep him on the leading-rein and jump him backwards and forwards over the jump, two or three times. Then we loose him off round the whole thing.' An especially difficult horse, he added, might need three lads and himself working with it at the same time.

The lad returned with the demonstration horse. It was a brown, four-year-old gelding, one from Nick Gaselee's yard. Head up, alert, he looked ready for the game. 'He really doesn't need any more of this,' Radclyffe chuckled. 'He's already finished off. He's done enough and he's getting too bloody flippant.'

The horse was let loose. He sped away, circling the tight, sandy course, flowing over the jumps, as nippy as a gypsy boy's pony. He came pounding round a second time. Then a third. 'He'd go on for five minutes if he had it his way,' said Radclyffe and stepping out, arms waving, flagged down the horse. It pulled up, considered the awful prospect of his game being over for the day, wheeled round and plunged all the faster in the opposite direction. He was caught by the lad and led away.

The demonstration gelding had provided the ideal show.

Sondrio's script had proven a little more troublesome. 'He went all to pieces. He seemed to blunder through everything, hit everything,' said Radclyffe and, for a moment, I forgot he was speaking of a six-figure horse, a stable star, a hurdler that had already won at Haydock and Ascot this season and was headed for the Cheltenham Festival. 'He was just a *very* bad jumper. He didn't really know when to take off and finally, when we got the jumps off the floor, we had to take a lungeing-whip and gently drive him over them.'

Sondrio Meets the Captain

Sondrio had made slow progress. He was a one-captain, three-lad job. It was a matter of teaching an older horse new tricks and he *was* an older horse, 8 years old. Coaxed and handled patiently, Sondrio finally got the knack of the job and in twelve days he was skimming, undriven, round the track. Radclyffe shrugged, modest, honest, unsure of his abiding success with the horse.

'If we start a young horse off, absolutely from scratch, we reckon never to see it again. But we really do *not* have much success with older horses, 8 years old and upwards,' the captain admitted. 'We find we can put them right for one race and probably *one* race only before they're back to their old ways.

'When Harry Thomson Jones had jumpers, I had all his horses here. He had one, wherever it ran, whether or not it won, whether it was Liverpool or down in the West Country, it always came back here for a week's refresher. But a lot of modern owners and trainers, if their horse wins, they think it's a frightful waste of time and money sending it back here.'

The captain paused, poised to go off on a digression. 'There are an *awful* lot of people now who own horses who wouldn't recognise their horse when they saw it. And when it's won a race at the right price it can go for slaughter,' he said. 'I feel sorry for a lot of trainers. They've got a gun to their heads.'

Anyway, to me, the demonstration gelding had shown an interesting bit of behaviour. It first had run anti-clockwise then, unbidden and willingly, clockwise. I wondered if Sondrio, who almost unfailingly jumped out to the left, had gone both ways round by the time he was finished. Radclyffe said he had. But that didn't mean much, he added, which was interesting. 'We have had horses that really *would* only go one way round the school. We've tried hours and hours and I've finally accepted it and never *ever* has it made any difference on a race course. Absolutely *not*. Why? I haven't any idea.'

Radclyffe squeaked down the pulleys of his ingenious jumps. He bumped a pole in place on the ground. He smiled to himself, recalling something from the past. 'We had a horse of Fulke Walwyn's here once who simply wouldn't jump an open ditch,' he said. 'So I got some railway sleepers, which I painted orange, and I made a really good, life-sized open ditch. And I started with my sleepers really close-up and took it back, day by day, until it was a proper open ditch. Eventually, that horse did win quite a lot of races.'

He seemed satisfied. But that was enough about him. Walking back to my car, Radclyffe mentioned Mole Board, only recently shifted to Jim Old's yard in Somerset, and how *brilliantly* he had jumped in the loose school. He mentioned Morley Street, his other prized horse he had bought as a yearling. He was with Toby Balding. 'That horse,' he said, 'is supposed to be the best young hurdler in England.' They would be interesting to watch at Cheltenham.

Mostly, the captain wanted to talk about Scudamore. 'A most amazing young man,' he said. 'The other day I watched him walk from the weighing-room to the paddock at Ascot. That's a long way at Ascot, and yet *literally* every ten yards a kid would stop him for an autograph. And never, ever, *once* did he tell one to push off. I can't get it out of my mind. *Marvellous*. That's the sort of chap he is.'

In the captain's eyes, Peter would do. So, obviously, would Sarah, the film producer. As for Sondrio, aged 8, he'd been put right. Once. He'd been given a last polish over tiddly hurdles with a lad on his back and sent back to Somerset. Whether he would revert to his old, swerving ways – well, that was another matter. We'd have to see.

Dead But Not Buried

Whenever I think of Scudamore's sensational win on Bonanza Boy in the Racing Post Handicap Chase, achieved in what appeared to be sucking mud around the tight corners of Kempton Park, I think of an American basketball player named Bill Bradley. Bradley, a former Rhodes Scholar at Oxford, now a US Senator – and quite possibly the next President of the United States – once spoke of his game in *The New Yorker* magazine.

'When you have played basketball for a while, you don't need to look at the basket,' said Bradley who, for years shone first for Princeton and later for the New York Knicks professional team. 'You know where it is. You develop a sense of where you are.'

On February 25, 1989 Scudamore knew where he was, for every one of the three hundred and eighty-six seconds of what, by common consent, was his most memorable and dogged riding performance of the 1988–89 season. Later, Scudamore was quick to point out that his victory that day was more a tribute to his workmanlike slogging than to finesse but, apart from that, he agreed with the American basketball player.

'I can see exactly what he means and, like he says, it comes with practice,' Scudamore said later. 'Horse-racing is different from basketball, obviously, in that every course I ride is slightly different from the next. Yet there are certain points, differing from course to course, where you can sense your position and know if you can still win.'

Kempton Park is flat, the turns sharp. 'It's a difficult track to come from behind on,' said Peter, 'you can't easily make up the ground. There are two points in the 3-mile chase at Kempton where I can sense my position. You've got to be in some sort of reasonable spot as you pass the 2½-mile gate, at the beginning of the back straight. And again at the fourth last because it's not a very long straight and the horses don't come back to you a lot.'

Scudamore laughed, considering his much-acclaimed ride. 'Things went wrong,' he said. 'I didn't ride a brilliant race because I was meant to be up there in front and I couldn't. So I had to make the best of a bad situation.'

What happened was this:

Heavy rain had fallen the previous day, presumably enhancing the strong little gelding's chances, but there were other factors that unsettled the jockey. Walking the track, Scudamore felt the 'soft' ground would still be too fast for the plucky little stayer. There is 'soft' and 'soft' on race tracks.

' "Soft" around Kempton,' Scudamore said, 'isn't the same as "soft" around Chepstow.' The going had been 'soft' at Chepstow on December 27 when Bonanza Boy, responding to extensive schooling from Scudamore, smashed some classy opposition to win the Welsh Grand National, a 3m 6f haul, by a dozen lengths. Scu, moreover, would have liked a longer distance than the mere 3 miles presented at Kempton.

More worrying, Bonanza Boy had fallen heavily at Ascot seventeen days earlier and Scudamore, frankly, had assumed much of the blame. 'I was rushing him along at a downhill fence,' said Peter, 'and he hit the top and really bowled over himself. I was afraid the fall might have frightened him because last year, when he hit fences, it all became too much for him. We had to school him back over hurdles.'

And finally, Scudamore felt there were too many front-runners in the 12-horse Racing Post field for his liking: If he lined up on the inside horses like Seagram and Cuddy Dale would squeeze out Bonanza Boy, no speed merchant, and Scu would have to hitch up and drop in behind them. Straightaway he'd lose a half dozen lengths.

'It would be like coming down the M5 and hitting a traffic jam,' was the way he put it much later, watching video tapes of the race. 'So, I decided it was better going down the A40, which is farther, but a smoother, uncluttered run.'

So, his thinking was made up of a complex set of components. Scudamore lined up on the middle-inner, set off, hoping to go wider before dropping onto the inside rail. Bonanza Boy jumped the first fence well: one problem met. Scudamore kept him in the middle but at considerable cost for, clearing the next obstacle, the first open ditch, he had fallen far behind. In fact, Scudamore was dead-last and as he swung through the immediate right-hander towards the back straight he felt briefly: no chance, I'm going backwards.

'What worried me was that I was behind the joint-favourite Bishop's Yarn,' he said, referring to a good, heavy-weather horse, with a reputed finishing pace. 'I wouldn't be able to accelerate around him. I was not having the clearest, easiest run. I was going to get chopped off.'

Deep down, Peter nonetheless enjoyed a glimmer of hope. The field was going at too quick a gallop for the ground. The quick pace would, he knew, allow his durable stayer to stick with it. 'If we'd got off at a slow pace,' he said later, 'I'd have had *no* chance whatever. Not from out at the back. The others were going to stop at some stage. The question was whether I could hang in there long enough to take advantage of it. I didn't want to leave too much to do.'

Going past the stands, about half way through the 3-mile race, Scudamore was off the television screen: his exact place in the field was open to debate. Was he 20 or 30 lengths off the pace being set by the young Irishman, Conor O'Dwyer on Cuddy Dale? 'At that point I'm still thinking negative,' Scudamore said later – and added illogically, 'but I'm still very hopeful.' Pipe, watching, gave up. 'I wouldn't have been at all surprised,' the trainer said later, 'if Peter had pulled him up at that stage.'

Scudamore had no such notion. 'I've been farther back than that and won,' Peter said later. 'I've fallen off and won.' Furthermore, he, like Bradley, the basketball player, was experienced enough to have a sense of where he was. He was, in fact, now moving for the second time towards the open ditch and the sharp right-hander into the back straight. 'I wasn't watching the whole field,' he recalled. 'My eye was on Bishop's Yarn. He had a good chance. He was my marker. I could sense the other horses getting tired.'

Bonanza Boy passed a clump of four or five horses as they went under the 2½-mile gate the second time. This, as Scudamore had said, was the first crucial point to take stock of where you are at Kempton. His heart leapt up. Four are in front of me, he said to himself, way out in front. But they can be taken. They're back-pedalling.

Scudamore now knew the horses ahead of him: Cuddy Dale, Gainsay, Ballyhane and, nearest to him, Seagram. I know Gainsay, he thought, I can have him. He reckoned that at least one of the other three would tire; they had started to race too early. That left him to drive for the third spot. Bonanza Boy, supremely economical, stayed on the rail and, as the horses passed the fifth from home, Gainsay took over the lead from Cuddy Dale.

Ten lengths adrift, Bonanza Boy pounded down towards that crucial, fourth-from-home fence. 'I remember thinking,' Scudamore recalled, 'if I jump the last fence on the back straight well, really well, I'll win this race.' He didn't. Shit! 'Then I looked up,' he went on, 'and I hadn't lost any ground.' Seagram, in fact, was coming back to him.

Scudamore swung off the rail to overtake Seagram and dropped back on the rail. On the bend the other three horses swung wide but not Bonanza Boy – 'they're not as handy as my little horse' – and, hugging the rail, the bay gelding hit a fortuitous good patch of ground and in a few bounds made up three or four lengths on Gainsay, Cuddy Dale and Ballyhane. 'I knew I could beat Ballyhane,' Peter recalled. 'That kept me going.'

Bonanza Boy's head was by now stuck out. Scudamore was aware of it. 'What a fighting horse,' he recalled, chuckling with affection. 'He was determined to get up that rail. It was his guide. He was tired and it was keeping him straight. All he had to do was concentrate on keeping his legs going. He was *really trying* for me but he wasn't getting anywhere.'

Bonanza Boy was still in fourth spot at the second last. 'He has a job to stand off,' Scudamore remembered, in his excitement switching the tense of his narrative to the present. 'All he can do is get popping and running and every time he gets running a fence comes in his way and it slows him down. He's still third, still third over the last, still third.' Ballyhane came back, beaten.

Into the last, Cuddy Dale was toiling hard and, from either side Gainsay and Bonanza Boy mounted their attacks. Over the fence, and Scudamore's horse, wobbling, battled for the lead. His head was out, the rail by his side. It now was a two-horse race. 'When he gets to Gainsay he runs more because he's got even more hope,' said Scudamore, picking up the story. 'He's got this surge of confidence which is inexplicable. He's quickened up again when he's got no more to give.'

He gave it. Bonanza Boy, gathering his last gasps of willpower, driven on under Scudamore's stick, got his nose in front some 60 metres from home. Stretching, heaving, he was there to stay. A stride back, Gainsay fought off a final challenge from Ballyhane. The race, though, was over. Bonanza Boy had swept past the post.

In the winner's enclosure, the gallant, mud-spattered gelding appeared to waver on his legs, exhausted. Then his head went up, his ears forward, responding to the thunder ringing round him. Within the hour, according to his stable lass Donna Cornforth, he was ready to run again. Scudamore, reflecting much later on the famous run, picked the key moment. 'The sharpest point of that bend was the crucial point of the race,' Scudamore said later. 'That's where we won the race.'

"That,' said Pipe, 'was the best race I've seen for a long, long time.' Corals, the bookmakers, agreed. Bonanza Boy was made their favourite, 12-1, for the Grand National.

Dad

On March 1, Scudamore helped Pipe reach another milestone: he rode Beau Ranger to victory through hoof-deep turf at Worcester to bring the Somerset trainer his 150th win of the term. In a two-horse race against Panto Prince, the Cheltenham hopeful had made heavy, labouring work of it. Peter steered all over the course, searching far and wide for good footing, before finally pushing on in a late, faltering rush to win the Hardanger Properties Chase by five unconvincing lengths.

In the winner's enclosure, Pipe put on a brave face. The ground, he said, had been horrible and, besides, Beau Ranger hadn't jumped any better when he beat Panto Prince a year ago in the same race. Beau Ranger, he said, needed the race.

The victory represented Scudamore's 169th of the season. It put him in many minds over his Gold Cup choice, or at least his preference, for Cheltenham. 'This sort of ground isn't ideal for Beau Ranger,' he brooded. 'It only adds to my problems.' Who would it be for the Big One? Increasingly, it looked less like Beau Ranger, more like Rusch de Farges or Bonanza Boy. The bookmakers seemed even less certain: Corals were quoting Rusch de Farges at 12-1, Beau Ranger at 14-1 and Bonanza Boy at 16s.

At that, punters were hardly breaking their legs to back any of these Pipe horses. Desert Orchid was Corals clear, 5-2 Gold Cup favourite, with Ten Plus 7-2. Other bookmakers elected to make these two horses the co-favourites, at 3-1. Support was gathering, too, round The Thinker, Cavvies Clown and Golden Freeze, the big Irish horse now being trained by Jenny Pitman.

Of the ill-destined Ten Plus, his veteran trainer, Fulke

Walwyn, was bullish. 'I think Ten Plus is as good as any of my previous Gold Cup winners,' he told John Karter of *The Independent*. That was heady talk indeed for his previous winners had been Mont Tremblant (1952), Mandarin (1962), and those great ones Mill House (1963) and The Dikler (1973). Looking forward a year or two, Walwyn added of Ten Plus, 'He's certainly bold enough for Aintree.'

Despite this sentimental support for Walwyn and his horse, the great grey Desert Orchid was the true favourite in every sense of the word. Even the jockeys referred to him merely as the Grey One. Apart from Peter and Martin Pipe, he was the only other star of the season. His owner had repeatedly expressed reservations about running at Cheltenham, but would he really be able to stand against the tide of popular feeling that wanted the all-conquering hero to run, and win, and prove himself in the Arkle class?

Anyway, all this Cheltenham talk could be diverting from the job at hand, and on March 2, a bleak Thursday, Scudamore found his dance card just about full: he had four Pipe runners at Lingfield, one of his favourite tracks, as bottomless as the going might prove.

For myself on March 2, I had an appointment with Pipe *père*.

Dave, who lives in a bungalow at the top of the gallops, had been up at 6:30, sitting in bed with the specially delivered racing papers and listening to the soft ruffle of the horses as they swept up over the wooden chips of the all-weather gallops. The gallops end not far from his bedroom window. 'If a horse gets loose, I can hear it,' he says. 'I can be out the door in a minute to help.'

Dave had then gone down to the yard. He had helped as the horse boxes were loaded up and then settled in to man the car-phone connections throughout the day. Martin went off to Lingfield with a box of four horses while Chester Barnes was already trundling on up to Ludlow where a small, modest ('workmanlike', was the *Timeform* term) 4-year-old gelding named Fetcham Park was favourite in a novices' hurdle.

Fetcham Park's jockey was Peter's friend, Lars Kelp, over from Denmark for experience as third jockey in the Pipe yard. Kelp, who had only ridden three times so far for the guv'nor, had been thoroughly briefed by Scudamore on the perilous whims of the sharp Shropshire track. 'Sit tight,' said Peter. The Dane, what is more, was sat tight in Pipe's living room and shown films of the course and, with Barnes, he was got to the track in plenty of time to walk it. The horse didn't run until the last race, the 5:15.

Pipe senior's phone rang early, urgently, that morning as he waited in the yard. It was Martin. He had bad news. The horsebox had broken down on the M4, mercifully near the Lambourn exit, which meant help was not far away. David phoned hurriedly to LTR, the Lambourn horse transport firm. LTR dispatched aid to the stranded trainer, and sent him on his way. That problem was solved.

Dave had hardly settled back when Martin was on the phone again. The message this time appealed more to his conspiratorial liking. There was a rumour – Martin had picked it up on his car phone – to the effect that in the last race at Ludlow there was surprising support, reflected in the betting, for a horse that the Pipe establishment hadn't considered a threat.

The rumour suggested nothing sinister, perhaps an owner's zeal, perhaps a spot-on morning blood count. Nevertheless, it demanded attention. It was standard practice, according to Pipe's planning, for his jockeys to know the two 'danger horses', the principal pair of threats, in a race. The 'X' horse hadn't been thought a danger. Kelp, inexperienced, might be in need of an update. Martin wondered if Dad would check out the weight of betting upon, and the form of, this sudden new 'danger' horse?

David, aged 63 and keen as a yearling, set to work. He phoned the ever-ready Hawkins who thumbed through the form books, searching for clues that might justify such unforeseen support for this new outsider. A mud-lark, perhaps? A strange, inexplicably poor recent performance? What weight did he carry? New jockey? He found nothing to suggest a minor racing renaissance in the making for 'X'. Dave likewise found nothing significant in the shift of odds. He reported as much to his son, by now near to Lingfield.

Dave then called Ludlow. Whatever you hear about 'X', he told Barnes, a man fond of keeping a portable phone on his person, don't worry. Who is 'X', wondered the perplexed former table tennis star? Never mind, said Dave. Don't worry about

'X'. Dave, reassured, then drove down to his betting shop in town and, checking the trade, holed up in a dark back room with Hawkins, the form man. They would spend the afternoon watching the racing on SIS close-circuit television. I joined them.

Up and down, jabbing at his thick-lensed spectacles, sucking at his teeth, shouting encouragement at the screen, smiling only as the custodian of some secret insight can smile, Dave Pipe was the antithesis to Hawkins. Hawkins sat as still as a stick in the corner. His form books were to hand.

The first race that concerned them from Lingfield was the 3 o'clock, a novices' hurdle. Martin Pipe was running Kumakas Nephew in its debut over hurdles. 'Nothing out of the ordinary,' said *The Racing Post*, 'but is sure to have been well schooled and no Pipe runner can be ignored.' Dave Pipe began to fidget. The horse ran a blinder, winning by twenty-five lengths. Pipe senior rubbed his hands. Scudamore: 170 winners. Pipe: 152.

Their next Lingfield race, a handicap chase, was a disappointment. Tarqogan's Best was pulled up, two out, by Scudamore. Dave Pipe walked out of the room. In retrospect, the race would be remembered for the painful, muddy unseating of Ray Goldstein by Hettinger, his ride-to-be in the Grand National. Dave Pipe returned. In the following novices' hurdle, the 4 o'clock, Pipe's Forest Flame, the favourite, was soundly beaten into third place which was another disappointment, which called for a look at the betting shop out front. Finally, at 5 o'clock, Pipe was on his feet in front of the quivering screen. He was shouting home the joint-favourite hurdler, Might Move, ridden by Scudamore.

Pipe considers himself a good judge of jockeyship and Scudamore, not just in deference, thinks this is true. In this light, it was interesting to hear the bookmaker's comments as Peter, in pink with a black cross of Lorraine, got away slowly and moved up through the field. 'Look at his hands. They're quiet, see,' commented Pipe, now more at ease as he concentrated on talking. 'He's not pushing the horse. Come on, push on. Push on!'

Scudamore, as though responding to the vibes shimmering from faraway Taunton, pushed on. 'Look,' said Pipe. 'He's not happy. See him change those hands. He's trying to get him to go up. He's asking him to go up.' Might Move, true to his name, was now two flights from home. Peter and the horse drew neck-and-neck with the leader. Pipe, seated again, was now wriggling his stretched-out toes, speechless with excitement. Scudamore tried to press his attack. The horse made no response. 'Oh, Peter's going to get done. Oh, Peter's going to get done,' said Pipe, over and over, in a low, mournful West Country keening. 'He's going to get . . .'

Peter did get done. By a neck. Pipe jabbed back his glasses and shook his head in despair. It was several moments before he could speak. 'I know what Peter's going to tell me,' he said. 'He's going to tell me he had time because Lingfield's got a long run-in and I'm going to tell him he was never going to do it. Not on that ground. Too heavy. He was carrying too much weight. He left it too late.'

Pipe heaved a sigh, rose, and moments later the Ludlow race, Kelp riding Fetcham Park, was flickering before us. Pipe returned to watch. The race, happily, was less shot through with excitement. Kelp, following Martin Pipe's orders, transmitted through Chester Barnes, went to the front. Fetcham Park made all. He coasted home, ten lengths the winner. No danger, known or unknown.

The darkened room fell silent. In the corner, Roy Hawkins remained quiet, undoubtedly running the results into his mental form book. Pipe was seated again, all passion spent. Watching him, I made a swift, approximate calculation: the man, 63 years old, fervent and a bit overweight, must already have watched something approaching 400 of his son's races this season. And if you took into account Scudamore riding other men's horses, that pushed the grand total towards 500. How much longer could he take it?

'It's in my blood,' he replied. 'I'd be a dead man without it.' He grinned. 'And, we're not finished yet.' He explained that the day had hardly begun at Pond House Farm. In a couple of hours, his son and Barnes, maybe even Peter, would be back at the yard. They would all have coffee, with Carol, and well into the night they'd study the race films from Lingfield and Ludlow.

One of the Boys

'I always watch the boys go round,' said Ray Cochrane, the flat jockey who years ago was one of the jumpers. 'I love jumping. I still love to hunt in the winter.' On 11 March he was at home in Newmarket, feet up in front of a telly, watching the boys at Sandown Park. The race that was to stick in his mind was the 4:10, the William Hill Imperial Cup, a two mile handicap hurdle.

He had a special interest in the race. His father-in-law, Johnny Gilbert, had won it in the past and, besides, one of the runners that day was a filly that he himself would ride in a month on the flat. 'It was a very hot race and it was going to be fun, watching that filly,' he remembers thinking afterwards. 'I'd seen her run on the flat and she was practically a novice in a handicap hurdle.'

The filly was called Travel Mystery. Her trainer was Pipe. Her jockey, fresh off a helicopter after winning the 1 o'clock hurdle at Chepstow, was the irrepressible Scudamore. She was fast. She was durable. On 23 February at Warwick, she had come off a five-month lay-off to win a handicap hurdle on sticky, tiring turf, belting through a flight or two on the way.

What's more, she was plucky and that day at Sandown she would need to be: Travel Mystery was 10 lbs out of the handicap. To be fair to the handicapper, there wasn't much to go by: her last National Hunt race had been a hurdle, which she had won, twenty-three months earlier at Ludlow.

According to reports, she wasn't jumping well, but Peter had schooled her diligently in Somerset and, in Cochrane's view, there was no jockey more diligent than Peter. He's a great

137

admirer of Scudamore. Their careers barely overlapped but Cochrane remembered the brash youngster.

'What I'll always remember about Peter was a handicap hurdle he won at Warwick, years ago, when he was an amateur with David Nicholson,' he recalled. 'He was riding this thing into the straight, a fence or two out, three or four in a line. What this horse needed was to be got hold of and Peter set down, just as he does now, and gave it a few cracks and it won well. I remember thinking, "This kid is tough, this kid can ride." I picked him out that day at Warwick.'

The Sandown ride that day would be one of Peter's strongest and most dramatic of the season. Travel Mystery was the 3-1 favourite. She didn't set out that way. She stood off from the third flight of hurdles and landed on her nose. Scudamore, holding on to the buckle of her reins, fought her back onto her feet. Cochrane, watching on the box, was amazed. 'How Peter stayed on,' he said later, 'I'll never know.'

Travel Mystery fell back. Slowly, patiently, still jumping badly, she moved back into the race. Nearing the end of the back straight Scudamore got her in the thick of the battle. She took the lead at the last and Peter drove her out to win by six lengths. 'I hope her jumping improves,' he said afterwards, 'so that she can go onto better things.'

For Cochrane, watching on television, Scu's ride had been exemplary. 'When things are going right, the race ticks over nicely for any jockey,' he observed. 'But when something goes wrong, especially in jumping, a lot of jockeys will panic. They'll try to rush it to get back into the race. Peter didn't do that. The filly had flattened a hurdle and missed the next two. He needed to nurse her along, get her back on an even keel and jumping again and he did it, I think, with great skill.'

On the evidence of this race, of the many races he'd seen through the season, did Cochrane think Peter was riding any differently now than he was years ago? 'No,' said Cochrane. 'He's just riding with more confidence. He's intelligent and his skill comes with confidence.'

Travel Mystery's win thrust her into the forefront of Pipe's and Scudamore's thinking for the Cheltenham Festival: Here was their horse for the closing race of the meeting, the Racegoers Club County Handicap Hurdle.

Ray Cochrane, a top jockey who has experienced both codes of racing. In 1988, he won both the English and Irish Derbys on Khayasi.

Cochrane rode Travel Mystery on 22 May in the Group 3 Insulpak Sagaro Stakes at Ascot. 'I thought to myself,' he said later, ' "this will be a good ride. She'll be as fit as a flea, as game as a pebble", and when I got on her, I thought, "She'll do for me." ' She did. She took the lead on the home turn and, perhaps fitter from her brief National Hunt season, stormed in to win by half a length. The victory was yet another milestone for Pipe: it was his first group race winner.

The Festival

In Cheltenham, there once was a pub, an unexceptional watering-hole called the Bath Hotel. But now during Festival Week a new sign swung out over its red door. Brightly painted, it showed a horse, ears pricked, jumping over a hurdle. Underneath, against a field of green, curled the words: 'Dawn Run'.

A big, dark mare, Dawn Run holds a unique place in National Hunt racing. In 1984, she won the Champion Hurdle and in 1988, still only eight years old, she returned to take the Gold Cup and pass into legend as the only animal – man, woman or eunuch – to win the Cheltenham Double, the most prestigious pair of hurdle and steeplechase races in the sport.

If Arkle was a gentleman, his successor in the hearts of the Irish was a tramp, a street-fighter, a roughneck who once tried to savage an overtaking horse. 'Dawn Run was the Tamara Press of National Hunt racing,' my Somerset neighbour Jim Old, the trainer, once told me, referring to the swarthy Soviet shot-putter. 'She would never have passed a sex test.'

Old was joking but, as he was the first to admit, he was prejudiced. It was his horse Cima, with Scudamore aboard, which under controversial circumstances lost that 1984 Champion Hurdle. Scudamore, at 66-1, had ridden a brilliant race. Dawn Run jumped the last flight one-and-a-half lengths clear of the gaining Cima but, little more than a neck in front up the run-in, she bore sharply across the other horse and passed the post three-quarters of a length to the good.

Would Old, asked the Press, request a stewards' inquiry? The trainer, who hadn't seen the incident clearly, asked Scudamore. 'No,' Peter said. 'Not in the Champion Hurdle.' Old was more

Mole Board – backed with more hope than confidence for the Champion Hurdle.

sensible. 'If a stewards' inquiry had so much as been held,' he said later, 'the Irish fans would have burnt down the stands.'

With this famous incident in mind, I crossed the threshold of the Dawn Run pub on the eve of the Festival and into a maelstrom of Irish racing fans. A long-legged fiddler, straight out of Yeats, whittled away in the corner. At the bar, with all still to play for, punters carried on a lively debate. The Irish, once a reckoning force, had won only one race in each of the past two Festivals. How would their thirty-four horses do this year?

Discussion centred on tomorrow's opener, the Supreme Novices' Hurdle, a race in which no fewer than seven horses, one third of the field, were both bred and trained in Ireland. The topic at the moment was Granville Hotel, a five-year-old gelding, of late trained by Mouse Morris in Tipperary. 'At Punchestown,' somebody was saying, with utter disdain, 'he run like a donkey.'

'At Thurles,' said another, 'and I seen it, he run worse.'

'Tosh,' retorted a young man in a white, roll-top jersey, a Dublin veterinary student, I later learned. 'I maintain he's always been short of a run. Mouse will have him ready for Cheltenham.'

Into Granville Hotel, a great amount of Irish emotion was being poured. A home-bred horse, for whom an Irishman had recently paid IR£100,000, maybe more, he was seen as something of a tourniquet to staunch the flow of potential Cheltenham winners from Ireland to England. Golden Freeze was gone. Don Valentino was gone. And now Granville Hotel, on recent form – a bust. He'd not won, in truth had *lost*, his last two races with the winning post in sight.

'I seen him at Thurles. Ten lengths.'

Mouse Morris would have him ready, assured the young vet, with stunning authority as he sipped his whiskey. Silence fell. A snort of scorn tumbled down the bar. 'I tink we ought to look no further than Elementary,' retorted a wizened, check-capped observer, seeking support for a big colt trained by Jim Bolger, another of their countrymen. 'Jim Bolger,' said Check-cap, 'is the only trainer at the moment in Ireland who operates on the teery that if you've got the best horse, you've got to get the best jockey.'

'I will dispute with you who is the best jockey,' said the vet. 'But true. If Peter Scudamore gets off a Pipe horse, he must tink he can win on the other one.'

'The switch,' someone agreed, 'is a tip in itself.'

I knew all about the switch: Peter abandoning the bad-jumping Sondrio after the Kempton Park fiasco, then being approached by Paul Green, Elementary's owner, who also kept horses with Pipe. Scudamore, what is more, had huge respect for Jim Bolger: as an amateur, he had worked for six months in the Irishman's yard and considered him the best, most *thorough* trainer, excepting Pipe, in the business. Blood-testing. Brilliant gallops. Bolger, once an accountant, shared Pipe's cool, clinical approach to the business of winning horse races.

Scudamore hadn't so much as sat on Elementary, let alone jumped him, until this morning when he rode him across the infield, 'the polo field', at Cheltenham. It was cold, bright. Cloud shadows sped across the landscape and a sharp, drying wind sliced down from Cleeve Hill. Two Irish race writers, appearing overwhelmingly *au fait*, stood with their hands in their pockets. Scudamore came by. He said he liked the horse. They wrote it down and went to find Bolger.

Scudamore then walked the course. No, with a Norwegian

friend and myself in the back, he drove a Range Rover to key points on it; an acupuncturist, seeking the pressure points. He was embedding his heel in the turf, a rugby-player again, kicking points. What seemed so astonishing was the swift efficiency of the reconnaissance. 'What persuaded me to take the ride was the Form Book,' he said, as faithful as ever to reason. 'Elementary was the highest-rated horse in the race.'

As I was reflecting on Scudamore surveying the course that morning, the Dawn Run brigade had got round to the big race the following day, the Champion Hurdle. The Irish found little to cheer about. They hadn't won it since Dawn Run in 1984 and this year the prospects were poor. Condor Pan, trained by the same Bolger, was their best bet, especially with prospects of good, dry going.

The boyos didn't warm to Condor Pan. Their hearts lay instead with Mole Board. Mole Board, to a man, was their horse. I, too, had an allegiance to Mole Board and I'd have been happy if he came second to Scudamore on Celtic Shot. Mole Board had been one of Radclyffe's yearlings, a *brilliant* jumper when he left the captain's yard. Also, he was now trained by Jim Old. Yet, with sore shins and much in need of a run, the lean gelding was a rank outsider. Corals had put him at 33-1, something like ninth-favourite in the early prices. Did they know something new about Mole Board?

'He just changed hands for a lot of money,' said the student vet. 'A quarter million, I hear.'

That, I knew, wasn't true.

'Owen O'Neill once had him,' added Check-cap and another man, breaking in helpfully, brought me nearer to the heart of the matter. 'Owen's got a yard near Cheltenham,' he said. 'He's an Irishman. He drinks with us here in the pub.'

The Start

The opening day at Cheltenham was peppering with rain and Captain Michael Sayers, the Senior Starter, could think of only one thing as he drove that morning from his home in Warwickshire to his last Cheltenham before retirement. After all these years, he thought, let's hope the luck doesn't run out. Let's hope they get away to a good, clean start in the first race. That'll set the pattern for the day.

The rain would be a bit of a bore, teeming down on his heavy mackintosh, rubber boots and the bowler, his tell tale mark of authority, while he did up the girths of the milling horses. Oddly enough, though, rain often made for a better start. 'The jockeys seem more relaxed in the rain,' chuckles the captain, retired from the Royal Horse Artillery. 'I suppose they're so miserable it takes their minds off the race.'

Capt. Sayers should know. He's been a Jockey Club starter for twenty-two years, the last six as the Senior Starter. A tall man, erect and unflappable, he commands authority. 'Unless you have to deal with an accident,' he says, 'you must never ever appear to be in a hurry. Always be the same from day to day. It's no good being ratty one day and hail-fellow the next. In that way the jockeys can rely on what you're going to do.' Capt. Sayers always commutes to Cheltenham, always parks in the same spot in the car park.

For Scudamore, the outlook for the afternoon was sunny and clear. 'Peter Scudamore, who has broken more records than a petulant disc jockey this season . . .' John Karter began his report in *The Independent* and went on to tip Peter for a double, Sabin du Loir and Calapaez, with 'good chances' on Elementary

145

and Pukka Major. The thought of four winners didn't enter Peter's head: just one, maybe two, would do.

In the Supreme Novices' Hurdle, the brothers Oliver and Simon Sherwood, trainer and jockey, had the favourite, Cruising Altitude. But Scudamore was second-choice and confident on Elementary. His reject, Sondrio, was also rejected by the 'experts': none of the tipsters in the thirteen national dailies fancied the errant jumper but, deep in Somerset, hope was aglow. Sondrio, now back from Captain Radclyffe's remedial jumping classes, had schooled immaculately the previous morning.

'It was a transformation,' Pipe said later of the brief warm-up over the Nicholashayne flights. 'Sondrio jumped brilliantly. I faxed his owners, Jim and Geraldine Ryan, to tell them the good news but, although I had seen it myself, I still couldn't believe it.' Scu was spared a copy of the fax.

The first race of the Festival got off to a perfect start. Sondrio, with his jockey Jonothan Lower following Pipe's instructions, made the running. Captain Radclyffe, on the grandstand lawns, watched with satisfaction his recent pupil's foot-perfect performance. Scudamore made a game-plan with Bolger. 'I would settle my horse in early on,' Peter said later, 'and if he jumped the last upsides we were home.'

They never got to the last. Three flights out, Granville Hotel came down and with him the frail dreams of my Irish friends from the pub. Alekhine went too, mortally breaking a shoulder and, in the mayhem, Blitzkrieg was brought down as well. 'One fell on the inside of me and I pulled round, trying to avoid it,' recalled Scudamore, 'and I hit the grey trying to get up.' The grey was Blitzkrieg, yet another Irishman.

Scudamore, down on the turf, watched Sondrio sweep up the hill towards the post. An ambulance bumped towards him. Was he alright? asked the medic. 'No, I'm not all right,' said Scudamore, as Richard Pitman of the BBC and *The Sunday Express*, reported, 'There goes another of my winners.' Sondrio won by two lengths. He had learnt his jumping lessons well and, on the lawn, the emphatic Captain Radclyffe could be heard repeating over and over: 'marvellous, marvellous, just *marvellous*.'

Scudamore was by now changing into the green emerald shirt, with the scarlet-hooped sleeves: the colours of Sabin du

Loir, no stranger to the winner's enclosure at Cheltenham. Six years ago, while under the tutelage of the great Michael Dickinson, he had won the race just gone by, the Supreme Hurdle, beating Dawn Run and West Tip among others. Today, at 2:50, Sabin was just about everybody's favourite in the Arkle Challenge Trophy Chase.

New to chasing, unbeaten in his four starts this season, including a twenty-length February demolition of an outsider called Waterloo Boy, Sabin had plenty of fans, and they had only one misgiving: he was ten and if he won today he'd be the oldest horse ever to win the Arkle. He didn't. So he wasn't – but not without putting up a gallant battle: twice Sabin got fences wrong, three times he came from behind to nose into the lead, only to lose by a length to Waterloo Boy, driven in by Richard Dunwoody.

'Sabin could be the greatest horse I've ever sat on,' Scudamore had said at Christmas, following the horse's debut over fences, but today, as Peter said, 'it wasn't to be. No excuses. He didn't jump very well but he doesn't know how to run a bad race.' As Peter had said on the opening day of the season: 'You think about these horses – and they never work out as you think.'

Sabin's connections were nonetheless pleased. Brian Kilpatrick, one of the gentlest of owners, leant on his stick and looked downright delighted by his horse's performance. 'Sabin got home in one piece,' he said, 'and that's all that matters.' Besides, once again, and as Kilpatrick always insisted, Peter hadn't hit his horse once with a whip.

For Scudamore it had been two races, no winners. Disappointment, not wholly unexpected, was to follow only minutes later in the blue riband event of the day, the Champion Hurdle. Of this race, I'm tempted to remark, as the golf writer Bernard Darwin once did when abandoning an important match: 'and then it was time for tea.' Celtic Shot, of course, was defending the title but on form, puzzling form, he wasn't in with a sniff. 'Last year we knew he was well enough, but was he good enough?' Peter had said. 'This year we know he's good enough, but is he well enough?'

He now stood looking out at the hammering-down rain from inside the doors to the weighing-room. 'Very nice,' he said solemnly. 'We could do with a lot more of it.'

Both sensible and sentimental money was on Kribensis – grey was the flavour of the week – who was trained by Michael Stoute and ridden by Richard Dunwoody. The leggy five-year-old, youngest in the field, was tipped to become the first Festival horse to go from a Triumph to a Champion Hurdle victory in successive seasons since Persian War did it in 1967–68. It seemed an oddly difficult double but, according to one theory, the Triumph, open only to four-year-olds, simply burns out the young beasts for three or four seasons.

In the event, Kribensis duly tired and Celtic Shot 'just didn't have the pace'. As Peter explained, 'I lost my race from the water jump to the top of the hill. I got pushed wider than I wanted to go.' Celtic Shot finished a length behind Celtic Chief, three behind Beech Road. It was to be the surprise of the day. At 50-1, the seven-year-old Beech Road joined the 1965 winner, Kirriemuir, as the longest-priced Champion Hurdler in history. Mole Board, who had shortened at 20-1, gave what he could, disputing the lead as late as third from last. He finally came sixth and I thought I caught the whispering sound of Irish stubs being torn to shreds. Indeed, as Peter was saying, horses never work out as you think.

Ah, but sometimes they do. After Calapaez pulled out of the Stayers' Hurdle, due to the ever-softening ground, Peter went on to clock out from his day at the office with a winner. On Pukka Major, 4-1 joint-favourite, he took the Grand Annual Handicap Chase but only after 4 minutes 10.3 seconds of hard labour.

Scudamore was riding for the young trainer, Tim Thomson Jones, whose father, I recalled, had been the man who kept sending his horses back to Captain Radclyffe's school for refresher courses. Young Thomson was aiming for his first Festival winner. 'Peter,' he advised his jockey, 'don't give up on the horse.' To pass on such instructions to Scu seemed massively unnecessary but, no matter. The champion never gave up and he later explained his success. 'Pukka Major is a bit of a character,' he said. 'He doesn't always consent to run. This time he consented to run.'

That night gloom settled over the Dawn Run pub. It had been a bad day for the Irish: no winners in six races. The young veterinary student in the white roll-top jersey, perhaps humbled by his arrogant faith in Granville Hotel, was gone. Scudamore and Elementary escaped censure for, deep down, there was a fugitive, communal guilt that it had been the Irish horse Blitzkrieg or maybe even Hotel himself who had brought down Peter and the Bolger horse. The fiddler struck up.

In the Champion Hurdle, Condor Pan was excused on the grounds of the ground: it was soft, all wrong. The Irish sorrow lay elsewhere. 'We're sick about Mole Board,' summed up a man called Frank Clarke, a drinker of Guinness, a Cheltenham travel agent, an ex-pat lately of Dublin. 'But Beech Road was the real sickener. He's originally from Ireland.'

The Second Day

The Cheltenham weather brightened on the second day of the Festival. Scudamore was still favoured to win the Ritz Club trophy as the leading Festival jockey – Corals had him at 2-5 – but his luck was to dry up.

In the opening race, the Sun Alliance Hurdle, he had his choice of the Somerset stable's top novice hurdler for the second day running. It was either Sayfar's Lad, the proven mudlark on which he had won twice this term, or Pertemps Network, already winner of eight races this season, six of them with Peter aboard. 'There isn't much between them,' he said. 'I'll go for Pertemps, on the strength of Newbury.'

It was at the Berkshire track eleven days earlier, powering through patches of heavy going, that the strong, dark gelding had played his part in Pipe's historic six-winner-out-of-six-runners coup, winning by eight lengths over the three miles. Sayfar's Lad, on the other hand, had carried Peter to a 20-length heavy-going victory over 2m 5f in February at Warwick.

In soft going, Pertemps went to the post at 6-1, the third favourite. Sayfar's Lad, carrying Mark Perrett who had come up at the last minute from waterlogged Newton Abbot, was next at 12-1. The favourite was Josh Gifford's Green Willow, 5-1, followed by the unbeaten Morley Street, who was not only a 'seriously good horse', according to his trainer Toby Balding, but a *cum laude* graduate of the Radclyffe School of Straight Jumping.

It was to be a strange race for Peter. He went immediately to the front, as expected, and along the inside. Perrett kept Sayfar's Lad handy while the two favourites, Green Willow and Morley

Beau Ranger – a great servant to his trainer and his owner, a man who knows a thing or two about horsepower.

Street, pounded safely wide in the twenty-two horse field. 'Pertemps then seemed to begin losing his power,' Peter reported later, 'and down round the water jump we started to go backwards.' Suddenly, conclusively, he knew he was out of the race.

Meanwhile, in the fast-paced field, Perrett pushed his spare ride to the front at the sixth flight and beat off the well-bunched challenge led by Trapper John, from Mick Morris's Irish yard, and won by five lengths, with the outsider Knight Oil a further five lengths back and half a length in front of Morley Street.

Pertemps came seventeenth, probably *fifty* lengths in the wake of his stablemate. Scudamore, puzzled by his horse's performance, swung from the saddle. He looked down at the creature's forelegs. There it was. A shoe was gone, picked clean from the hoof. 'I don't know when it went,' said Scudamore. 'You rarely know when a horse loses its shoe but somewhere, probably down by the water, he began to feel the ground.'

With that, he scooted into the weighing-room and slipped into the light-blue – Ford-blue, in fact – colours of White Brothers, the Taunton car dealers who owned Beau Ranger. The great Beau presented a problem. In terms of distance, he was a horse that fell between two stools. For him, two miles was too short, three miles too long and two-and-a-half miles just right. Sadly, though, there were no level-weighted, championship races at two-and-a-half miles. What to do?

The handsome chestnut gelding, now eleven years old, had been entered in the two-mile Queen Mother Champion Chase, the big race of the middle day of Cheltenham, and in the Gold Cup, the even bigger race on the following afternoon, an event in which he had come third in 1988. The Whites had nursed hopes that their horse might go again for the big prize but, on his regular Sunday visit to Nicholashayne, Peter White got the news: barring an unlikely good long-range weather forecast, Bonanza Boy, who fancies a bit of give in the ground, would be the stable's choice for the Gold Cup. So the two miler it was.

At the post Beau Ranger, at 11-4, was second favourite to Barnbrook Again, 7-4, a classy, durable 8-year-old trained by David Elsworth and ridden by Simon Sherwood. Scudamore's plans were simple: take the inside and go flat out for, over this distance, he would need to milk every drop of speed out of the old boy. It was their best chance.

Beau Ranger got away fast, took the lead and, travelling at high speed, the shape of his jumping flattened out. He hit the first two fences hard, recovered to fly the next two safely. He kept the lead until the ninth, four from home, when Barnbrook Again got his nose in front. Beau Ranger was toiling by now and, with Barnbrook keeping command, Scudamore was forced to drive hard to sweep into third place, eight lengths behind Sherwood, four behind Hywel Davies on the long-shot Royal Stag. 'It was a pure matter of speed,' Scudamore said later, 'my horse just had to go faster than he wanted to go.'

The fourth and, for Scudamore, the third and final race of the day brought further disappointment. This time it was on Pharoah's Laen in the three-mile Sun Alliance Chase. Peter had already steered the leggy and sometimes awkward 8-year-old to victory during the season but the gelding, third favourite, wasn't in the same class as the winner, Envopak Token, trained by Josh Gifford and ridden by Peter Hobbs, nor Nick the Brief, who chased home the leader. Pharoah's Laen came a faraway ninth.

'That's probably about as good as he is,' said the champion, empty-handed for the day. He then phoned Marilyn at a Bristol hospital where their son, Michael, had undergone an operation to remove some excessive tissue on the right side of his face. Michael was fine; he even spoke from his bed to his father. He would be back home in the morning which, for Peter, was the only good news of the day.

At the Dawn Run that evening, there was only one horse in the Gold Cup, as far as the Irish were concerned. And it wasn't Desert Orchid, pin-up boy of the racing world. The Irish preferred Carvill's Hill, one of their own, a novice, a youngster at seven years old, but for all that a handsome threat. This season, on either soft or heavy ground, he had won all his four races, save for the one on Boxing Day, when he fell at Leopardstown. 'He's the best horse since Arkle,' said someone. 'Even better than Arkle. He's in the same class as a novice as Golden Signet. It's just a matter of keeping your ticket and collecting your money.'

The Judge

Racing is full of dynasties. Take, for example, the Judge, the man who stations himself at the finishing post and officially determines the winner. Michael Hancock is the Senior Judge of the Jockey Club; his father and uncle, Malcolm and John, were Senior Judges before him and *their* father, Alfred, was a freelance Jockey Club judge at the turn of the century.

Malcolm, who was to die on May 7, 1989 at the age of 92, was probably the most famous judge in the history of racing, a man 'who played a major role in the administration of racing for fifty years,' as *The Times*' obituary put it. He certainly left the most indelible imprint. No stranger to the game – his father-in-law, a Senior Starter, was often at the other end of the track – Lieutenant Colonel Hancock got the top post when the then senior judge, the luckless C. A. Robinson, blew the finish of the Cambridgeshire at Newmarket in 1927.

It was a terrible, if understandable error, given the great width of the course at Newmarket. Robinson was watching one side of the track where a pair of horses, Niantic and Medal, strained towards the finish. Meanwhile, a horse called Insight II, running up the rails and outside Robinson's field of vision, pounded barely noticed past the finish line. The crowd, in hysterical unison, acclaimed Insight II the winner.

So did a well-placed, professional observer. 'Indeed, as they went past the post I thought he had won,' wrote the man from *The Times*, 'but the judge, who alone could see, decided that Medal and Niantic, who finished very fast, had caught and beaten him and run a dead-heat for first place.'

Judge Robinson's decision stood, for in those days, there was no official film against which to check a result. The Jockey Club gave lip-service support for Robinson but, without so much as a mention of the incident in its minutes, he was replaced by Hancock as Senior Judge at the close of the season.

Judge Hancock, a slender and immaculate man, soon restored the public's faith. He was said to possess the keenest eye in Jockey Club memory, a vision enhanced by a small pair of British-made No. 6 binoculars – 'Never use No. 8s,' he would say, 'they pull your eyes out of their sockets' – which during World War I he got off a German prisoner who, in turn, had got them off a British prisoner of war. Malcolm Hancock also had a limp and a distorted toe, which required a special boot. These were the legacies of a bullet taken in the right leg during the Gallipoli campaign in 1915.

He is best known in judging circles, however, for his Notebook and his System. The notebook was designed by Hancock and specially printed by his father-in-law, the race course manager and stakeholder John Pratt. It was sturdy, waterproof and of a size to fit into a man's pocket.

On the third day before the Gold Cup Hancock, the senior judge, walked round the weighing-room. He took in all of the walls with a glance, assembling the jockeys' vast array of shirts and sleeves and caps in his head. Notebook and pencil in hand, pausing to jot down a note, he looked like a traffic-meter man, though a bit classier. The spectrum of colours, light to dark, were foremost in his mind. Pink and white, he thought, glancing at Bonanza Boy's colours. At the top of his page he wrote 'pink' and beside it the number that Scudamore's horse would be wearing: '2'.

The two predominantly yellow colours – Pegwell Bay's yellow with black spots and Yahoo's yellow with white epaulets – gave Hancock not a moment of doubt. The first would be 'spots' followed by its number '9' and the other would be 'yellow' accompanied by '14'. Hancock moved on. West Tip would *not* be called 'blue' and certainly not the accurate, but two-worded, 'light blue'. The light blue took its rightful place down the spectrum, to be sure, but it bore no colour description. 'To me powder blue always means Peter Luff, the owner,' Hancock explained. 'So I call his horses "Luff".' So, beside the word 'Luff' went his horse's number: '13'.

And so it went, down the page, enough to send a Martian back home: Carvill's Hill, wearing common red, was called 'chevrons' but written down as an inverted 'V'. Slalom, with its emerald green and white quartered shirt, became mere '1/4'; Cavvies Clown's green and pink cross-belts 'X'; Charter Party's emerald green and white stars 'Stars'. Finally, but one, came the dark blue and grey of the great Desert Orchid. 'I call him "Burridge", after the owner,' said Hancock and then, with an unscientific twinkle in his eye, he added, 'but don't worry. I always recognise The Grey Horse when I see him.'

The Big One

As Simon Sherwood, Desert Orchid's jockey, had driven through the swirling snow towards Cheltenham on Thursday morning, he was taken by the notion that the Gold Cup might be declared unplayable that day. There were precedents for such a decision. In 1937 the race had been cancelled by snow and in 1968, again due to snow, it was put off until April. In 1987, a year he didn't ride, snow again nearly ruined the foremost race of the steeplechase season.

'To be totally honest, I rather hoped it would be put off this time,' Sherwood said later. 'By the time I got to the weighing-room, there was a rumour going round that the race would be run in a month, possibly at Sandown. That would have suited us a treat.'

That Desert Orchid prefers firm ground, rather than slop, is a commonplace. That the four-legged fighter, who leads with his left, is better on such right-handed tracks as Sandown, is an equally known fact. Sherwood brooded and, changing into his colours for the first race of the day, the *Daily Express* Triumph Hurdle, he was struck by the most unsettling rumour of all: it was said that the filmwriter Richard Burridge, who owned Dessie, might withdraw his grey gelding from the Gold Cup, which was to be staged at 3:30.

Scudamore, returning from a spell in the weighing-room sauna, noticed his friend's consternation and played on it. 'The ground out there is much too heavy,' advised Scudamore, tongue-in-cheek, for his own Gold Cup entry was Bonanza Boy, a proven runner in mud. 'You'd better not run The Grey Horse.' Jockeys, as much in awe of Desert Orchid as the public, often call him 'The Grey Horse'.

On the way to victory – Simon Sherwood and Desert Orchid jump the twelfth fence in The Tote Cheltenham Gold Cup Chase.

The Grey Horse had been under guard for a fortnight at the Hampshire yard of David Elsworth and now he was in the race course stable with his lass, Janice Coyle. She wouldn't leave his box. 'You never can tell what somebody might feed him,' she said. 'If you know what I mean.' What she meant was to be made clear only about an hour later on the BBC *World at One* programme when David Barons, who trained the 1988 Gold Cup favourite Playschool, claimed his horse's lacklustre performance in the race that day had been due to surreptitious doping.

Earlier, Burridge had walked the wet course in the snow. He dwelt at the second last fence where the fire brigade pumped away surface water and, in gloom, squelched up the famous final hill. 'It's fit for flippers, not racing plates,' he said and in the interest of his beloved horse, a living national monument, he was indeed doubtful about running him.

'I'm starting not to enjoy this at all,' he said. He spoke with the respected writer and television commentator, John Oaksey, a former rider himself, who pressed him to pull the horse out. 'I talked to about twenty people,' he said later, 'and they all advised me to pull the horse out.' Trainer Elsworth's minority opinion nevertheless prevailed. 'He's the best horse in the race,' Elsworth said simply. 'He can handle the ground and next year, who knows, it might freeze or he may not be fit. If the chance is there, we have to take it.' Sherwood, mindful of the owner's anxiety, promised he'd soon pull up if the going got dangerous.

In the parade ring, Elsworth was even more bullish about Desert Orchid's prospects. He was fit and he would win, he told Sherwood. He wouldn't be bothered by uncertain footing: he was the best-balanced horse in the field. He then gave the jockey his usual free-rein instructions. 'You know the horse,' he said. 'You know how to ride him. Do your thing.' Burridge's final instructions were of a less technical nature. 'Look after him,' he said, 'he's not only mine. He's Public Horse Number One.'

Indeed, Dessie was already the best-loved steeplechaser since Red Rum, a decade ago, and burdened down by the sentiment of punters, he went to the starting post 5-2 favourite. The Irish gelding Carvill's Hill was fancied next at 5-1, with the ill-fated Ten Plus, ridden by Kevin Mooney, next at 11-2. Scudamore's Bonanza Boy, an accomplished mudlark, was 15-2, the defending champion Charter Party, Dunwoody up, closed at 14-1. The Irish jockey Tom Morgan and Yahoo, who hadn't won a race in his last six outings over two seasons, were far back in the pack at 25-1.

The official going was heavy as they reached the start. Captain Sayers described by O'Sullevan as being in particularly fine voice in this, his retirement year, prepared to get his last Gold Cup under way. At the other end of the course, his great friend Hancock was moving up to his box.

Sherwood has standard plans for mud-running. 'I hold onto his head a bit more,' he said later, 'and obviously I don't do anything so quickly in the mud. It's also always in the back of my mind not to ask him to do too much too early in the race. He's got to get home. Besides, there would be lots of carnage as a result of the ground.' That last remark, while not meant literally, was to be prophetic: of the thirteen starters, one was to be killed, seven more would not finish.

As the starting tape leapt up, Dessie went to the front of the field. 'He was jumping well,' recalled Sherwood, 'but he was labouring. There was no spring in the ground and he didn't like it.' Meanwhile, jockey Kevin Mooney got away slowly but by the third fence he and Ten Plus were laid up in touch with the leader.

Mooney was thrilled. At thirty-four, this was his first Gold Cup and 'maybe you get only one Gold Cup in your life.' He was also confident. Ten Plus, while not very clever, was an honest 'gentleman' in the eyes of his rider. Together, they had won their last four chases. Still, deep in his mind, Mooney remembered their last trip over fences at Cheltenham.

It had been horrifying. 'It was in January, 1988,' the jockey recalled later. 'He turned a somersault over the second last. Ignored the fence completely. Just crashed into it. I landed under him but luckily neither of us got hurt. It knocked the confidence out of the horse, though, and it was hard putting it back.'

Ten Plus, moving nicely, had taken the lead at the fourteenth of the twenty-two fences which, in truth, had brought no great distress to Sherwood. 'No bother at all,' he later recalled in a throw-away, public school manner. 'It gave my horse a chance to have a bit of a rest. Glad to let someone else do the hard work.'

Then, last circuit, down the hill, third fence from home and fate struck again. Ten Plus, leader by three lengths, met the birches wrong. 'He got in a bit short and just hit the top and couldn't get a leg over. Eight times out of ten he'd have got away with it,' Mooney recalled much later. 'But this time he didn't get away with it.' The jockey's memory then became a muddle: Ten Plus plunging on to his head, sitting back on his hind legs, struggling up and galloping in herd spirit after the other horses, his near hind leg hanging down. 'I got up and asked people hanging over the fence and they said he was all right.'

Battle was joined now between the new leader Yahoo with Morgan – 'I was sorry to see Ten Plus go,' said the Irishman. 'I was going to need his help against Dessie' – and the great toiling Grey One. Yahoo had a half-length lead over the final fence and then up the merciless, final hill they went. Sherwood sat patiently and Dessie clawed back. The jockey had devised a plan for the run-in. 'I was going to edge to the right,' the jockey said, 'so we could have the help of the running-rail on the right.'

Dessie wouldn't have it. He closed over leftwards, against his natural right-moving instincts, and towards Yahoo. Morgan, catching the Grey One out of the corner of his eye, was intimidated and thought: Simon is coming to get me. He's showing Dessie the fight.

Desert Orchid's odd drift may, as some experts think, have been brought on by fatigue or, as his owner Burridge contends, because 'Dessie hangs that way.' Sherwood, who ought to know, has a different explanation and one suited to the legend growing round The Grey Horse. 'He was running *at* the other horse,' explained the jockey. 'This may sound cranky, but to be totally honest I'm convinced he went over to shout, "Push off, mate, this is my race," and to elbow him out.'

Sherwood had witnessed this behaviour before. 'In all the times I've ridden him, he's never run at a horse unless he's been very close to getting beat,' he said. 'He does it at home on the gallops and a couple of months ago at Ascot he swerved, this time to the right, over the last twenty or thirty yards, when we beat Panto Prince by a head.'

Sherwood chuckled. 'If I hadn't taken a hold, he'd have ridden Yahoo off – and I'd have lost the race. I mean it.' As it was, Desert Orchid lunged forward, consuming the ground in great, raking strides and swept past the line a length and a half clear. The stands exploded in cheers.

Charter Party, the 1988 winner, came third. Bonanza Boy and Scudamore dribbled in fourth. High above in the judge's box, Hancock passed the news officially to the commentator.

Of the 51,500 fans, a record, few could have heard the official confirmation. Burridge wrapped his arms round the two strangers beside him. Hats were flung in the air and grown men wept in the Press box. John Karter of *The Independent* overheard one fan say, 'Dessie's got another gear,' and another reply, 'No, he's got another heart.'

In the hysteria of victory, the death at the foot of the hill was forgotten. Ten Plus, his near hind leg swinging, its fetlock broken, had had to be shot. His jockey Mooney broke down and wept on the weighing-room steps when told. 'He was a slow-learner,' he said later. 'He was just learning his trade. He hadn't got it all together. But he was a gentleman.'

Much later, in darkness, the fans were still cheering their hero as he stood outside the open ramp of his horsebox. It was cold. Desert Orchid was trembling but, great showman that he is, was reluctant to leave the stage until his owner led him into the box.

As Dessie disappeared, a drunken voice rang up. 'You're lucky. If Ten Plus had stood on his feet, you'd have been slaughtered.'

Burridge, a compassionate man, was struck cold by the grotesque remark. Thinking of his own misgivings about running Dessie that day, thinking of the deaths of other brave horses, he fell silent. 'Success is a funny thing,' he said at last, not smiling for the first time in hours. 'It sort of dissolves in front of you.'

Overture . . .

Beside the first fence at Aintree stood a Mercedes lorry. In the back a winch rose above the high sides. On the cab door, written in Old English script, were the words:

Stan Waite, Ltd.
Licensed Slaughterers
The Tannery
Garstang, Lancs.

This, in the grim parlance of Aintree, was the 'knacker's cart'. The driver, a gaunt man, sat relaxed, waiting in his cab. It would be his job to follow the horses round the Grand National and winch the shot or otherwise dead ones into his lorry. He had, he said, carried off many dead horses in his day: Alverton, the favourite in 1979, Dark Ivy in 1987. He felt that it was the first fence that was the sure indicator of how his work would go.

'If they come over the first all fanned out you won't see much trouble – at least early on,' he said. 'But if they're bunched up, you'll get the fallers. Soon enough, and lots of them.'

It was the morning of the National. The sun poured down. It tightened the raw Northern turf, less cultured but deeper, springier than the grasses of Cheltenham. It cast a carnival cloak over the most famous of steeplechase courses. Acrobats tumbled for charity and down by the first open ditch a collie dog climbed a ladder and jumped through a hoop. A vintage car gave rides.

Into the bright air rose the friendly, metallic voice of a Tannoy. It spoke of parachutists to come. It gave a tip to the fans. 'It takes an hour to walk the course,' said the voice and, as though to remind them that other races were taking place that day, it went on to say, 'Please be back by one o'clock.'

Sightseers, some in singlets, some carrying beer packs and hampers, took advantage of the invitation. They crunched over the cinders of the Melling Road and strolled along the four-and-a-half miles of track. They peered at the sixteen fences, thirty in all for the National, for some would be jumped again on the second time round. The fences, as in a museum, were roped off and attended by watchmen. To many of these racegoers, Aintree was less a museum than a chamber of horrors. It was a wonder of the world, delicious to see.

The first fence, four-and-a-half feet of thorn, seemed straightforward. It excited little interest. Such an innocent view was misplaced. After all, the knacker-cart man had considered it as a sure indicator of trouble.

Over coffee that morning, Peter's father had warned of its dangers when taken fast, whips up, in a cavalry charge. I gazed at it: the fence stood quiet, arrogant, composed. It would have something to say to the riders.

Continuing down the course, past the second fence, I was reminded of what Mark Todd, the Olympic Gold Medal event rider, had told me in general about the layout of the National. He and some of the other top eventers had ridden it a week earlier for charity. Going cautiously and keeping clear of each other, they had got round. Nonetheless, it had been a sobering experience for the laid-back New Zealander.

'My first impression was that it was different from what I had expected, because of the TV cameras,' Todd said. 'The cameras always get the back view of the fences and I was quite surprised that on the take-off side they had such a nice, inviting apron on them.' Todd had voiced respect for the third fence, the open ditch, down where the collie was now climbing the rungs of a ladder. Then Todd had grinned. 'The fences are big. Very unsettling. The thought of lining up with forty others, to me, would be horrifying.'

Approaching the sixth fence, I crossed a path and, in the blue sky beyond, a television gantry could be seen pointing back towards the action. A crowd had gathered on the other side of the fence, on the 'outer' and, due to the angle of Becher's, many of the fans appeared to be on the racetrack itself. I recalled

Richard Dunwoody telling me how that colourful, shouting, point-blank corner of spectators could put off a horse. He reckoned it had brought him down when he was leading second time round on West Tip in 1985. 'When he fell and his head hit the floor,' recalled Dunwoody, 'his ears were still pricked. He was looking over that way at the crowd.'

Down the left, a row of firs ran like a wing to the fence. Todd had liked those trees: they led him nicely to the obstacle. A youngster, nipping round the guards, was snapping off a fir twig: a souvenir. An older spectator, camera in hand, moved a friend to a place in front of a sign. The sign read: 'Becher's Brook'.

So, this was the notorious Becher's. It appeared vivid, as Centre Court and the Road Hole at St Andrews appear vivid at first sight. In itself, it looked harmless, too: a wall of dark thatching, spruce from the Welsh Mountains, as neatly-woven as the roof on a calendar cottage. Then I thought of the much-photographed drop on the far side of the fence. Becher's seemed like a shot-gun suicide: the face looked fine but the back of the head was blown off.

It had been here where Scudamore's best chance of winning the great race, after seven starts and a third-place finish in 1985 on Corbiere, came to grief. It happened last year on that maddening, inattentive Strands of Gold, the strong gelding who had dumped Peter so unceremoniously in December at Ascot. Peter once recalled that Aintree spill on Strands. 'The problem was much the same as it was at Ascot,' he said. 'He just hit the fence too low. He suddenly misses a fence out. It's a matter of concentration.' I could remember the photographs of Peter getting up from the fall: no fear, no injury, just anger and disgust.

Today, an odd business was going on at Becher's. A guard and a policeman watched a sniffer dog work. He clambered over the fir boughs and moved swiftly, haltingly, along the edge of the brook. The dog's purpose, and the image it evoked, was spectacular, unthinkable: could it actually be that a time-bomb was buried in the brush, set to explode under the horses? Carnage, man and beast, would be witnessed by 300 million television viewers round the world.

Terrorists? I asked an official. 'Fergie,' said a guard, tightly smiling. 'We're expecting a visit from the Royal Family.' Presently her car rolled up. Plain clothesmen piled out and then the Duchess of York herself, all in green, and her husband Prince Andrew. The guards looked at the crowd. Fergie and Andy looked at the fence. Bob Davies, Assistant Clerk of the Course and National winner on Lucius in 1978, was in place to tell them about Becher's. In his day he always took it just outside the middle, he explained, where the drop is less severe. Andrew nodded. Fergie said she'd bet on Lucius as a little girl.

Davies, unaccustomed as he was to entering the Royal House-hold, walked with the couple to Foinavon, the smallest fence on the course, the scene of the famous 1967 pile-up, and onwards to the Canal Turn, which he also explained. Fergie and Andy then rejoined their car and the spectators who had followed them returned to take up their places at Becher's. Becher's was the place to be. It might have been Tyburn.

The jockeys, too, were walking the course and far out in the country, beyond the Canal Turn, the lanky Devonian Jimmy Frost was having a look. A distinguished point-to-point rider – he won his first at the age of 13 in Cornwall – Frost had turned National Hunt jockey late in his career. He was to ride Little Polveir, only recently taken on by his guv'nor, the trainer Toby Balding. Frost had first sat on the horse four days before. He was a comradely jockey, much respected by his fellows, and jokingly maligned by Balding. 'Jimmy has everything a jump jockey needs,' Balding said later in a much-cited quote. 'Long legs and no brains.'

Frost, in turn, regarded Balding, the public schoolboy, with a mixture of puzzlement, respect and, at the moment, anger. The previous day at Devon and Exeter, Frost had ridden a horse trained by Balding, the 5-2 favourite. It finished fourth. In the evening, as Frost drove with other jockeys up the motorway towards Liverpool, Balding buzzed in on the car phone and roasted him for what he took to be a poor ride. Frost was furious. 'If there hadn't been a lady in the car,' Frost said later, 'I'd have told Balding to stuff his Grand National.'

Such a threat would have been hard to believe. Frost lusted for the ride. It was his first National, or at least his first *bona fide* National. Years ago he had played the part of an extra, a jockey, in the film *Champions*, the story of Bob Champion's battle against cancer and his victory on Aldaniti in the 1981 National.

'In the film, we jumped only the first three fences and the Chair,' Frost said. 'And they didn't have the spruce on them. They were just the bare sticks and you had to fill in a bit with your imagination.'

His imagination was chock-a-block. In his view the Grand National layout, for example, was like an historic building, perhaps the Coliseum in Rome: 'I felt like a Christian,' he said, 'come to have a look at where I'd get fed to the lions.' Frost, aged 30, had actually dreamt of riding in the celebrated race since boyhood. 'I was really steeped in it. The only book I ever read was Bill Curling's *Grand National*,' he said, referring to the illustrated history of the event by the one-time 'Hotspur' of the Daily Telegraph. 'I could tell you every winner of the National since 1900.'

Frost studied Valentine's Brook, the ninth and twenty-fifth fences on the course. Valentine's, like Becher's, was named after a competitor; in this case it was a horse that had reared up and miraculously twisted over the fence in 1840, the year after Capt. Becher's unceremonious dunking. Its size is almost identical to Becher's but, without the cruel drop, the dangers are less. Still, it commanded respect: two horses had died there since the Second War.

Frost found it more upright than he had expected. He'd pop over it, he decided, play it steady. Then, with a pang, his imagination was filled with the next fence, a 5-ft wall of gorse. It was here at the 26th fence, five from home in 1988, that Little Polveir had parted company with his jockey, Tom Morgan. If I get this far, Frost thought, I'll have reached a milestone.

He moved on. The second open ditch, fences 11 and 27, was 'trappy' as they say in the trade. The takeoff board, a yellowish strip, is all but buried in the turf. It is difficult to see. It demands care in presenting the horse because, as Frost recognised, the animal doesn't properly see it until he's on top of it. Immediately after the takeoff board, Frost noted, there was 'this great big awesome hole' six feet of it, in fact, in front of the fence. In the past, horses had misjudged the takeoff, foundered in that big, awesome hole.

Frost continued and, beginning to turn for the stands, he passed three negotiable fences before arriving at the Chair. Although jumped only once, on the first circuit, the Chair perhaps commands more respect than any obstacle at Aintree.

The Chair, Frost thought respectfully, is not the same fence I saw in the Bob Champion film. On his feet, and Frost is a tall man for a jockey, it looked massive – and narrow. Little Polveir will know what to do, he reckoned. It was his job to present him properly and, at the time they passed over the jump, to hope they would find that the traffic was light.

Frost finished his tour of the fences with the Water Jump, fifteen feet across, big. What's more, it had a niggling drop where an unsuspecting horse might peck and lose balance. Frost had walked the circuit for the first time and he concluded that in real life, the Grand National course was a good deal bigger than it had been on celluloid.

With that he set the National from his thoughts for, rising to occupy his mind, was the hurdle course. He had better hurry and walk that one off for, in truth, that's where his hopes lay for the day. Little Polveir might get round but he'd never win the Grand National. Frost's deepest concern was to survive the race unhurt and be ready for his ride on Morley Street in the Novices' Hurdle at 5:10. Morley Street, certainly more than Little Polveir, was his banker for Liverpool.

If the tall, self-effacing West Country boy had glanced over the rails towards the infield that moment, he might have seen a young girl, pacing head-down between the Chair and the Water Jump. She was Donna Cornforth, stable lass to Bonanza Boy, Scudamore's ride in the National. She was tired and in anguish. Worried over the National, she had not eaten a morsel the previous day and in the transporter with the horse that morning she had fretted the entire five-hour journey from Somerset.

At Aintree, Miss Cornforth had plaited Bonanza Boy straight away and soon left him in his box, happy and head-up, listening to the Tannoy. She joined another stable lass for a walk round the big course. She started, and stopped, at the Chair, too frightened to go on. There was no way, she concluded, that her little monkey was going to get round the Grand National.

A breeze had sprung up across the race course and, wandering back to the weighing-room and Press area, I thought of another of Peter's Grand Nationals. In it he had experienced a weird, surreal sensation. It took place in 1984 when he was aboard the free-running Burnt Oak, a fellow that pulled like a dray horse.

'He'd run away with me down the first few fences and I was about twenty lengths clear,' Scudamore recounted, 'and this breeze was blowing in such a way that I could hear a great wind whistling in my ears. Nothing else. Just the wind. Then when I turned back on the race course, all alone and still way clear, the wind suddenly stopped. Deadly silence. I must have been going at the same speed as the wind.' Panic briefly seized him. 'I thought, "Oh dear, you prat! You've gone the wrong way."'

It wasn't the first, nor would it be the last, time a jockey worried about going the wrong way, turning up the Mildmay steeplechase course at that very point at Aintree. As for Burnt Oak, he was soon to be burnt out. Peter had pulled him up just after Becher's.

Only Peter, I thought, could pull up a horse just *after* Becher's.

. . . And Beginners

Captain Martin Becher, born in 1797, occupies a unique spot in the sport. 'More than any other person,' wrote Michael Seth-Smith in *The History of Steeplechasing*, 'he is the connecting thread between the earliest days of steeplechasing and the emergence of Liverpool as the greatest steeplechase course in the country.'

Son of a retired Army officer, Becher was raised on a farm in Norfolk where he learned to ride and, after a brief Army fling, to break and train horses. A dandy in side-boards, a fellow whose footing and balance were so sure he could circle a room on its skirting, he went on to achieve national acclaim as a cross-country rider.

On 26 February, 1839, the first Grand National, then called The Grand Liverpool Steeplechase, was staged at Aintree. The going, heavy that day, added to the brutal riding assignment that included a 5 ft stone wall, a 'Table Jump' where the landing was 4 ft higher than the take-off and an early obstacle, jumped out of a ploughed field, which was especially testing.

That early obstacle was made up of 'a post and rails in front of a fence with a six-foot ditch on the landing side', according to The Lonsdale Library's *Steeplechasing*. Other sources claim the fence was three-and-a-half-foot high, the ditch eight foot wide, with an overall carry of twenty-three feet.

Peter Scudamore had laughed when I read out the dimensions of the original National. 'That's not a steeplechase course,' he said, 'that's for cross-country eventers. Mark Todd could handle it better than us.'

Anyway, it was here that Captain Becher, aged forty-two, fell into everlasting fame. His horse, Conrad, hit the rails hard, stopped and pitched his rider into the brook. Becher's humiliation is captured in an engraving of the day which shows him in the brook, cowering under the hooves of oncoming horses.

He remounted, fell again, and never rode in another National. But from that day the fence was called Becher's Brook.

Over the years Aintree and Becher's have evolved. Becher's now is the sixth and twenty-second fence on the course: a four-and-a-half foot obstacle of tightly-packed spruce, with a drop of five-and-a-half feet into a 45 degree slope. Rightly or wrongly, it has the reputation as the most murderous of steeplechase fences. From the end of World War II through 1988, it had claimed the lives of seven horses.

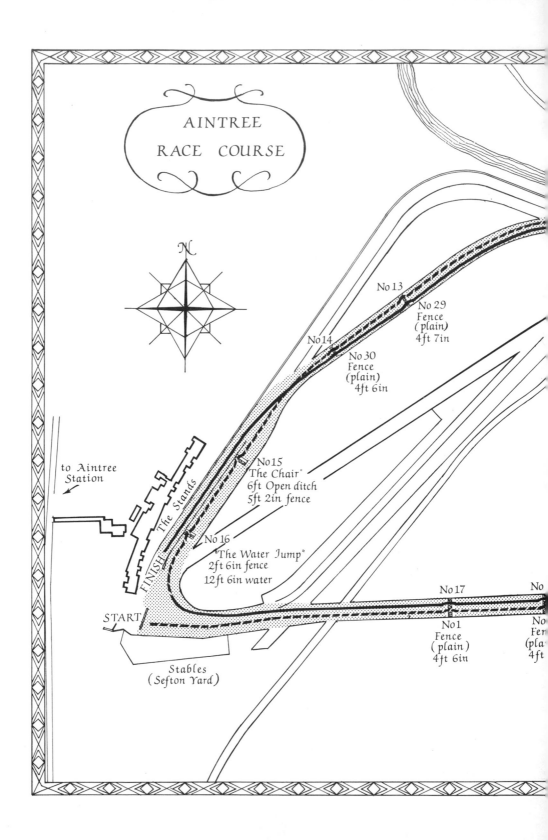

AINTREE
RACE COURSE

N

to Aintree
Station

FINISH The Stands

No 13

No 29
Fence
(plain)
4ft 7in

No 14

No 30
Fence
(plain)
4ft 6in

No 15
"The Chair"
6ft Open ditch
5ft 2in fence

No 16
"The Water Jump"
2ft 6in fence
12ft 6in water

No 17

No

START

No 1
Fence
(plain)
4ft 6in

No
Fen
(pla
4ft

Stables
(Sefton Yard)

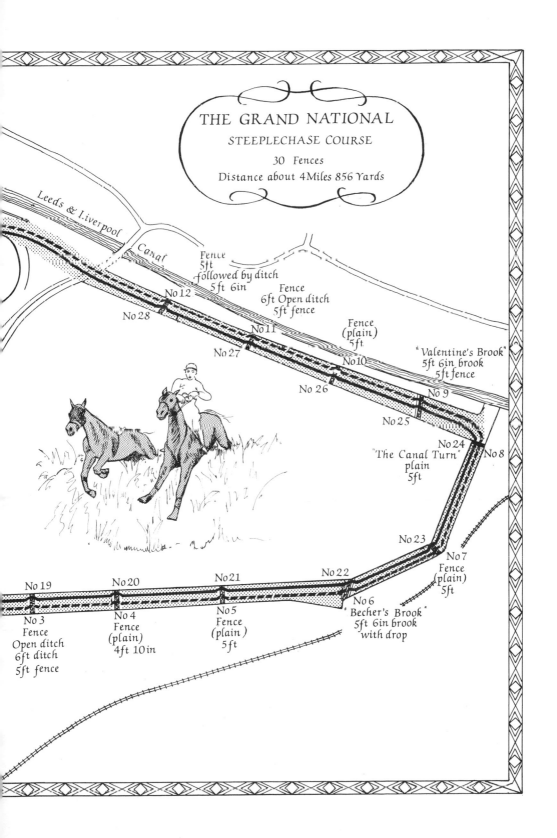

THE GRAND NATIONAL

STEEPLECHASE COURSE

30 Fences

Distance about 4 Miles 856 Yards

Leeds & Liverpool

Canal

Fence
5ft
followed by ditch
5ft 6in

Fence
6ft Open ditch
5ft fence

Fence
(plain)
5ft

"Valentine's Brook"
5ft 6in brook
5ft fence

No 12

No 28

No 11

No 27

No 10

No 26

No 9

No 25

No 24
"The Canal Turn"
plain
5ft

No 8

No 23

No 7
Fence
(plain)
5ft

No 19

No 20

No 21

No 22

No 3
Fence
Open ditch
6ft ditch
5ft fence

No 4
Fence
(plain)
4ft 10in

No 5
Fence
(plain)
5ft

No 6
"Becher's Brook"
5ft 6in brook
with drop

The National

'The thing about Liverpool was, and still is, to keep out of trouble,' he said and, chuckling softly, stirred the milk in his coffee. 'I ought to know.'

The speaker, Michael Scudamore, sat in the lobby of the Royal Clifton Hotel in Southport, the place where old riders gather to relive their past glories. It was the morning of the 1989 Grand National and he was recalling his debut in the race, back in 1951, when he still rode as an amateur. That was the year of the premature start, when the field of thirty-six horses, including East A'Calling with Scudamore on board, were still milling round for position when the barrier went up.

'I was in the middle somewhere,' he said, 'and I can still remember a mass of hooves and when I crossed the Melling Road the ashes and stones coming back in my face. Everybody had their whips up. We were all going too fast. So some of the horses over-jumped the first fence and the rest of us fell into the backs of them.'

Scudamore chuckled again as he recalled the chaos, the eleven horses down round him, the briefness of his maiden Grand National ride, perhaps forty-five seconds. 'Funny, I was looking at photographs of the pile-up the other day. Pat Taaffe, Brian Marshall, myself – all on the floor. And between us we went on to win five Grand Nationals.'

Taaffe and Marshall each won two and Scudamore one, on Oxo in 1959. He told of how his colours and a chocolate horse had decorated the victory dinner-dance that evening at the old Adelphi Hotel in Liverpool. He recalled the race, how on the second circuit his friend Tim Brookshaw had broken a stirrup as he dropped over Becher's Brook, kicked out of the other iron, and in high spirits shouted curses on ahead as he chased Oxo home. Brookshaw was later to break his back in a hurdle race at Aintree. 'So sad,' said Scudamore, 'Tim was a great character, lovely man. Very tough.'

Scudamore had been tough too. There was a scar on his chin and of course that dead left eye, hardly noticeable, which was the legacy of the terrible fall under the horses at Wolverhampton. The fall had brought an end to his jockey days, finished his long Grand National run: five finishes and, perhaps imperishably, sixteen consecutive appearances, a longevity record unmatched in the 150-year history of the most famous steeplechase race in the world. He smiled. 'I didn't always manage to keep out of trouble.'

Keep out of trouble. Those indeed were the riding instructions for Liverpool, a unique track but, when taken once round at a leisurely pace, no killer at all, even with its hidden drops on the landing sides: a week earlier, heavy with rain, it had been popped round by Olympic cross-country riders. On Grand National day, however, it can turn nasty: ridden twice round, it is four-and-a-half miles long, with 30 fences, taken flank-to-flank in a cavalcade of upwards of forty horses. Basically, it is to be tackled in one of two ways: along the outside route, avoiding the heavy traffic until it thins out, or fast up the inside, staying ahead of the fallers.

Scudamore Senior was a confirmed 'outsider' and before his son's first National ride, on a horse named Cheers in 1981, he advised Peter to follow that more prudent path on the first circuit. 'He did it for his first three or four Nationals but then, in 1985, he rode Corbiere and Mrs Pitman said go up the inner. He had a marvellous run, finishing third, and he's been up the inside ever since.'

Warming to the memories, Scudamore, now 57, spoke of his two other fine finishes, second on Legal Joy in 1952, third on Irish Lizard in 1954. 'Irish Lizard, now there was a horse,' he said, his spoon tinkling in his coffee cup: 'If you kicked him to stand off, he'd go in close; if you wanted him to go in close, he'd stand off.' Scudamore laughed: 'You'd best let *him* get on with the job.' He gazed out the tall windows towards the dunes, towards the sands where everybody will tell you Red Rum used to exercise. Then he returned to the topic at hand.

Little Polveir and Jimmy Frost complete a fabulous month of big winners.

The ill-fated Enemy Action, winner of four races in the season.

'I often think Becher's cost me another National,' he said. 'It was in 1964. I was on a horse called Time. I'd done awfully well going round on the outer and, with the field thinning out, I dropped over onto the inner second time round. I was lying about fourth or fifth. Just cruising. Then we met Becher's. He jumped it too well and the drop caught him out. He didn't fall, mind. He just slithered along on his belly and by the time we got up the race was over.' In retelling the story Scudamore, the most modest and generous of men, had fallen into a common jockey's trap: *he'd* done awfully well, but the *horse* had been beaten.

Beaten by Becher's: Aintree's sixth and twenty-second fence: a four-and-a-half foot obstacle of tightly-packed spruce, with that blind drop of five-and-a-half feet into a leg-buckling 45-degree upslope. Becher's indeed had been Scudamore's stumbling block, through falls, on two other National occasions. Come to think of it, Becher's had foiled his son only last year; Peter had fallen there, second time round, when he was leading the field on Strands of Gold.

'If he'd been out in the middle he might have won the National. I don't know. Nobody will ever know. But, between you and me, and I haven't spoken to him yet, if he comes to me for advice, I'll tell him to stay away from the inner. I'd remind him of the way to get round Liverpool. Stay out of trouble.'

Of the forty runners in the 1989 Grand National, two were considered by the jockeys to be the danger horses, *literally* the danger horses. There was the lunatic gelding Hettinger, who last year had fallen at the first Grand National fence and who, in fact, had fallen a total of six times in the season. He was a horse who, without a blind bit of notice, might run straight into a fence but it was almost moral blackmail for the owner to enter him for charity: £140 for each fence cleared to go to a leukaemia fund.

Hettinger was to be avoided at all costs. The race programme said as much. 'Even the indestructible Ray Goldstein,' its tipster wrote, 'will do well to complete the course on this one.'

In 1988, the fallen Hettinger had nearly brought down Rhyme 'N' Reason and Brendan Powell, who together went on to win the race. This time Powell was on the brown gelding Stearsby, another strong contender. He wasn't amused at the prospect of dealing with the creature again. He wasn't amused either at the thought of his jockey: although popular, the dark, hirsute Goldstein is the 'Italian Stallion' among his fellow jockeys, a Rambo by looks and a Rambo by nature in the saddle.

In the weighing-room Powell spoke to Goldstein. 'Fancy a 36-year-old like you, riding in his first National,' said the Irishman. 'And on a horse like Hettinger. Ray, you'll never get round. This is going to be your last race of the season.'

Getting round was all Goldstein wanted. No stranger to the inside of ambulances, he was nervous. 'I think Hettinger will make it,' he said. 'There's only one way of finding out. By going out there.' He pulled on his pink shirt, with the emerald green cross belts: Hettinger's colours; his fellow jockeys all knew them well. For all that, Goldstein was to be excused, pitied perhaps, for at his age the offer of a ride in the National doesn't come often.

David Pitcher was another matter. Pitcher was an amateur, a 54-year-old businessman who had taken up the game at the age of 48. In the weighing-room, he changed by himself, without the aid of a valet. 'I've got the best tack that money can buy,' he will explain, 'and I don't trust it in anybody's hands but my own.' He is especially proud of his Australian saddle, the tree of which has a 'breaking strain of 3,500 pounds'.

Pitcher's horse, Brown Trix, was his own. He had bought it for £25,000 two years before from Fred Winter, who had made it into a good chaser. Together, Pitcher and Brown Trix ran in the 1987 National: he fell, the horse didn't and, riderless, went on to beat the winner Maori Venture to the finishing post. In his other National, Pitcher had also fallen. Yet today his plan of attack was untrammelled by doubt.

'Go like stink to the Melling Road and take a pull. Then get over the first half dozen fences,' he said, ignoring any intricate view of Becher's, the sixth. 'Then "hunt" the first circuit and put yourself in the race the second time round.' What about Becher's? 'I've jumped fences bigger than Becher's out hunting.' Pitcher hunts with the Berks and Bucks but he's not everybody's stirrup cup. Before the race, Scudamore was generous towards the bumptious man, harsh towards his riding.

'Unbelievable,' the champion jockey said simply beforehand. 'Unbelievable.'

Scudamore was late to the parade ring. He had ridden in the previous race, the Sandeman Aintree Hurdle, and come third on the faltering favourite Celtic Shot, beaten once more, and conclusively so, by Richard Guest and Beech Road. It was for the moment a blow but hurriedly changing into his National colours, he swept the defeat from his mind. 'Celtic Shot's race was gone,' he said later. 'It was history.'

Such a dismissive remark is a common cliché among sportsmen. Scudamore was either speaking the truth or profoundly fooling himself but, whatever, it didn't much matter. Among those who pursue sport, none has a better-refined gift of finding a clean sheet after failure. And the failures were piling up: Scudamore had now gone twenty-two races without a win, his worst run of the season.

In the parade ring, he noticed Bonanza Boy's stable lass in distress. He told her Bonanza Boy looked fine. The National is the National, seldom run to plan, and Pipe gave no instructions as Scudamore, mounted, turned towards the race track. 'Look after yourself,' said Donna Cornforth. 'Come back safely.' She was speaking to Bonanza Boy.

Red Rum, full of the occasion, led the horses past the stands, past the big television screen in the infield. Scudamore blocked out the din of the Aintree crowd. He blocked out the instinct to find himself up on the screen. Celtic Shot truly was history. Instead, he homed in on the race at hand. In his mind he went through the Form Book, horse by horse, with composure and in remarkable detail.

Lastly, gazing round the field, he attached colours to horses, a safety device especially crucial in the National. He then put it all into practical theory.

Stearsby wouldn't win, not after his recent run-out at Wincanton. He probably wouldn't even get round. Yet he'd have an influence on the race. This was because Brendan Powell was riding him. Last year Powell had taken the outside route round the course and won on Rhyme 'N' Reason. He'd go outside again and other people would go outside; outside was the flavour of the season. Mind the traffic, Scudamore told himself, and noted Stearsby's colours: black and red.

West Tip, with Richard Dunwoody, was a bit old at twelve. Couldn't see him winning. He was nonetheless sure-footed;

after all he won this thing in 1986 and came fourth in 1987 and 1988. The horse was safe. If Richard doesn't take him up the inside, reckoned Scudamore, I'll track him. Light blue and black.

Monanore, with McCourt, wouldn't be a bad horse to track either; he'd got round Aintree the past three times. In the Grand National, more than in any other race, you look for a safe horse to follow. Dark blue.

Gainsay, with Mark Pitman, sometimes over-jumps. He'll be going up the inside. Jenny Pitman always sends her horses up the inside at Aintree. She sent Scudamore up the inside on Corbiere in 1985. Orange with a black star.

Mearlin, with Simon McNeill. The last mare to win the National was Nickle Coin, way back in 1951, but Peter was not dismissing her because of her gender. Still, *Timeform* had it pretty much right: 'quite a modest chaser'. Pink, purple.

Dixton House, with Tom Morgan, was something else again. He was Father's horse – he'd trained him in his early days – and Scudamore felt certain he'd get round. Father's horse, which was the way Scu viewed Dixton House, whosoever trained him now, was the danger horse in the National. On form, if this had been an ordinary handicap 'chase round Cheltenham, he'd be the only horse favoured to beat Bonanza Boy. Dark green and light blue.

Little Polveir. 50 to 1. Scudamore had no worries about Little Polveir, probably the smallest horse save Scu's own Bonanza Boy in the race. He'd had a bad season and, what's more, he tended to unseat his riders in the National. What Little Polveir had going for him was Jimmy Frost, his jockey, a very good horseman. Blue and black.

The horses cantered off for a look at the first fence. Chris Grant, on the joint-favourite Durham Edition, sidled up to Scudamore. 'Bloody hell,' said Grant, gazing down from the heights of his big chestnut. 'You'll never get round on that little thing.'

'Thank you. Now piss off,' replied Scudamore, beside him on the dark little horse, near enough black.

'Bit small, isn't he, Scu?' added Graham McCourt, with that sly grin of his, as he walked past Scudamore on Monanore. Bonanza Boy was the target of much friendly ridicule among jockeys, especially those with a fair chance of completing, for, indeed, he looked small for the Aintree task. He stands just under 16 hands high, the smallest horse in the field, and no really small – by the measuring stick even Red Rum wasn't *really* small – horse has won the National since Battleship, 15.2 hands, in 1938.

Scudamore's thoughts were elsewhere. Bonanza Boy. He had to be here with a chance. After all, he had won the Welsh Grand National like a good horse. Still, his jumping was sometimes flawed: next time out after Chepstow he had taken a header, a nasty fall at Ascot that *really* unsettled Miss Cornforth, and later, in that richly disappointing performance, he clattered the fences when he came fourth in the Cheltenham Gold Cup.

Bonanza Boy's turn of foot wasn't all that blinding, either, and Scudamore had watched helpless in the weighing-room as pounds of lead were slipped into his saddle cloth. Bonanza Boy was second top weight at Aintree. On the other hand, he had plenty of heart, to be sure: remember Kempton Park.

Bonanza Boy was Scu's kind of horse: they don't know when they're beaten.

'There's Bonanza Boy to the right of the picture. And the stars of Peter Scudamore, 30-year-old Peter, enjoying an absolutely fantastic season, with 189 winners. In his ninth National which his father won, of course, on Oxo . . .' chattered Peter O'Sullevan, the BBC veteran. *'With West Tip on his far side. Two of the best riders we've seen for years. Peter Scudamore and Richard Dunwoody.'*

Dunwoody appeared in that erect, deep seat of his, his usually long leathers looking oddly short: walking round, Dunwoody always rides with his toes in his irons, pushing his legs up and, besides, it took a lot of leg to get round that great bulk of West Tip. The Ulsterman was speaking to Scudamore. He was unusually ebullient. 'I've never known this horse in better form,' he said, restraining his mount from breaking into a canter. 'He's *really* well. Whoever beats me will win.'

'Dixton House 10 to 1. Bonanza Boy 11s. West Tip 12 to 1 and opened at 16s, remember. Stearsby . . .'

Little Polveir had settled at 28-1, fifteenth favourite in a field of forty. Frost circled, considering the tips he had got from Morgan, who had been unseated by the horse the previous year.

'He's a lazy horse,' said the Irishman. 'He likes to go his own pace. But keep him a bit handy.' Frost had come to much the same conclusions, having the past four evenings studied the video tape of the 1988 National. Yes, he would stay up there in touch and, as Balding had instructed, he'd wait until late in the race before making his move.

Scudamore sought out Goldstein. Other jockeys sought out Goldstein. 'I was the most popular bloke at the start,' Goldstein said later. He explained to each of his colleagues that he'd take Hettinger down the middle. Scudamore spoke with Pitcher. Pitcher planned to take Brown Trix down the outside. Bloody hell, Peter said to himself, cantering back to the start. I'll have to go down the middle-outer. There's no other place left.

At the start, the field of riders began milling round in two roughly equal circles: those, like Scudamore, who would go down the outer and those who chose the inner. On the starter's stand, Captain Keith Brown, who for seventeen years had been starting races at one level or another and had now succeeded Michael Sayers as the Senior Starter, was handling his first National. He was struck by the deafening crowd noises that drowned out the usual chat between starter and riders. He picked up a signal from the handler of Gala's Image: the horse had spread a plate. A farrier was summoned and, with pit-stop speed, the shoe nailed back into place.

'Mr Pitcher, 54 years old . . .'

'Line up, Gentlemen,' shouted Capt. Brown. The waiting, the joking was over. Scudamore moved into place, pleased that his mount never needed relaxing; he was that sort of horse. 'Good luck,' said somebody. 'Safe journey,' said someone else. Safe journey. Safe journey, a soft, whispered incantation. Scudamore closed his eyes: God, may we all get round in one piece. 'Wait!' screamed Capt. Brown. But the chestnut Bob Tisdall broke. He broke the tape. He veered off towards the inside rail. 'Back! Back!'

The gatemen gathered up and tied the broken tape. Scudamore again shut his eyes. He *hated* breakaway starts. 'It's the roar of the crowd,' he says, 'and then nothing happens. It's terrible.' Brown shouted: 'Wait! Wait! Wait!' And then suddenly, as though in an after thought, the starter cried – 'Come on!' They were off. This time Bob Tisdall cocked his jaw and veered outwards towards the starter's stand, as though he had a score to settle with Captain Brown. Brown, transfixed, watched the errant horse.

Scudamore heaved forward on Bonanza Boy. And then: What's this? The starting tape, a fine webbing, was hooked over Bonanza Boy's ears. It swarmed across Peter's chest. *Christ*, I'm going to get pulled off, he thought. *Christ*, the horse is going to get tangled in tape. This had never happened before – and now, in the Grand National. He snatched at it, flung it away.

The tape ensnarling Scudamore also frightened Carl Llewellyn on Smart Tar. 'When I saw Scu trapped in the stuff,' Llewellyn later recalled, 'I swung wide.'

'Brown Trix making ground on the far side . . .'

As the horses pounded towards the Melling Road, Scudamore sought West Tip to track, but Dunwoody had swung too far inside. Okay. Bonanza Boy settled in, up near the front, and Scudamore was pleased. We're not going that quick. But we're not losing ground we'll have to make up. As he passed the road, ashes flicking into his face, he prepared with exaggerated care to present his mount perfectly at the first obstacle: a 4 ft 6 in. thorn fence.

Up! Bonanza Boy flew it, technically speaking jumped it too big. They landed a bit too steep. Fine, thought Scudamore. But we can't do that at Becher's. If we land too steep there, we'll fall.

'The only faller there is Cerimau.'

Peter Hobbs, Cerimau's jockey, had felt the fall coming. It was the classic, run-of-the-mill fall. The horse, pounding along, had got a good look at the fence, taken caution, backed off and 'ballooned' it without so much as touching a twig. Once up in the air, without much impulsion, he came down too steeply, failed to get his forelegs out and skidded about three strides on his belly before capsizing. Hobbs was harmlessly spilled on the turf. End of story for horse and jockey.

'And Brown Trix, Mr Pitcher, 54 years old, on the far side leads the National field. Stearsby right up with him . . .'

The amateur Pitcher sped on, as he had planned, 'like stink'. He kept the lead over the second fence and Powell found himself directly behind those dark blue colours. Powell thought: he's pushing his horse's head off. This is a nightmare. Not another Hettinger.

The Irish horse Cranlome, carrying Kevin O'Brien, hit the second low, as if it were a soft Irish fence, and tipped over. Two horses gone. Then three when, as my then-colleague Brough Scott at *The Sunday Times* put it so nicely, 'Bob Tisdall, who had set out sulkily in hopeless pursuit, drew stumps at the second.'

At the third, the big open ditch, Scudamore muttered to himself: this is the crunch, little horse. Bonanza Boy cleared it well and Scu looked around for someone to track. In the weaving horses, he found nothing. Squeezed, he swung wider. He was happy enough. The horses weren't going fast and, like the other riders, he was already thinking three fences ahead to Becher's.

'Brown Trix made a bit of a mistake . . .'

Over the fourth and fifth fences the field began to swing in a stream to the right. They would attack Becher's from the outside, where the drop is less punishing. Bonanza Boy resisted the flow. Go with the tide, thought Scudamore, steering him firmly. Or we'll be jumping across people, into people. They joined the flow, well back in the pack.

Meanwhile Powell, on Stearsby, was taking a decision: he had hoped to drop in a half dozen horses off the lead but, maddened and frustrated by Pitcher and Brown Trix in front of him, he changed his mind. He accelerated into the fourth, a negotiable 4 ft 19 in. gorse fence, and overtook the dreaded pair. Reluctantly he had the lead for a while and then, throttling down, still well ahead of Brown Trix, he settled into fifth spot as the field cleared another gorse fence.

'And now as they race down to Becher's Brook with Stearsby in the lead. Stearsby on the wide outside . . .'

In the middle group, West Tip's nose moved slightly in front of Dixton House and Dunwoody, mindful of the horse's fall when going alone into the fence in 1985, swiftly reminded himself: the crowd on the right. Too many horses have fallen here, distracted, when they think they're in front. We'll need company going over. He held up his horse, just fractionally. West Tip dropped back, upsides Tom Morgan on Dixton House. 'If Tom hadn't been there,' Dunwoody said later, 'I'd have taken a pull and found somebody else.'

Becher's was on them. 'About four or five strides out,' Powell recalled later, 'I knew I was going to meet it spot-on. So the only thing to do was to give him a kick and get him out over the brook.' Powell gave him a kick. Stearsby not only got out over the brook but, by Powell's estimation, moved farther ahead of three or four horses in the air.

Scudamore, well back, caught a glimpse of the row of firs leading into Becher's on the left. About sixty yards out, he saw the path across the track. The path, not to put too fine a point on it, is rather like a marker on a fast-bowler's run-up. It was a signal to Scudamore to quicken up and as he swept over it he also began to feel for his horse's strides into the famous fence.

Scudamore met Becher's perfectly, heard the single word 'down' stick out like a spike from the commentary. Rising, he heard the rattle of hooves on the guard rail and the fir boughs crackling like gun-fire round him. He leant back on his horse, more than over any obstacle anywhere, for 'there's no way, certainly not there, you want to land up round his ears.' Dropping over, Scu saw a split-second flash of green-and-blue colours: Tom Morgan. Dixton House is down, he noted, and, with a jump of hope, he filed it away in his mind. The danger horse was out of the race.

Touching down, Scudamore counted the fall of his own horse's hooves: one-two-three-four. All legs down. Good. Aided by an encasing flow of horses, he eased himself round the crumpling Dixton House. The first problem was over. Becher's, he thought briefly, and allowed himself a grin. What's all this crap about Becher's?

'And another faller at the back is Brown Trix. He's down . . .'

Scudamore hadn't seen the crash of Brown Trix, the horse twisting and shouldering the fence, flinging out Pitcher like a rag doll. He hadn't seen Seeandem's fatal fall. He hadn't seen Tom Taaffe, thrown from Sergeant Sprite, bouncing along the floor, his left boot still hooked in his iron, nor the plight of Goldstein and Hettinger. For Goldstein, it was only a blur: another horse (Mr Crisp, he learned from the video tape) leaping into his path, Hettinger's head against its flanks and Goldstein, plunging straight downwards, already constructing a defence of his horse: we fell, like you all said we'd fall, but it wasn't his fault. Then, as Goldstein later recalled: 'black-out'.

Scudamore's mind, as he galloped to the Foinavon fence, scene of the 1967 pile-up, was on the turn ahead. He attempted to track leftwards to attack the Canal Turn fence on the inside. 'Don't come across!' shouted a rider behind him. 'Don't come across!' Squeezed up, denied a fluent run at the fence, Bonanza Boy merely popped over it. Forced to ease off, Scudamore dropped in towards the rail.

Ahead, Powell and Stearsby were in the lead, motoring, as he might have put it. The Irishman is fond of automotive analogies. 'Stearsby has a lot of scope,' he will say. 'He's got a high cruising speed and he corners very well for a big horse.' Powell cornered the big horse very well through the Canal Turn and steered him sweetly over Valentine's Brook.

'And West Tip and Stearsby dispute the lead . . .'

'How's he going?' asked Dunwoody, upsides Stearsby on West Tip.

'Pretty well,' said Powell, setting up for Fence No. 11, a 6 ft ditch followed by a 5 ft fir fence. 'I hope he keeps going.'

'And Stearsby is gone at that one . . .'

It was one of those equine aberrations. Stearsby put in a short stride where a long one was due. He ran straight into the open ditch in front of the fence: no fall, just a spectacular refusal. Powell, meanwhile, flipped over the wall of fir boughs and crashed onto the ground. Gathering his wits, he began to scramble to his feet and *wham* got hit by a horse. It was Smart Tar.

'I saw the horse and the fence and I saw Brendan go over in front of me,' Llewellyn recalled later, 'and then I could see Brendan on the floor below me and, shit, I landed right on top of him. I thought I'd killed him. I thought about it for a few seconds. But there's so much going on that I soon forgot about him.'

It was Powell's arm, but it wasn't too bad. He got to his knees and suddenly felt an odd surge of elation: it was all over. He wasn't hurt. He guessed his horse wasn't hurt. He wasn't going to win two Nationals in a row and that was fine. He darted off the course and remounted Stearsby for his journey back to the finish line.

Hywel Davies, who had been thrown from his horse first time round, was making his way back from the country on foot. He tried to cadge a lift on the back of Stearsby. Powell turned him down. 'Stearsby was still full of himself,' he said later. 'Wouldn't it have looked stupid, a horse running away with two men on his back. Besides, I wanted to get back to see who was going to win the National.'

'As they go towards the Melling Road on the first circuit, the leader is West Tip from Newnham. Then Little Polveir . . .'

At this point, a half dozen horses behind West Tip, Scudamore reckoned it could be he himself who won. Round him, flicking through his mind were Mithras – I could have ridden that horse. Lastofthebrownies – Tommy Carmody – riding short. You've got the hard bit done, he told himself, you're going really well. Just keep jumping, three more up to The Chair. Monanore – McCourt.

A loose horse on Scudamore's right. Stop pissing about, he tells it quietly. Don't start running down the fence. Scudamore prudently drops back. Still, he's in a tidy position. Still, he's laying up well.

The loose horse didn't go to a corner, didn't run out as Scudamore's experience told him was likely. He seemed set to jump The Chair. To avoid trouble, Scudamore committed himself, overtook on the inside and drove towards the narrow obstacle. Still a dozen horses off the pace. Over The Chair really well, over the Water Jump. A horse (Mr Crisp) down. Down in the water: unusual, Scudamore thought in passing, as he swept past the stands, swung out onto the second circuit.

'It's Little Polveir and West Tip disputing it . . .'

Scudamore, tucked in and still a half dozen horses off the pace, was already thinking six fences ahead: Becher's. On a little horse like Bonanza Boy, who surely was tiring, he didn't want to take Becher's on the inside, on the big-drop side. And yet . . . and yet . . .

It wasn't until months later, in the tranquillity of the close season, that the fiercely competitive jockey could discuss, indeed could even remember, the unworthy flicker of temptation that darted through his mind at that moment as he moved down towards the famous fence.

'Deep down, I was still angry with the people who said I shouldn't have taken Strands of Gold down the inside when he fell,' he recalled. 'I knew *damned* well I'd done the right thing and, for a moment, I thought "*Stuff* 'em! I'll take up the challenge. I'll go down the inside with Bonanza Boy." And then I thought, "Sod it, I don't have to prove anything to anybody. I'll do what's best for my horse." '

Still far away from Becher's second time, swinging away from the stands, Scu started to drift out. 'Not yet!' It was Carmody, half-joking, blocking the way. 'I'm not letting you out yet!'

Dunwoody, upsides Little Polveir, meanwhile asked Jimmy Frost how he was going. Frost grinned. 'I've had a great round,' he said. 'Hope the second goes as easy.' Dunwoody, eyes forward, replied loud enough, 'A bit steady for me. I'd like it a bit quicker.' Scudamore heard Dunwoody's last remark and was encouraged by it. The pace was fine: any quicker now, he thought, and we'll start making mistakes. McCourt, now upsides, began a conversation with Scudamore. 'Shut up!' Peter cut in. 'I can't talk now. Too busy. Too frightened to talk.' His confidence, nevertheless, was bubbling. I'm going to win this race, he told himself. Away we go.

Little Polveir began pulling away, unbidden, and despite an awkward, tucked-up jump of the open ditch, the nineteenth fence, he extended his lead to three, perhaps four lengths. All at once, Frost felt alone. He'd struck the front too soon. Where was Dunwoody? He cleared the twentieth fence, two short of Becher's. 'Suddenly, I got this little image of me guv'nor standing on top of the stand,' Frost said later, 'and he's thinking, "What's he doing that far in front?" and I thought, "if I don't win this race, I'm in for a real bollocking." ' '

A few seconds later, Scudamore saw Smart Tar fall at the 20th, with Carl Llewellyn aboard. This put the onrushing Bonanza Boy, Scu thought, into second place. I'm in second place and I haven't made my move. Actually, he was third, behind Little Polveir and Lastofthebrownies but going like a train. I'll jump Becher's and then the Canal Turn, he thought. Then I'll be headed for home.

'*Little Polveir still leading the Grand National field Lastofthebrownies in second, Bonanza Boy getting much closer now West Tip going really well . . . as they come down to Becher's for the second time . . .*'

Frost, eyes down, looking for the path beneath him, suddenly glanced up. A figure was in the track, gesturing, shouting: 'Go

middle! Go middle!' It was the official Bob Davies – although
Frost didn't know it – directing them between the two fallen,
out-of-sight horses. 'The third time I heard it, it rung with a
serious tone,' recalled Frost, 'and then I saw the orange discs.
One on the outer, one on the inner. I didn't have to change my
line. I was going up the middle anyway.'

His next feeling was bliss to remember. 'I could feel Little
Polveir strengthening under me,' he recalled. 'He shortened his
stride slightly, put his hocks underneath him and angled over
the fence. We'd taken off well and I prayed, "will we land well?"
and then he's gone away and he hasn't even nodded. Fantastic!
There was a dead horse on the inside and all I remember
thinking was, "there goes a dead 'un," and that was that.'

Dunwoody, with West Tip's nose now slightly in front, took
in the orange-disc warning. However, quite independent of
Davies, he was considering another move. He considered it all
in a split-second: leading alone into Becher's second time
round, West Tip had fallen in 1985, maybe distracted by the
screaming crowd that faced him over the fence. Too many
horses have fallen at Becher's while out in front, Dunwoody
thought – Scu last year – and we're going to need company
going over that fence. He checked his horse ever so slightly. It
came back, just a tad, and dropped in upsides Carmody on
Lastofthebrownies. 'If Carmody hadn't been there,' Dunwoody
said later, 'I'd have taken a pull and looked round and found
somebody else.'

At Becher's, now plainly in second place, Scudamore was
puzzled by the orange disc raised at the outside of the fence. He
didn't, of course, hear Julian Wilson's television commentary
that offended millions of viewers. '. . . and they're being forced
to the right to avoid a dead horse . . .' The BBC cut out the
dead-horse reference in its evening transmission.

His inner-rather-than-middle temptation had been banished
from his mind. Scudamore took Becher's inner-middle. He
didn't see the fallen horse as he cleared the fence. In the heavy
traffic, he couldn't swing left to prepare for the Canal Turn
down the course. He began to lose ground over Foinavon.
Nearing the Canal Turn he could nurse only one desperate
hope: they'll stop. They'll come back.

'. . . as they come to the Canal Turn for the second time. Little

Polveir. West Tip over in second. Monanore third. Lastofthe-brownies fourth. Bonanza Boy on the outside . . .'

It didn't happen. The other horses didn't come back. Scudamore held his spot, fifth, then sixth place as the field flowed over the twenty-fifth fence, Valentine's Brook. 'I was pushing him,' Scu said later. 'I was pushing him with my arms and my legs and my ass. No response.' The little horse had nothing left. For Bonanza Boy the Grand National was over. Scudamore reluctantly knew it.

'Little Polveir jumps the fifth from home. That's the one he went at last year. This time he's all right . . .'

The next fence, the fourth from home, was easy for Scudamore, who tried to rekindle his hopes. Powell and Stearsby had knocked a hole through the gorse of the fence on the first circuit and Peter steered Bonanza Boy through the gap. Two fences out, Simon Sherwood passed him on The Thinker and Scudamore, in a final effort to leave his mark – somehow – on the race, called out: 'Go on mate! You can win it from there!'

Up front, Frost, having passed his 'milestone' twenty-sixth fence, was in deep concentration, careful to jump one fence at a time. As he passed Anchor Bridge and swung towards the final two fences, he felt a second task had been accomplished. It was a simple, modest, oddly sufficient achievement. One day, he thought, Daniel will have a story to tell. 'When he goes to school,' thought the leader of the field, 'he'll be able to say his Daddy led the National over Anchor Bridge.' Daniel is nineteen months old.

Apart from the pressing threat from the following horses, Frost was soon to face two unsettling obstacles. Both were shared by millions of television viewers. The first was a spectator, the shirtless nutter who burst onto the track. He danced about and waved his arms at Little Polveir as the horse pounded round the final corner and headed for home. The stunt might have ended in catastrophe.

'We were running along the rails, Little Polveir and me, and this lunatic leapt out in front of us on the bend and I thought, "Shit, what's *this*?",' Frost recalled later. 'He was only about four strides away from him, maybe a second in time – that's all – and it took a split-second for the guy to register. If he'd been in a straight line ahead, it would have been easy to shift direction.

But when the horse is on the right leg and leaning round the turn, you can't do it so easily. You'll put him in all sorts of trouble.

'My instant reaction was to get hold of my horse and steer him round the obstacle and then I realised: this is a *fucking idiot*! I thought, "I'm going to take you with me, boy. I don't care. Come along with me." And I kept going.'

The spectator nipped clear.

I later asked the jockey, 'Couldn't the spectators have brought them all down, Little Polveir, Frost and the idiot himself?'

'I doubt it,' replied Frost, still angry a month later. 'I would have hit him close enough, side-on, just to wing him. Luckily, he didn't put the horse off. But my moment's hesitation probably cost me – like half a length.'

That wasn't all. The loose horse, Smart Tar, swinging upsides and outside of Frost, presented a different problem. Frost, being a Devonshire boy, a regular rider at Newton Abbot, felt a fear of loose horses in his bones. Hadn't he called for mounted stewards last August, when Scudamore nearly crashed head-on into two loose horses? At Aintree now, Frost fixed the newcomer in the corner of his eye.

'The loose horse was definitely coming round me and it looked as though he was going to cut across my front and go up the Mildmay course,' recalled Frost. 'So I looked down at him and I leaned Little Polveir towards him slightly to hold him off. My only worry was that he'd turn me up the other course. But then we got past the gap in the rail.' He laughed at the memory. 'At that point, I should have been having a nice, easy time of it.'

The dash to the post, indeed, appeared to Frost to be between only Little Polveir and the loose horse. Frost jumped the second last. Nobody but the loose, he thought, has got to me yet. *'As they come down to the final fence it's Little Polveir from Durham Edition,'* O'Sullevan rattled on and far back Scudamore and the other jockeys, like millions of other listeners, strained to hear the commentary. It was impossible: strange, verbal graffiti written on a wall of sound from the stands. *'There's little between the two . . .'*

Then the last fence, successfully jumped. There is nothing left but this famous, freaking run-in, thought Frost – Dick Francis going splat on Devon Loch – where everything happens. I've got the better ground, Frost comforted himself. I'm on the outer. I can do nothing. I can only go for home as hard as I can and pray that nothing touches me for speed.

He and Little Polveir went into a tunnel of noise. The riderless Smart Tar, like some bay Horse of the Apocalypse, joined in again and as the two animals moved close together Little Polveir responded. He quickened up. Frost felt the surge. I'm flying, he thought, and later he said: 'You don't finish like that at the end of four and a half miles and get beat.' He said later still: 'The loose was my enemy turning for home and my friend coming up the road.'

There was, at the kill, more than eighteen lengths between the two, Little Polveir and Durham Edition, as the challenger fell away and O'Sullevan called out the finishers: Little Polveir, West Tip, The Thinker, Lastofthebrownies, Durham Edition, Monanore, Gala's Image . . .

Bonanza Boy finished in eighth place. It was a result that pleased Scudamore. The little horse had had just too much weight. Donna, his lass, rushed up, bursting with tears of relief and Peter sought to reassure her that he'd always be safe in his hands. 'He's a good little horse. Look after him,' he said. 'He's got all the heart in the world.' Peter indeed was genuinely happy and so was his son, Thomas, who grinned under his checked-hat round the weighing-room. 'He's the littlest horse ever to get round the Grand National,' said Thomas and you didn't have the heart to point out that long ago, before his father was born, there once had been a tiny horse called Battleship.

It had been a brutal National, Seeandem and Brown Trix were killed following their falls at Becher's Brook. In Seeandem's death his jockey, Liam Cusack, sustained neither injury nor criticism. In Brown Trix's fall, Pitcher suffered a broken nose, teeth driven into his gums and the slings and arrows of his outraged fellow riders and the media.

Scudamore didn't spare the whip. 'I like David Pitcher. He's a nice man and as a person I've got a lot of time for him. But, in my view, he had no right to ride in the Grand National,' said the champion jockey after watching video tapes of the race. Scudamore's belief was later substantiated by the new regulation that all amateur riders must be approved before competing in the

National. 'He's a bad tactician and, as far as I could see, he had no race plans. He just rode like a maniac down over those first three or four fences and, to me, that's not fearless. It's brainless. He rides a horse like he's swinging from the heels against West Indian fast-bowling.'

Pitcher, for his part, had no self-recriminations about the fatal fall. 'There was nothing I could do about it and, with all due respects to Freddy Winter and all the other good jockeys in the past, there was nothing *any* human being could have done about it,' he said. 'It was Brown Trix's fault. I was exactly where I wanted to be. I was stoking him up as much as possible and I was going at exactly the speed I wanted to go. I saw my stride. I got hold of him to lift him and he backed off. He just didn't get high enough.'

'Once you're in the air, other than being unseated or un-balancing the horse, there is nothing *any* human being can do about it,' Pitcher said and added, 'and what could the best jockey in the world do about his horse falling back into the ditch? In National Hunt racing, you learn to live with dead horses.'

The dead horse total, already three for the day, was to rise to four after the final event, the Novices' Hurdle in which Frost was going for his double for the day on Morley Street. It was a thrilling race. Scudamore, on Enemy Action, straightaway put the Pipe stamp on the running: he drove the handsome 4-year-old gelding to the front and stayed there until three hurdles from home. He then faded badly, finishing fourth, as Frost came on late to win by one-and-a-half lengths.

It had been a disappointing race, an empty meeting for the champion. As he walked Enemy Action into the stableyard, he felt the horse shudder beneath him. He slid from the saddle and swiftly loosened the tack. But the animal was beyond help. He had suffered a heart attack and slumped dead at the jockey's feet.

I saw Scudamore minutes later as he walked, head down with his saddle under his arm, towards the weighing-room. He passed by and said nothing, just clapped me sadly on the shoulder. I continued unawares through the stabling area where Enemy Action lay under a tarpaulin, his stable lass cradling his head. The tableau was complete with the Mercedes lorry: *Stan Waite, Ltd. Licensed Slaughterers*, its winch already grinding.

'It was no doubt a very exciting spectacle,' wrote the *Liverpool Mercury* after the event, 'but we can be no more reconciled to it on that account than we are to cockfighting, bullbaiting or any other pastime which is attended with the affliction of wanton torture to any living being.'

So wrote the local paper after the inaugural event in 1839, at which a horse was killed (not at Becher's), and similar hues and cries have been raised ever since. Down the years, eleven horses had been killed through falls at Becher's and, following the deaths of Seeandem and Brown Trix, the public outcry reached the floor of the House of Commons. The most dramatic changes were made to the world's most dramatic steeplechase fence. While the drop was retained, the foreleg-jarring slope was filled in and the ditch all but filled in. One inch of water would now trickle through the famous brook.

Scudamore, together with most jockeys, was furious over the change. 'The National was unique, it was a test and now they've spoiled it,' he said. He then added darkly 'and you know, now Becher's may become even more dangerous. Without the drop, everybody's going to stampede down the inner and one day there is going to be a horrible pile-up.'

221

Independent Television News made the arrangements. Peter, Marilyn, the boys and Fee Moore would go by car to Hereford where a news crew would meet them and get footage of Peter in his races. Then, while Fee took the boys over in the car, Peter and Marilyn would take a laid-on helicopter to Towcester where he was riding in the evening. A cherished moment in racing history would later be put out on ITV news.

It was the morning of April 27, 1989. Scudamore was on 197 wins and he seemed certain to reach his double-century sometime during the day: after all, he had four rides at Hereford and three more at Towcester in the evening.

'Four more at Towcester,' corrected Peter, meeting the TV boys as he arrived at Hereford. He'd only just got word of a fourth evening ride over his car phone: Jimmy Duggan called to say he was 'struggling'. He couldn't do the weight in the 7:45 at Towcester. Would Scu ride the horse, a gelding called Gay Moore? Likes heavy going. He'll go close. Trained by Michael Robinson.

That lifted Scu's rides to eight for the day. He'd need three winners and, if the world took this for granted, he didn't: three of eight was pitching it a bit high since only two of his mounts were fancied. 'I was confident at the beginning of the week,' he told the Press. 'But now I'm getting cold feet. The races are much hotter than I reckoned.'

At Hereford, Scudamore drew a bust. No winners. What's more, in the opening race he made the wrong choice. He got off a winner, Brooks's Hello Steve, in order to ride Pipe's fancied novice hurdler Brilliant Future. In the event, Pipe's 4-year-old

The 200 up – Gay Moore wins at Towcester.

filly proved to be anything but brilliant: jumping indifferently, she ran out of puff second time round and came twelfth, with the blue and yellow colours of Hello Steve and Ben de Haan disappearing in the distance.

By late afternoon, buckled into his seat as the helicopter tilted forward and swept into a lowering sky towards Towcester, Scudamore had more reason to feel sick than the motion of the aircraft. A treble wasn't on. If he could pick up just one winner in Northamptonshire, perhaps on the hurdler Old Kilpatrick in the 5:45, there was tomorrow at Taunton, maybe Saturday at Worcester for the other two.

Scudamore brooded. Getting to the 200 mark was proving as sticky as the 150. He couldn't talk to Marilyn for the thrashing of the helicopter rotors overhead; instead, locked in his own thoughts, he gazed down over the northern ridges of the Cotswolds. He consulted *Timeform* for its views on his 'spare' ride, Gay Moore. 'Workmanlike gelding,' it said, '. . . 16-1, made a lot of the running when winning novice event at Bangor in December in chasing debut by 15 lengths . . . acts on soft going.' The report gave him heart. Gay Moore was a stayer, thought Scudamore, he'd make the three mile trip today.

The helicopter landed in good time for the opening Towcester race, the Tiffield Claiming Hurdle, and Scudamore hurried from the infield, saddle under his arm, bag over his shoulder and made his way to the weighing-room. His opening mount, Old Kilpatrick, had liked the heavy at Chepstow a month earlier and he was soon to like the heavy at Towcester. The dark, glistening gelding slopped to a 12-length victory as, incongruously, a calypso band rattled away to keep warm in the stands. Scu now had 198 winners. Two away from the target. Three rides to go. Hope flickered. Press photographers, in an agony of frustration, held up their light-meters in the gathering gloom.

His next race was the 6:15, the Wood Burcote Novices' Chase, and astride Canford Palm Scudamore rode his 199th winner, his 26th for Brooks for the season. The horse made the 2m 5f novices' chase look easy, running out the twenty lengths winner. One to go. Two chances to do it. First came the 7:45, a 3-mile race that bore the forgettable name of the City Trucks Handicap Chase.

Inauspicious, too, were both Scudamore's colours – brown,

with a pale yellow disc – as darkness silted down over the racecourse and the *Timeform* remark: 'workmanlike gelding'. Peter noticed, without gratification, that the 8-year-old's overnight backing, ninth in a field of eleven, had shortened with the news that he would be in the saddle. Gay Moore was to close at 10-1, fourth favourite. 'Thank God,' he thought. 'We're not over-fancied. Nothing *has* to be done in this race.'

In the weighing-room Duggan, who'd earlier in the season taken Gay Moore to his first victory over fences, gave Peter a last run-down on the horse. His verbal shorthand was brief and immaculate. 'He jumps like a buck,' said Duggan, 'but he's fairly one-paced. He won't be afraid of going in front. Keep him handy.'

In the paddock Scudamore first noticed, unavoidably, the other riders. 'There were a couple of girls riding,' he said, 'and you're always a bit wary of what they're going to do. You've got to keep an eye on them.' He then turned his mind to the gelding as it circled the ring: he's well-made, thought Peter. He's got a good head carriage. He carries it low. He'll look after himself which, first time on a horse, was always a comfort to know.

Mounted, Scudamore continued his assessment of the horse as he cantered down towards the three-mile start at the far side of the track. Gay Moore was nicely balanced. He spooked once at a hedge, but Peter was not disconcerted: at least, he thought, the fellow's going to be careful. What the jockey continued to like most about Gay Moore was the low head carriage. The horse took a nice amount of rein. Scudamore could ride him with his hands on the withers. He could get his legs behind, which was all the better for his own balance and for pushing the horse, driving him on. It's good, concluded Peter, I'll be able to attack.

'Thinking about the horse in such detail helped me to blot the 200 out of my mind,' Scudamore said later. 'I was thinking, at the back of my mind, "don't let it get to you or you'll make a mistake".'

At the start, a horse ran backwards, got loose and Scudamore's raw nerves briefly cracked. *Don't catch it* he roared to himself. *Make it go away.* 'Not being kicked by that horse,' he said later, 'just shows you how lucky I was all season.' Then, suddenly, they were off.

In the mud, the first fence had been dolled off. Scudamore guided Gay Moore round it and went downhill and into a plain fence, upsides in front but came out of it slowly with most of the ten-horse field now ahead of him. 'I don't know why,' he later recalled, 'but I was very confident. It was the feel of the horse.'

Dropping through Towcester's signature deep bottom land on the back straight, the going was sucking and Scudamore dropped away to second last but not hopelessly far off the pace. He was comfortable. He was having a good run on the inside. He stayed there, sensing the field was travelling too fast, and he remained happy, despite blundering in the greasy going over the second last first time round.

'That was my low point,' he recalled, 'things improved from then on.' Indeed they did and, slogging relentlessly on, Scudamore took up the challenge coming up the hill off the back straight. Good boy, he said, turning for home. The horse responded and, churning through the mud, Scu knew he'd win two fences from home. He took no chances, drove him on. 'Peter Scudamore . . .' screamed the commentator, and not for the first time this season, he was drowned out shouting. Peter kicked past the post, twelve lengths in front. The calypso band struck up.

'I've still got to ride until June 3. The season wouldn't be complete unless Martin didn't do it as well,' Peter said after thanking Jimmy Duggan for the ride and expressing his thrill at breaking a record, now a commonplace reply for the season. He then broke off and a half hour later rode his fourth winner of the day. It was Market Forces, trained by Nick Gaselee, which drew well clear on the run-in to win the Buckingham Novices' Hurdle and raise Scudamore's season total to 201 wins.

Peter stood in his damp shirt in the darkness and cold outside the weighing-room and for a half hour he signed programmes, autograph books and odd bits of clothing. Of all the sportsmen I had watched down the years only the golfer Arnold Palmer, perhaps the cricketer Derek Randall, had shown such patience and generosity towards their fans.

Scudamore, signing with left hand, the one wrapped in the velcro-and-leather, speculated that if he stayed in one piece he might reach 215 winners for the season. Marilyn, asked if she wished her husband might quit, said she loved it and hoped it would never end. She couldn't imagine Peter thinking of anything but riding winners.

There would be more winners that season – twenty of them – but for Scudamore the obsessional pursuit of numbers was over. 'If you told me at the start of the season that I'd ride 200 winners I'd have thought, "fantastic, I'll go out and get drunk the night when it happens". But when it actually did happen, I found that life went on just the same.'

It did, following the historic 201: another glass of champagne with Marilyn in bed early, back on his feet at 5:45 the next morning, into the car, onto the motorway where he gave a dawn, car-phone interview to BBC's Radio Four and then to Pipe's where he schooled horses through the morning.

'Martin didn't ask me to come down,' Peter said later. 'Getting up that early and going to work was a conscious effort to keep my feet on the ground. I'm not trying to be modest but at times I strike myself as being lazy.' Such a harsh view of oneself may seem odd in Scudamore's case, perhaps clinically odd, but it is true.

The target now was to help see Pipe to his double century. The Somerset wizard was on 183. His 200th came on May 19 at Stratford when he gave Scu a leg-up onto Anti Matter, the milestone-buster, who had taken Peter past Jonjo O'Neill's 149. Scudamore was to remember that race as vividly as any all season.

'It was quite funny, Martin's 200,' he later recounted. 'We wanted to get it over with. We were getting a bit tense and down at the start my colt got his head over the back side of a filly and I thought, "Here we go, he's going to get randy and we're going to get kicked and there goes the 200." Then a horse got loose, not once but twice. Then Hywel's horse pulled a plate off in front of me. So that's another holdup. I could picture Martin, with his binoculars in the stands, getting crosser and crosser and suddenly I started laughing.'

Off fourteen minutes late, the race went smoothly otherwise with Anti Matter a comfortable winner: Pipe, too, had reached his double century and then, oddly and unthinkably, both the Somerset sorcerer and Scudamore wound down for the season.

Pipe took a holiday in Portugal, telephoning back for news three times a day while Peter turned his mind to other matters.

First there were the match flat races – Scu v the Shoe – against the legendary Willie Shoemaker the next week at Cheltenham. Peter won the first two but somehow, perhaps sportingly, lost the third by a neck. Then there was a holiday in Jersey and the horse sales in Dublin, which he attended as chief executive of Peter Scudamore Bloodstock Ltd.

In this capacity, Scudamore had grown to take a new view of a horse. 'Being a jockey, I used not to look at the horse so much as the Form Book,' he said candidly. 'I could ignore certain defects in a horse because, at the end of the day, I could get away with them. But buying commercially is a different ball game. I'm buying for somebody else and the confirmation has got to be nigh-on perfection. And if it hasn't got pedigree, you won't sell it.'

Pedigree sold – pedigree bought. At the Doncaster Spring Sales, Peter Scudamore Bloodstock Ltd, got off to a purple start: Fulke Walwyn, acting for the Queen Mother, paid 23,000 gns.

Hazy Sunset, the last winner of an amazing year, would become the first winner, in the first race, of the 1989–90 campaign.

for the first horse the firm ever owned, a 4-year-old gelding by Monksfield. Pipe–Scudamore Racing PLC, a syndicate, soon had seven horses, 2,000 members and a capitalisation of £½ million.

The race-riding, meanwhile, had come to an end on June 3 at Stratford. There Scudamore laid a last milestone, embedded a last jewel, that would shine down through the ages. He rode his 221st, and last, winner of the indelible season.

The race was the Gambling Prince Steeplechase. The horse, trained by Brooks, was Hazy Sunset, a useful 12-year-old which, according to *Timeform*, 'occasionally has appeared temperamental'. In the race card, I found rosier portents: Hazy Sunset, like Beau Ranger's mare, was sired by the awesome Irishman, Menelek and, last time out, the gelding had won at Fakenham. Also, Scudamore was to carry number 1.

From the judge's aerie, a wooden hut on stilts, we watched the horses file out of the parade ring. As Peter dropped back to the end of the string, settling the 'temperamental' Hazy Sunset, Michael Hancock opened his slim judge's book. Notations – circles, diamonds, words – were entered for the race. Opposite horse number '1' the word 'red' appeared. 'I'm calling Scudamore's horse "red",' said Hancock, 'because that's his owner's dominant colour.'

The horses broke, exactly on time. Hazy Sunset took the lead. He was headed once, challenged on the back straight second time round, but looked a sure winner coming to the last. Scudamore had fallen here in October while going for his fastest 50. He cleared it this time and, deep in the saddle, swept past the post. 'Red,' Hancock muttered and, turning to the Tannoy man, said loudly, 'First. Number One.'

The winning was over or, as Paul Hayward put it in *The Racing Post*, 'the score-board stopped clicking.' At the end of the day, the weighing-room was strangely silent, the jockeys overtaken at last by exhaustion. Speaking to nobody and everybody, the senior rider Smith Eccles said 'one piece' and Scudamore, unzipping the velcro and leather support from his wrist, responded for all. 'One piece,' he said and they slapped hands, putting a full-stop to the season.

Appendix A

Reproduced from the *Racing Post* record 1988/89 Jumps Season

1988/9	RNRS	WNRS	WNS-RNS		2ND	3RD	4TH	UNPL	£PROFIT/LOSS
Hurdle	183	66	**127-389** (33%)		73	32	33	124	−£67.06
Chase	114	50	**94-274** (34%)		39	23	28	90	+£8.51
NHF	0	0	**0-0**		0	0	0	0	£0.00
All	285	111	**221-663** (33%)		112	55	61	214	−£58.50

FALLS: Hdles 4-389 (1%) **Chases** 19-274 (7%)
Close Finishes won 16 lost 15

BY COURSE				HURDLES			CHASES			NHF
Newton Abbot	**26-57**	(46%)	+£0.23	**12-37**	(32%)	−£7.09	**14-20**	(70%)	+£7.32	–
Haydock	**17-36**	(47%)	+£15.87	**7-21**	(33%)	−£4.66	**10-15**	(67%)	+£20.53	–
Devon	**17-38**	(45%)	−£6.59	**14-29**	(48%)	−£3.41	**3-9**	(33%)	−£3.18	–
Worcester	**15-34**	(44%)	+£3.05	**9-20**	(45%)	+£1.25	**6-14**	(43%)	+£1.80	–
Chepstow	**13-29**	(45%)	+£3.65	**9-17**	(53%)	+£3.82	**4-12**	(33%)	−£0.17	–
Newbury	**12-45**	(27%)	−£6.27	**1-23**	(4%)	−£21.20	**11-22**	(50%)	+£14.93	–
Cheltenham	**11-52**	(21%)	−£13.92	**5-27**	(19%)	−£14.67	**6-25**	(24%)	+£0.75	–
Warwick	**10-24**	(42%)	+£5.44	**7-12**	(58%)	+£7.07	**3-12**	(25%)	−£1.63	–
Taunton	**9-28**	(32%)	−£6.39	**6-18**	(33%)	−£5.43	**3-10**	(30%)	−£0.96	–
Wolverhampton	**8-16**	(50%)	+£9.60	**4-6**	(67%)	+£5.27	**4-10**	(40%)	+£4.33	–
Ascot	**8-32**	(25%)	−£13.41	**5-17**	(29%)	−£4.99	**3-15**	(20%)	−£8.43	–
Fontwell	**8-21**	(38%)	−£0.77	**7-17**	(41%)	+£0.23	**1-4**	(25%)	−£1.00	–
Lingfield	**7-23**	(30%)	−£4.73	**3-14**	(21%)	−£3.47	**4-9**	(44%)	−£1.27	–
Hereford	**7-23**	(30%)	−£5.19	**4-15**	(27%)	−£3.69	**3-8**	(38%)	−£1.50	–
Ludlow	**6-21**	(29%)	+£1.79	**4-13**	(31%)	+£5.07	**2-8**	(25%)	−£3.28	–
Bangor	**6-11**	(55%)	+£0.54	**4-6**	(67%)	+£0.92	**2-5**	(40%)	−£0.38	–
Huntingdon	**5-13**	(38%)	+£3.54	**3-7**	(43%)	+£5.13	**2-6**	(33%)	−£1.58	–
Leicester	**5-14**	(36%)	−£1.52	**4-9**	(44%)	+£1.64	**1-5**	(20%)	−£3.17	–
Kempton	**5-19**	(26%)	+£2.50	**3-11**	(27%)	+£1.50	**2-8**	(25%)	+£1.00	–
Towcester	**4-13**	(31%)	+£10.13	**2-6**	(33%)	+£1.13	**2-7**	(29%)	+£9.00	–
Stratford	**4-16**	(25%)	−£6.85	**3-9**	(33%)	−£3.35	**1-7**	(14%)	−£3.50	–
Nottingham	**3-13**	(23%)	−£5.58	**2-8**	(25%)	−£3.45	**1-5**	(20%)	−£2.13	–
Wincanton	**3-9**	(33%)	+£3.67	**1-3**	(33%)	−£1.33	**2-6**	(33%)	+£5.00	–
Southwell	**3-6**	(50%)	−£0.09	**1-2**	(50%)	+£0.88	**2-4**	(50%)	−£0.97	–
Sandown	**2-15**	(13%)	−£9.43	**2-6**	(33%)	−£0.43	**0-9**		−£9.00	–
Plumpton	**2-11**	(18%)	−£6.40	**1-7**	(14%)	−£5.27	**1-4**	(25%)	−£1.13	–
Market Rasen	**2-4**	(50%)	+£1.75	**2-3**	(67%)	+£2.75	**0-1**		−£1.00	–
Folkestone	**1-5**	(20%)	−£2.50	**1-4**	(25%)	−£1.50	**0-1**		−£1.00	–
Fakenham	**1-4**	(25%)	−£1.90	**0-1**		−£1.00	**1-3**	(33%)	−£0.90	–
Uttoxeter	**1-14**	(7%)	−£11.75	**1-9**	(11%)	−£6.75	**0-5**		−£5.00	–

Also: Liverpool (12), Windsor (4), Hexham (1)

BY RACE TYPE				HURDLES			CHASES			NHF
Handicap	62-278	(22%)	−£70.23	24-126	(19%)	−£51.26	38-152	(25%)	−£18.98	–
Sell/Clm	32-63	(51%)	+£12.48	32-62	(52%)	+£13.48	0-1		−£1.00	–
Conditional	–		£0.00	–		£0.00	–		£0.00	–
Ladies/Amateurs	–		£0.00	–		£0.00	–		£0.00	–
Feature/Champ	3-25	(12%)	−£15.93	1-15	(7%)	−£11.00	2-10	(20%)	−£4.93	–
Novice	149-382	(39%)	−£19.68	98-264	(37%)	−£23.12	51-118	(43%)	+£3.44	–
Hunter	–		£0.00	–		£0.00	–		£0.00	–

BY SP				HURDLES			CHASES			NHF
Odds On	90-133	(68%)	+£7.75	55-87	(63%)	−£1.92	35-46	(76%)	+£9.66	–
Evens−2/1	79-173	(46%)	+£24.75	43-97	(44%)	+£8.78	36-76	(47%)	+£15.98	–
9/4−6/1	48-233	(21%)	−£19.04	28-126	(22%)	−£7.92	20-107	(19%)	−£11.13	–
13/2−16/1	4-104	(4%)	−£52.00	1-63	(2%)	−£50.00	3-41	(7%)	−£2.00	–
above 16/1	0-20		−£20.00	0-16		−£16.00	0-4		−£4.00	–
Favourites	168-334	(50%)	+£19.11	101-212	(48%)	−£2.28	67-122	(55%)	+£21.39	–

Average SP: Runners 4.4/1 **Winners** 1.7/1

BY PRIZE MONEY				HURDLES			CHASES			NHF
below £1,000	34-81	(42%)	−£6.41	34-81	(42%)	−£6.41	–		£0.00	–
£1,000 to £2,999	142-396	(36%)	+£3.13	79-228	(35%)	−£10.94	63-168	(38%)	+£14.07	–
£3,000 to £5,999	26-99	(26%)	−£35.79	7-37	(19%)	−£23.93	19-62	(31%)	−£11.86	–
£6,000 to £9,999	7-36	(19%)	−£17.55	2-18	(11%)	−£13.22	5-18	(28%)	−£4.33	–
above £10,000	12-51	(24%)	−£1.93	5-25	(20%)	−£12.56	7-26	(27%)	+£10.63	–

BY WEIGHT CARRIED				HURDLES			CHASES			NHF
below 10-00	–		£0.00	–		£0.00	–		£0.00	–
10-00 to 10-07	24-87	(28%)	+£1.22	13-42	(31%)	−£7.26	11-45	(24%)	+£8.48	–
10-08 to 11-00	60-199	(30%)	−£43.46	40-145	(28%)	−£32.06	20-54	(37%)	−£11.40	–
11-01 to 11-07	84-204	(41%)	+£29.68	48-111	(43%)	+£1.17	36-93	(39%)	+£28.51	–
11-08 to 12-00	49-161	(30%)	−£42.09	26-88	(30%)	−£25.91	23-73	(32%)	−£16.18	–
above 12-00	4-12	(33%)	−£3.90	0-3		−£3.00	4-9	(44%)	−£0.90	–

Most Overweight: 4lb **Average Overweight:** 2lb
Lowest Weight Ridden: 10-00

BY TRAINER				HURDLES			CHASES			NHF
M. C. Pipe	158-359	(44%)	+£40.14	103-242	(43%)	+£7.42	55-117	(47%)	+£32.73	–
C. P. E. Brooks	28-95	(29%)	−£14.04	11-44	(25%)	−£12.17	17-51	(33%)	−£1.87	–
R. Akehurst	7-10	(70%)	+£6.65	3-4	(75%)	+£4.95	4-6	(67%)	+£1.70	–
B. Preece	6-18	(33%)	+£3.33	1-4	(25%)	£0.00	5-14	(36%)	+£3.33	–
T. Thomson Jones	2-5	(40%)	+£6.50	0-3		−£3.00	2-2	(100%)	+£9.50	–
A. J. Wilson	2-6	(33%)	+£2.25	2-6	(33%)	+£2.25	–		£0.00	–
Capt. T. A. Forster	2-5	(40%)	+£4.50	1-2	(50%)	+£0.50	1-3	(33%)	+£4.00	–
Mrs M. Rimell	2-14	(14%)	−£5.13	0-4		−£4.00	2-10	(20%)	−£1.13	–
J. L. Spearing	2-8	(25%)	−£1.20	–		£0.00	2-8	(25%)	−£1.20	–
M. H. B. Robinson	1-1	(100%)	+£10.00	–		£0.00	1-1	(100%)	+£10.00	–
J. G. FitzGerald	1-3	(33%)	−£0.13	0-1		−£1.00	1-2	(50%)	+£0.88	–
N. Tinkler	1-2	(50%)	+£1.00	1-2	(50%)	+£1.00	–		£0.00	–
B. L. Key	1-1	(100%)	+£2.00	1-1	(100%)	+£2.00	–		£0.00	–
Andrew Turnell	1-12	(8%)	−£8.50	1-6	(17%)	−£2.50	0-6		−£6.00	–
D. R. C. Elsworth	1-2	(50%)	−£0.67	–		£0.00	1-2	(50%)	−£0.67	–
D. Nicholson	1-5	(20%)	−£3.17	0-1		−£1.00	1-4	(25%)	−£2.17	–
J. A. C. Edwards	1-3	(33%)	−£2.00	1-1	(100%)	£0.00	0-2		−£2.00	–
N. A. Twiston-Davies	1-4	(25%)	+£2.00	0-2		−£2.00	1-2	(50%)	+£4.00	–
N. A. Gaselee	1-2	(50%)	+£2.50	1-2	(50%)	+£2.50	–		£0.00	–
I. A. Balding	1-2	(50%)	−£0.60	–		£0.00	1-2	(50%)	−£0.60	–
R. J. O'Sullivan	1-8	(13%)	−£6.00	1-7	(14%)	−£5.00	0-1		−£1.00	–

Also: M. Tate (6), P. O'Connor (5), R. Hollinshead (5), P. D. Cundell (5), Miss B. Sanders (4), M. Scudamore (4), W. G. R. Wightman (3), D. R. Tucker (2), G. B. Balding (2), N. D. Painting (2), J. R. Jenkins (2), S. Woodman (2), Mrs N. S. Sharpe (2), D. A. Wilson (2), G. A. Hubbard (2), O. Sherwood (2), D. J. Wintle (2), P. A. Kelleway (2), A. P. Ingham (2), N. A. Callaghan (2), T. J. Etherington (2), Mrs G. E. Jones (2), R. Dickin (2), A. Barrow (1), M. E. D. Francis (1),

Appendix A

P. Mitchell (1), W. E. Fisher (1), R. G. Brazington (1), R. G. Frost (1), D. H. Barons (1), R. J. Hodges (1), H. O'Neill (1), B. C. Morgan (1), M. H. Easterby (1), P. Howling (1), T. Casey (1), N. B. Thomson (1), T. Fairhurst (1), G. Richards (1), K. C. Bailey (1), G. M. Moore (1), R. Lee (1), Miss L. Bower (1), Denys Smith (1), J. S. King (1), C. Spares (1), W. T. Kemp (1), Kevin Connolly (1), O. O'Neill (1), H. J. Collingridge (1), J. S. Bolger (1), R. B. Francis (1), P. S. Felgate (1), P. G. Bailey (1), J. I. A. Charlton (1), Mrs D. Haine (1), G. Roe (1)

Appendix B

Peter Scudamore: 221 Winners in 307 Days

	DATE	COURSE	RACE & VALUE	TRAINER	WINNER	SP
1	30 Jul	NewAb	Dimplex Tango Handicap Chase £2,665	M. C. Pipe	Rahib	10/11F
2	1 Aug	NewAb	South Zeal Novices' Hurdle (Div 2) £933	M. C. Pipe	Benisa Ryder	4/1
3	3 Aug	Devon	Alwyn Trundle Memorial Challenge Cup Novices' Chase £2,108	M. C. Pipe	Big Paddy Tom	4/5F
4	3 Aug	Devon	Summer Selling Hurdle £737	M. C. Pipe	Celcius	7/4F
5	4 Aug	Devon	Telegraph Hill Novices' Hurdle £710	M. C. Pipe	Star of Kuwait	8/11F
6	6 Aug	Sthwl	J & B Rare Novices' Chase £1,122	M. C. Pipe	My Cup of Tea	4/6F
7	10 Aug	Fontw	Ladbrokes Sussex Young Cricketers Handicap Hurdle £2,469	R. J. O'Sullivan	Ruling Dynasty	EvensF
8	11 Aug	NewAb	Hotline Electric Fencing Selling Handicap Hurdle £745	M. C. Pipe	Maintown	7/2
9	11 Aug	NewAb	Ham & Huddy Novices' Chase £2,253	M. C. Pipe	Big Paddy Tom	2/7F
10	11 Aug	NewAb	Phoenix Print Novices' Hurdle £950	M. C. Pipe	Hi-Hannah	8/13F
11	11 Aug	NewAb	Brian Birchill Textiles Handicap Chase £2,616	M. C. Pipe	African Star	13/8F
12	12 Aug	Devon	Dawlish Claiming Juvenile Novices' Hurdle £672	M. C. Pipe	Brilliant Future	1/2F
13	12 Aug	Devon	Haldon Moor Novices' Selling Hurdle £745	M. C. Pipe	Celcius	4/7F
14	12 Aug	Devon	Weldon Memorial Cup Novices' Hurdle £815	M. C. Pipe	Pertemps Network	1/3F
15	15 Aug	Worcs	Pomp And Circumstance Novices' Chase £1,602	M. C. Pipe	My Cup of Tea	4/9F
16	24 Aug	Devon	Shell Rimula X Oils Novices' Hurdle £960	M. C. Pipe	Pertemps Network	4/6F
17	24 Aug	Devon	Shell Tellus Hydraulic Oils Novices' Hurdle £863	M. C. Pipe	Liadett (USA)	8/11F
18	24 Aug	Devon	Shell Tractor Super Engine Oil Novices' Chase £1,896	C. P. E. Brooks	Chalk Pit	13/8JF
19	26 Aug	Bangr	Marcher Sound Novices' Hurdle £685	M. C. Pipe	Hi-Hannah	10/11F
20	29 Aug	NewAb	English Riviera Visitor Juvenile Novices' Hurdle £1,083	M. C. Pipe	Afford	11/10F
21	29 Aug	NewAb	Goodhead Print Group Handicap Chase £2,820	M. C. Pipe	African Star	1/2F
22	29 Aug	NewAb	South Devon Business Review Novices' Chase £2,640	M. C. Pipe	My Cup of Tea	8/11F
23	31 Aug	NewAb	Tamar Novices' Hurdle £952	M. C. Pipe	Pertemps Network	8/11F
24	2 Sep	Hford	Michaelchurch Novices' Chase £1,896	C. P. E. Brooks	Chalk Pit	2/1
25	3 Sep	Strfd	Three Spires Claiming Juvenile Novices' Hurdle £685	M. C. Pipe	Brilliant Future	6/4F
26	7 Sep	Fontw	Fons Selling Hurdle £701	M. C. Pipe	That There	11/8F
27	7 Sep	Fontw	Fishbourne Novices' Hurdle £685	M. C. Pipe	Liadett (USA)	4/7F
28	8 Sep	NewAb	Britvic Corona Selling Hurdle £777	M. C. Pipe	Chiropodist	13/8F
29	8 Sep	NewAb	William Grant Challenge Handicap Chase £2,729	M. C. Pipe	African Star	1/5F
30	8 Sep	NewAb	Skol Novices' Chase £2,472	M. C. Pipe	My Cup of Tea	5/2
31	9 Sep	NewAb	Peplows Handicap Hurdle £2,595	M. C. Pipe	Dick's Folly	8/15F
32	17 Sep	Warwk	Harvey Fork Lift Hurdle £2,532	M. C. Pipe	High Knowl	4/9F
33	21 Sep	Devon	Business South West Novices' Chase £2,493	I. A. Balding	Insular	2/5F
34	26 Sep	Fontw	Sidlesham Selling Hurdle £868	M. C. Pipe	Celcius	3/1
35	26 Sep	Fontw	Eartham Novices' Hurdle £695	M. C. Pipe	Hi-Hannah	2/1F
36	28 Sep	Ludlw	Birdgnorth Novices' Selling Hurdle £728	M. C. Pipe	Chiropodist	EvensF

Appendix B

	DATE	COURSE	RACE & VALUE	TRAINER	WINNER	SP
37	5 Oct	Chelt	Colgate Oral Care Novices' Chase £3,688	M. C. Pipe	My Cup of Tea	11/4
38	5 Oct	Chelt	House of Palmolive 3-Y-O Novices' Hurdle £1,932	M. C. Pipe	Liadett (USA)	9/4
39	6 Oct	Chelt	Postlip Novices' Chase £2,960	C. P. E. Brooks	Chalk Pit	5/4F
40	7 Oct	Worcs	Flyaway Selling Hurdle £1,127	M. C. Pipe	Celcius	2/1F
41	8 Oct	Worcs	Inkberrow Hurdle £1,568	M. C. Pipe	Parlezvousfrancais	1/7F
42	11 Oct	NewAb	Miller Lite 4-Y-O Novices' Hurdle £1,256	M. C. Pipe	Chiropodist	11/4
43	11 Oct	NewAb	Courage South West Handicap Chase £4,164	M. C. Pipe	Tarqogan's Best	85/40F
44	12 Oct	Plump	Win With The Tote Maiden Hurdle £1,009	M. C. Pipe	Sayfar's Lad	8/11F
45	13 Oct	Wcntn	Shaftesbury Claiming Hurdle £1,103	M. C. Pipe	Afford	4/6F
46	19 Oct	Chelt	Rodborough 3-Y-O Novices' Hurdle £1,607	M. C. Pipe	Liadett (USA)	11/10
47	19 Oct	Chelt	Lydney Novices' Chase £3,707	M. C. Pipe	My Cup of Tea	7/4F
48	22 Oct	Strfd	Edgehill Novices' Hurdle £901	C. P. E. Brooks	Espy	8/15F
49	24 Oct	Fkngm	Garfunkel Novices' Chase £1,527	C. P. E. Brooks	Wolfhanger	11/10F
50	27 Oct	Wcntn	Witchampton Novices' Chase (Div 2) £1,391	M. C. Pipe	Pharoah's Laen	7/2F
51	28 Oct	Devon	Bass West Of England Juvenile Selling Hurdle £753	M. C. Pipe	That There	EvensF
52	29 Oct	Ascot	Binfield Juvenile Novices' Hurdle £2,352	M. C. Pipe	Afford	2/1JF
53	29 Oct	Ascot	Bagshot Handicap Chase £7,531	C. P. E. Brooks	Bajan Sunshine	15/8JF
54	3 Nov	Kmptn	Standard Life Novices' Chase £2,610	C. P. E. Brooks	Canford Palm	2/1
55	4 Nov	Bangr	Tilston 3-Y-O Novices' Hurdle £782	M. C. Pipe	Afford	2/7F
56	5 Nov	Chpsw	Corinth Novices' Hurdle (Div 2) £1,476	C. P. E. Brooks	Bruton Street	5/1
57	8 Nov	Devon	Whitbread Best Bitter Novices' Hurdle (Div 1) £840	M. C. Pipe	Sayfar's Lad	10/11F
58	8 Nov	Devon	Whitbread Best Bitter Novices' Hurdle (Div 2) £853	T. A. Forster	Fiddlers Three	6/4F
59	8 Nov	Devon	Whitbread Best Bitter Juvenile Selling Hurdle £624	M. C. Pipe	That There	4/7F
60	9 Nov	Nbury	Curridge Handicap Chase £3,837	N. A. Twiston-Davies	Donald Davies	5/1
61	9 Nov	Nbury	Halloween Novices' Chase £4,304	C. P. E. Brooks	Wolfhangar	11/8F
62	9 Nov	Nbury	Winterbourne Handicap Chase £2,820	D. Nicholson	Springholm	5/6F
63	11 Nov	MarRn	Levy Board Novices' Hurdle £1,786	M. C. Pipe	Lavrosky (USA)	6/4JF
64	11 Nov	MarRn	George Novices' Hurdle £1,635	M. C. Pipe	Blue Rainbow	9/4
65	12 Nov	Chelt	Mackeson Gold Cup Handicap Chase £22,141	T. A. Forster	Pegwell Bay	6/1
66	12 Nov	Chelt	Flowers Original Handicap Chase £5,811	J. L. Spearing	Run And Skip	4/1
67	12 Nov	Chelt	Flowers Fine Ales 3-Y-O Novices' Hurdle £3,335	M. C. Pipe	Liadett (USA)	8/11F
68	14 Nov	Wolv	Pendeford Novices' Chase (Div 1) £1,582	M. C. Pipe	Swing To Steel	6/4
69	16 Nov	Kmptn	Motorway Novices' Hurdle £2,091	C. P. E. Brooks	Penalty Double	4/1
70	16 Nov	Kmptn	Fairview New Homes Handicap Hurdle £2,750	C. P. E. Brooks	Admirals All	3/1
71	17 Nov	Taunt	Necktie Novices' Hurdle (Div 1) £784	M. C. Pipe	Blue Rainbow	4/9F
72	17 Nov	Taunt	JCR News Challenge Trophy Novices' Chase £1,841	M. C. Pipe	Golden Glitter	4/1CF
73	18 Nov	Ascot	Bingley Novices' Hurdle £2,639	R. Akehurst	Man On The Line	7/2
74	18 Nov	Ascot	Racecall Ascot Hurdle £13,552	M. C. Pipe	Sabin du Loir (FR)	1/2F
75	21 Nov	Leicr	Thorpe Satchville Hurdle £2,385	C. P. E. Brooks	Celtic Shot	1/6F
76	23 Nov	Hdock	Weaverham Novices' Hurdle £990	M. C. Pipe	Jabrut	9/4JF
77	23 Nov	Hdock	County Handicap Chase £3,493	M. C. Pipe	Tarqogan's Best	EvensF
78	23 Nov	Hdock	Edward Hanmer Memorial Limited Handicap Chase £9,056	M. C. Pipe	Beau Ranger	13/8F
79	24 Nov	Hdock	Hepworth Supersleve Junior Hurdle £3,558	M. C. Pipe	Enemy Action	8/11F
80	24 Nov	Hdock	St Helens Handicap Chase £3,590	J. L. Spearing	Run And Skip	4/5F
81	25 Nov	Nbury	Oxfordshire Novices' Chase £3,753	M. C. Pipe	Pharoah's Laen	8/15F
82	25 Nov	Nbury	Arlington Premier Series Chase (Qualifier) £3,028	D. R. C. Elsworth	Barnbrook Again	1/3F
83	26 Nov	Nbury	Hennessy Cognac Gold Cup Handicap Chase £29,544	M. C. Pipe	Strands of Gold	10/1
84	29 Nov	NewAb	Claude Whitley Memorial Challenge Cup (Handicap Chase) £3,753	M. C. Pipe	Bonanza Boy	8/11F
85	30 Nov	Hford	Dinmore Novices' Hurdle (Div 1) £680	M. C. Pipe	Go West	13/8F
86	30 Nov	Hford	Bishops Frome Novices' Handicap Hurdle £1,265	M. C. Pipe	Sunwood	10/3F
87	30 Nov	Hford	Dinmore Novices' Hurdle (Div 2) £680	M. C. Pipe	Sondrio	5/4F
88	2 Dec	Sand	Crowngap Construction Winter Novices' Hurdle (Listed Race) £3,785	R. Akehurst	Man On The Line	4/7F
89	7 Dec	Huntg	Long Sutton Handicap Chase £1,632	M. C. Pipe	Fu's Lady	4/6F
90	7 Dec	Huntg	EBF Novices' Hurdle (Qualifier) £1,324	C. P. E. Brooks	Espy	13/8F
91	8 Dec	Taunt	Bicknoller Novices' Hurdle (Div 2) £802	M. C. Pipe	Sunwood	6/5F
92	9 Dec	Chelt	Charlton Kings 3-Y-O Novices' Hurdle £2,057	M. C. Pipe	Enemy Action	EvensF
93	12 Dec	Warwk	Budbrooke Novices' Chase (Div 2) £1,844	Mrs M. Rimell	Deep Moment	15/8F
94	14 Dec	Hdock	Ashton Novices' Hurdle £1,518	M. C. Pipe	Sondrio	1/2F

	DATE	COURSE	RACE & VALUE	TRAINER	WINNER	SP
95	14 Dec	Hdock	Arlington Premier Series Chase (Qualifier) £2,794	M. C. Pipe	Rusch de Farges (FR)	16/1
96	14 Dec	Hdock	Ribble Novices' Chase £2,872	M. C. Pipe	Pharoah's Laen	4/9F
97	15 Dec	Hdock	HLH Timber Novices' Chase £3,002	M. C. Pipe	Stepaside Lord (USA)	EvensF
98	15 Dec	Hdock	HLH Timber Novices' Hurdle £1,954	M. C. Pipe	Voyage Sans Retour (FR)	1/2F
99	15 Dec	Hdock	Boston Pit Handicap Chase £3,202	M. C. Pipe	Fu's Lady	EvensF
100	20 Dec	Ludlw	Tanners Manzanilla Novices' Hurdle £680	M. C. Pipe	Sayfar's Lad	4/6F
101	20 Dec	Ludlw	Tanners Wines Novices' Chase £1,909	M. C. Pipe	Swing To Steel	11/10F
102	20 Dec	Ludlw	Tanners Claret Handicap Chase £1,865	B. Preece	Crowecopper	13/8F
103	26 Dec	NewAb	EBF Novices' Hurdle (Qualifier) £2,530	M. C. Pipe	Sayfar's Lad	4/6F
104	26 Dec	NewAb	Mid Devon Novices' Chase £3,127	M. C. Pipe	Sabin du Loir (FR)	1/2F
105	27 Dec	Chpsw	Finale Junior Hurdle (Listed Race) £7,375	M. C. Pipe	Enemy Action	8/15F
106	27 Dec	Chpsw	Coral Welsh National (Handicap Chase) (Listed Race) £21,818	M. C. Pipe	Bonanza Boy	9/4F
107	27 Dec	Chpsw	Wiseacre Handicap Chase £2,407	M. C. Pipe	Fu's Lady	5/6F
108	27 Dec	Chpsw	Scout Novices' Chase £1,580	M. C. Pipe	Elegant Isle	9/4
109	29 Dec	Taunt	Standard Life Novices' Chase £1,501	M. C. Pipe	Mareth Line	11/8F
110	29 Dec	Taunt	Hangover Novices' Selling Hurdle £508	M. C. Pipe	Delkusha	7/4F
111	30 Dec	Nbury	Weyhill Handicap Chase £2,950	C. P. E. Brooks	Bales	10/11F
112	31 Dec	Nbury	Hungerford Handicap Chase £2,794	C. P. E. Brooks	Battle King	7/2
113	5 Jan	Lingf	Sevenoaks Novices' Chase £1,861	R. Akehurst	Juven Light (FR)	4/5F
114	5 Jan	Lingf	Horley Novices' Hurdle (Div 1) £1,360	M. C. Pipe	Honest Word	3/1
115	6 Jan	Hdock	Federation Brewery Special Ale Handicap Chase £3,626	M. C. Pipe	Silver Ace	13/8
116	7 Jan	Hdock	Philip Cornes Novices' Hurdle (Qualifier) £1,947	M. C. Pipe	Rolling Ball (FR)	4/11F
117	7 Jan	Hdock	John Birchall Memorial Novices' Chase £2,587	M. C. Pipe	Mareth Line	2/7F
118	7 Jan	Hdock	Makerfield Selling Handicap Hurdle £1,184	B. L. Key	Stocksign (USA)	2/1
119	9 Jan	Wolv	Bescot Novices' Chase £1,801	M. C. Pipe	Elegant Isle	5/6F
120	9 Jan	Wolv	Bridgnorth Novices' Hurdle (Div 2) £1,088	C. P. E. Brooks	Battalion (USA)	6/5F
121	9 Jan	Wolv	Gorsebrook Handicap Hurdle £1,534	B. Preece	Baluchi	3/1F
122	10 Jan	NewAb	Bet With The Tote Novices' Chase (Qualifier) £2,610	M. C. Pipe	Out of The Gloom	4/11F
123	10 Jan	NewAb	Ellacombe Handicap Chase £2,794	M. C. Pipe	Rusch de Farges (FR)	4/7F
124	10 Jan	NewAb	St Marychurch Handicap Hurdle £2,023	M. C. Pipe	Might Move	11/8F
125	11 Jan	Plump	Pevensey Novices' Chase £1,925	C. P. E. Brooks	Roscoe Harvey	15/8F
126	13 Jan	Ascot	Thunder And Lightning Novices' Chase (Feature Race) £9,903	M. C. Pipe	Sabin du Loir (FR)	6/5F
127	14 Jan	Ascot	Philip Cornes Novices' Hurdle (Qualifier) £2,700	M. C. Pipe	Pertemps Network	8/11F
128	14 Jan	Ascot	Durham Ranger Novices' Hurdle (Div 1) £2,427	M. C. Pipe	Sondrio	2/7F
129	17 Jan	Worcs	Bransford Novices' Hurdle (Div 1) £1,088	M. C. Pipe	Fetcham Park	2/1JF
130	17 Jan	Worcs	EBF Intermediate Chase £2,490	Mrs M. Rimell	Celtic Flight	5/1
131	18 Jan	Ludlw	Welshpool Novices' Hurdle £1,224	M. C. Pipe	Kings Rank	2/5F
132	19 Jan	Lingf	Thornfield Securities Novices' Chase £1,958	R. Akehurst	Juven Light (FR)	1/3F
133	19 Jan	Lingf	Keep Novices' Hurdle (Div 2) £1,360	M. C. Pipe	Honest Word	8/15F
134	20 Jan	Kmptn	Ashford Novices' Hurdle £1,926	C. P. E. Brooks	Battalion (USA)	5/2F
135	21 Jan	Hdock	Premier Long-Distance Hurdle (Feature Race) £10,047	M. C. Pipe	Out of The Gloom	3/1
136	21 Jan	Hdock	Steel Plate And Sections Young Chasers Qualifier (Novices' Chase) £3,948	C. P. E. Brooks	Bruton Street	7/4
137	24 Jan	Chpsw	Partridge Novices' Chase £2,651	C. P. E. Brooks	Canford Palm	5/2F
138	24 Jan	Chpsw	Levy Board Novices' Handicap Hurdle £1,072	A. J. Wilson	Elvercone	4/1
139	25 Jan	Wolv	Compton Handicap Chase £2,175	B. Preece	Baluchi	2/1
140	25 Jan	Wolv	Kidderminster Handicap Hurdle £2,637	Andrew Turnell	Protection	5/2F
141	26 Jan	Taunt	Pickeridge Novices' Claiming Hurdle £1,114	M. C. Pipe	Le Cygne	15/8F
142	27 Jan	Wcntn	Craftsman Handicap Chase £2,709	T. Thomson Jones	Pukka Major (USA)	11/2
143	31 Jan	Leicr	Golden Miller Novices' Hurdle (Listed Race) £3,720	M. C. Pipe	Tel-Echo	11/10F
144	31 Jan	Leicr	Marshall Handicap Chase £1,716	B. Preece	Baluchi	5/6F
145	31 Jan	Leicr	Charnwood Claiming Hurdle £1,562	M. C. Pipe	Celcius	4/1
146	1 Feb	Hford	Leominster Novices' Chase £2,466	C. P. E. Brooks	Admirals All	EvensF
147	2 Feb	Lingf	Edenbridge Novices' Chase £1,475	M. C. Pipe	Wingspan (USA)	11/10F
148	6 Feb	Fontw	Pagham Selling Hurdle £1,072	M. C. Pipe	Delkusha	11/8F
149	6 Feb	Fontw	Bet With The Tote Novices' Hurdle (Listed Race) £4,386	C. P. E. Brooks	Battalion (USA)	10/11F
150	7 Feb	Warwk	Ryton Novices' Hurdle £1,360	M. C. Pipe	Anti Matter	EvensF
151	7 Feb	Warwk	Regency Hurdle £4,080	M. C. Pipe	Pertemps Network	6/4
152	8 Feb	Ascot	Daniel Homes Novices' Chase (Listed Race) £10,380	M. C. Pipe	Sabin du Loir (FR)	1/2F
153	10 Feb	Nbury	Aldermaston Novices' Chase £2,213	R. Akehurst	Juven Light (FR)	4/7F
154	11 Feb	Nbury	Chaddleworth Novices' Chase £2,252	C. P. E. Brooks	Admirals All	15/8F

Appendix B

	DATE	COURSE	RACE & VALUE	TRAINER	WINNER	SP
155	13 Feb	Nttm	Charnwood Novices' Hurdle (Div 2) £1,360	C. P. E. Brooks	The Gaelcharn	7/4F
156	14 Feb	NewAb	Corndon Tor Novices' Chase £2,402	M. C. Pipe	Wingspan (USA)	8/15F
157	14 Feb	NewAb	Palace Hotel Torquay Handicap Chase £2,924	M. C. Pipe	Let Him By	7/4F
158	14 Feb	NewAb	Hound Tor Novices' Selling Hurdle £1,128	M. C. Pipe	Avionne	4/9F
159	15 Feb	Worcs	Westbury Homes Silver Jubilee Handicap Chase £3,623	B. Preece	Baluchi	15/8F
160	15 Feb	Worcs	EBF Novices' Hurdle (Qualifier) £1,436	M. C. Pipe	Sayfar's Lad	4/6F
161	16 Feb	Leicr	Vicarage Claiming Novices' Hurdle £1,360	M. C. Pipe	Au Bon	11/8F
162	18 Feb	Nttm	Nottinghamshire Novices' Chase (Feature Race) £10,227	J. G. FitzGerald	Phoenix Gold	15/8F
163	20 Feb	Fontw	John Rogerson Memorial Challenge Trophy Handicap Chase £2,898	M. C. Pipe	Let Him By	2/1
164	22 Feb	Warwk	Coventry City Novices' Trial Hurdle (Listed Race) £7,068	M. C. Pipe	Sayfar's Lad	9/4
165	22 Feb	Warwk	Highfield Road Novices' Chase £7,133	M. C. Pipe	Pharoah's Laen	7/2
166	22 Feb	Warwk	Vice Presidents Handicap Hurdle £2,783	M. C. Pipe	Travel Mystery	6/4F
167	23 Feb	Folks	Hythe Novices' Handicap Hurdle £1,088	M. C. Pipe	Go West	6/4F
168	25 Feb	Kmptn	Racing Post Chase (Handicap) (Listed Race) £23,217	M. C. Pipe	Bonanza Boy	5/1
169	28 Feb	Nttm	Junior Selling Hurdle £1,142	M. C. Pipe	Le Cygne	4/5F
170	1 Mar	Worcs	Hardanger Properties Chase £6,324	M. C. Pipe	Beau Ranger	40/85F
171	2 Mar	Lingf	Swanley Novices' Hurdle £1,408	M. C. Pipe	Kumakas Nephew	4/1
172	4 Mar	Ilford	Newent Chase £2,259	M. C. Pipe	Silver Ace	1/2F
173	4 Mar	Hford	Bromyard Novices' Handicap Hurdle £1,170	M. C. Pipe	Go West	11/10F
174	4 Mar	Nbury	Philip Cornes Nickel Alloys Novices' Chase (Listed Race) £4,644	C. P. E. Brooks	Admirals All	EvensF
175	4 Mar	Nbury	Philip Cornes Saddle Of Gold Hurdle (Final) (Listed Race) £10,034	M. C. Pipe	Pertemps Network	4/5F
176	11 Mar	Chpsw	Swish Hurdle £3,460	M. C. Pipe	Fetcham Park	8/15F
177	11 Mar	Sand	William Hill Imperial Cup (Handicap Hurdle) (Listed Race) £16,798	M. C. Pipe	Travel Mystery	3/1F
178	14 Mar	Chelt	117th year of The Cheltenham Grand Annual Chase Challenge Cup (Handicap) (Listed Race) £15,842	T. Thomson Jones	Pukka Major (USA)	4/1JF
179	17 Mar	Wolv	Whiston Four Year Old Fillies Selling Hurdle £1,212	M. C. Pipe	Le Cygne	4/7F
180	17 Mar	Wolv	Mitton Handicap Chase £2,700	B. Preece	Mithras	6/1
181	18 Mar	Lingf	Bic Lady Shaver Handicap Chase £2,872	M. C. Pipe	Silver Ace	6/4F
182	22 Mar	Worcs	Pitchcroft Novices' Hurdle (Div 1) £1,088	M. C. Pipe	Temple Reef	3/1
183	22 Mar	Worcs	St Barnabas Novices' Chase £1,644	M. C. Pipe	Fandango Boy	11/10F
184	22 Mar	Worcs	Portland Walk Claiming Hurdle £1,674	M. C. Pipe	Celcius	4/7F
185	23 Mar	Taunt	Pitminster Juvenile Handicap Hurdle £1,072	M. C. Pipe	Anti Matter	8/11F
186	27 Mar	Chpsw	Welsh Champion Hurdle (Listed Race) £10,432	C. P. E. Brooks	Celtic Shot	1/7F
187	27 Mar	Chpsw	Castle Novices' Hurdle (Div 2) £918	M. C. Pipe	Go West	1/7F
188	27 Mar	Chpsw	Castle Novices' Hurdle (Div 1) £1,340	J. A. C. Edwards	Hilarion (FR)	w/o
189	28 Mar	Chpsw	Easter Selling Hurdle £946	M. C. Pipe	Old Kilpatrick	4/11F
190	29 Mar	Worcs	Racing Post Series Handicap Hurdle £1,772	A. J. Wilson	Elvercone	9/4JF
191	13 Apr	Ludlw	Tote Novices' Hurdle £1,155	M. C. Pipe	Just Rose	12/1
192	15 Apr	Bangr	Alfred McAlpine Minerals Novices' Handicap Hurdle £2,110	M. C. Pipe	Au Bon	8/11F
193	15 Apr	Bangr	Alfred McAlpine Construction Novices' Chase £3,392	M. C. Pipe	Wingspan (USA)	2/1
194	18 Apr	Devon	West Of England Homes Ltd Novices' Hurdle (Div 1) £1,088	M. C. Pipe	Old Kilpatrick	6/4F
195	20 Apr	Chelt	Cheltenham Juvenile Novices' Hurdle £2,233	M. C. Pipe	Voyage Sans Retour (FR)	9/4
196	22 Apr	Uttox	Bayer UK Selling Handicap Hurdle £1,254	M. C. Pipe	High Bid	5/4F
197	24 Apr	Sthwl	Rainworth Selling Hurdle £1,380	M. C. Pipe	Avionne	15/8
198	27 Apr	Towcr	Tiffield Claiming Hurdle £1,716	M. C. Pipe	Old Kilpatrick	13/8F
199	27 Apr	Towcr	Wood Burcote Novices' Chase (Div 2) £1,800	C. P. E. Brooks	Canford Palm	4/1
200	27 Apr	Towcr	City Trucks Handicap Chase £2,390	M. H. B. Robinson	Gay Moore	10/1
201	27 Apr	Towcr	Buckingham Novices' Hurdle £1,088	N. A. Gaselee	Market Forces	7/2
202	28 Apr	Taunt	Peter Blackburn Memorial Challenge Trophy Novices' Chase £2,071	M. C. Pipe	My Cup of Tea	4/6F
203	5 May	NewAb	Tetley Bitter Juvenile Handicap Hurdle £1,254	M. C. Pipe	Anti Matter	4/7F
204	6 May	Warwk	Hawtal Whiting Novices' Handicap Hurdle £1,702	R. Akehurst	Raahin (USA)	15/8F
205	9 May	Chpsw	Crystal Ball Claiming Hurdle £2,024	M. C. Pipe	Au Bon	11/10F
206	10 May	Worcs	Graham Dilley And Graeme Hick Novices' Selling Hurdle £1,282	M. C. Pipe	Rastannora (USA)	8/13F
207	12 May	Taunt	May Juvenile Novices' Hurdle £1,072	M. C. Pipe	Aimee Jane (USA)	4/7F

209

	DATE	COURSE	RACE & VALUE	TRAINER	WINNER	SP
208	13 May	**Warwk**	Charlecote Novices' Handicap Hurdle £1,640	M. C. Pipe	**Fatu Hiva (GER)**	7/2F
209	13 May	**Warwk**	Eastgate Handicap Chase £2,532	R. Akehurst	**Dudie**	2/1
210	17 May	**Worcs**	Colin Davies Novices' Chase £1,730	M. C. Pipe	**Al Misk (USA)**	10/11F
211	17 May	**Worcs**	Formsnet Novices' Handicap Hurdle £1,716	M. C. Pipe	**Fatu Hiva (GER)**	EvensF
212	18 May	**Huntg**	Abbots Ripton Novices' Selling Handicap Hurdle £1,324	N. Tinkler	**Hanseatic**	2/1F
213	18 May	**Huntg**	Papworth Novices' Handicap Chase £1,579	M. C. Pipe	**Dusty Diplomacy (USA)**	7/4
214	18 May	**Huntg**	Brent Leisure Handicap Hurdle £2,215	M. C. Pipe	**Melendez (USA)**	11/2
215	19 May	**Strfd**	Fairclough Four Year Old Novices' Hurdle £1,548	M. C. Pipe	**Anti Matter**	8/13F
216	20 May	**Bangr**	Dee Novices' Hurdle £1,696	M. C. Pipe	**Chic Carolyn**	EvensF
217	20 May	**Bangr**	St Johns Handicap Chase £2,005	M. C. Pipe	**My Cup of Tea**	8/13F
218	27 May	**Sthwl**	Roy Allen Print Novices' Chase £1,254	M. C. Pipe	**Dusty Diplomacy (USA)**	4/11F
219	29 May	**Devon**	Mamhead Claiming Novices' Hurdle £1,156	M. C. Pipe	**Mighty Prince**	1/3F
220	29 May	**Devon**	Howard And Howard Life Pensions Ltd Selling Hurdle £1,100	M. C. Pipe	**Avionne**	1/2F
221	3 Jun	**Strfd**	Gambling Prince Chase £2,490	C. P. E. Brooks	**Hazy Sunset**	5/2